# TREASURES FROM PAUL

# *Corinthians*

## *The First Letter*

## KEN CHANT

# TREASURES FROM PAUL

## *Corinthians*

## *The First Letter*

### KEN CHANT

Copyright © 2013 by Ken Chant.

ISBN 978-1-61529-115-1

All rights reserved worldwide.

Vision Publishing
1672 Main Street E109
Ramona, CA 92065
www.booksbyvision.com

## A NOTE ON GENDER

The English language unfortunately does not contain an adequate generic term (especially in the singular number) that includes without bias both male and female. So "he, him, his, man, mankind," with their plurals, must do the work for both sexes. Accordingly, wherever it is appropriate to do so in the following pages, please include the feminine gender in the masculine, and vice versa.

## FOOTNOTES

A work once fully referenced will thereafter be noted throughout the remainder of the book either by "*ibid*" (the same) or "*op. cit.*" (a work previously cited).

## TRANSLATIONS

Unless otherwise noted, all scripture translations are my own.

# TABLE OF CONTENTS

4

# ABBREVIATIONS

Abbreviations commonly used for the books of the Bible are

| | | | |
|---|---|---|---|
| Genesis | Ge | Habakkuk | Hb |
| Exodus | Ex | Zephaniah | Zp |
| Leviticus | Le | Haggai | Hg |
| Numbers | Nu | Zechariah | Zc |
| Deuteronomy | De | Malachi | Mal |
| Joshua | Js | | |
| Judges | Jg | | |
| Ruth | Ru | Matthew | Mt |
| 1 Samuel | 1 Sa | Mark | Mk |
| 2 Samuel | 2 Sa | Luke | Lu |
| 1 Kings | 1 Kg | John | Jn |
| 2 Kings | 2 Kg | Acts | Ac |
| 1 Chronicles | 1 Ch | Romans | Ro |
| 2 Chronicles | 2 Ch | 1 Corinthians | 1 Co |
| Ezra | Ezr | 2 Corinthians | 2 Co |
| Nehemiah | Ne | Galatians | Ga |
| Esther | Es | Ephesians | Ep |
| Job | Jb | Philippians | Ph |
| Psalm | Ps | Colossians | Cl |
| Proverbs | Pr | 1 Thessalonians | 1 Th |
| Ecclesiastes | Ec | 2 Thessalonians | 2 Th |
| Song of Songs | Ca * | 1 Timothy | 1 Ti |
| Isaiah | Is | 2 Timothy | 2 Ti |
| Jeremiah | Je | Titus | Tit |
| Lamentations | La | Philemon | Phm |
| Ezekiel | Ez | Hebrews | He |
| Daniel | Da | James | Ja |
| Hosea | Ho | 1 Peter | 1 Pe |
| Joel | Jl | 2 Peter | 2 Pe |
| Amos | Am | 1 John | 1 Jn |
| Obadiah | Ob | 2 John | 2 Jn |
| Jonah | Jo | 3 John | 3 Jn |
| Micah | Mi | Jude | Ju |
| Nahum | Na | Revelation | Re |

* *Ca* is an abbreviation of *Canticles*, a derivative of the Latin name of the *Song of Solomon*, which is sometimes also called the *Song of Songs*.

# OUTLINE OF I CORINTHIANS

## *INTRODUCTION*

- See 1:1-9; and note that Paul had heard a **report** (1:11; 16:7); and received a **letter** (7:1). His letter is largely a response to those two items.

- Paul's introduction –

- The salutation (1:2)

- The greeting (1:3)

- The thanksgiving (1:4-7a)

- The promise (1:7b-9).

## *PART ONE*

# FROM THE *"REPORT"*

FACTIONS (1:10-4:21)
INCEST (5:1-13)
LAW (6:1-9a)
CHASTITY (6:9b-20)
FREEDOM (9:1-10:13)
EUCHARIST (10:14-11:1; 11:17-33)
RELATIONSHIPS (11:2-16)

## *PART TWO*

# FROM THE *"LETTER"*

MARRIAGE (7:1-40)
MARKET (8:1-13)
CHARISMATA (12:1 - 14:33a)
WOMEN IN MINISTRY (14:33b-38
RESURRECTION (15:1-58)
GIVING (16:1-4)

## FINAL COMMENTS

16:5-21.

*PREFACE*

# ON WRITING A BOOK

Here is what Thomas Carlyle felt about people who write books --

> Wondrous indeed is the virtue of a true Book. Not like a dead city of stones, yearly crumbling, yearly needing repair; more like a tilled field, but then a spiritual field: like a spiritual tree, let me rather say, it stands from year to year, and from age to age (we have Books that already number some hundred and fifty human ages); and yearly comes its new produce of leaves (Commentaries, Deductions, Philosophical, Political Systems; or were it only Sermons, Pamphlets, Journalistic Essays), every one of which is talismanic and thaumaturgic, for it can persuade men. O thou who art able to write a Book, which once in the two centuries or oftener there is a man gifted to do, envy not him whom they name City-builder, and inexpressibly pity him whom they name Conqueror or City-burner! Thou too art a Conqueror and Victor; but of the true sort, namely over the Devil: thou too hast built what will outlast all marble and metal, and be a wonder-bringing City of the Mind, a Temple

and Seminary and Prophetic Mount, whereto all kindreds of the Earth will pilgrim. [1]

I will never be such a writer nor compose such a book as Carlyle had in mind, but I can take to myself something of his remarks. Assuredly, I would prefer to write a book than burn a city, or even build one, and I have no envy of any man, except perhaps one who can write a better book than I. But of this present work I may at least hope that you will find it, as Carlyle said, "talismanic and thaumaturgic"!

What you won't find here is a complete commentary on Paul's *First Letter to the Corinthians*, of which better writers than I have done a better job than I could do. As in the other books in this series of *Treasures from Paul*, I have concentrated upon a few key themes, with special attention given to Paul's injunctions on **divorce and re-marriage**, on the **charismata**, and on **women in ministry.**

I hope you will find my approach to those debates reasonable, fair, and above all biblical. But if perchance you cannot agree with me, then I beseech you, restrain your wrath and continue to look upon me kindly. The world will not collapse because there are diverse opinions on these matters, nor will the church decay into ruin, nor will the scriptures be rendered futile. You should at least allow that my arguments are reasonable, even if you do not find them persuasive.

The simple fact is people of good will, who love God and the Bible, do examine the biblical data and then arrive at different conclusions as to what God is saying. I will echo

---

(1)   Sartor Resartus, Book II.8; J. M. Dent & Sons Ltd, London, 1913. The title means "The Tailor Re-tailored". Beginning as a series of essays, it was first published as a book in 1836.

Paul (Ro 14:5) and suggest that *"every reader should make up his or her own mind on the matter"*. But when you have decided, please continue to respect the integrity of those who may choose to differ from you. After sixty years of adult ministry and constant study, I am weary of stubborn dogmatists who insist that their view and theirs alone on any matter is valid. I am even more weary of people who have nothing better to do than to scorn, deride, and abuse those who differ from them.

"Ha!" someone says accusingly, "You have been known to be dogmatic yourself on occasion." Yes, I have been and will be again, but never, I hope, with bitter anger or denigrating insult, but always with respect for sincere Christians who may disagree with me. After all, none of us is infallible. Inerrancy in doctrine is an attribute of the Bible alone. Neither scholar, nor denomination, nor college, nor anyone else may claim absolute truth in dogma, free from any fault or folly.

The Bible is a marvellous book. It vividly reflects all the drama, emotion, diversity, confusion, and ambiguity of daily human life. It is the Word of the Almighty. How then can it be surprising if we mortals, with all our limitations, cannot always agree on what its pages are teaching? We do disagree, and no doubt will continue to do so until the end of the age. But we should never quarrel about the need for kindly grace, and for love in our dealings with others who, like ourselves, truly are servants of the Lord, and yearn only to do his will as they understand it.

I will love anyone, even if we deeply disagree on some issues, for whom Christ is truly Lord, honouring him as the only Saviour, and committed to serving him above all others.

"A happy heart," says Sirach (13:26), "is marked by a cheerful face. But inventing proverbs is painfully hard work!" So is writing a book like this. Nonetheless, I send it to you with a merry heart, a cheerful face, and a prayer that these pages will bring you pleasure and enlightenment. May they also bring honour to the Master. And may we all continue to grow in grace and in the knowledge of the Lord, until we are carried safely from earth to glory, to rejoice before his throne for ever.

## *INTRODUCTION*

# THE CHURCH AT CORINTH

The city of Corinth in southern Greece was founded by Julius Caesar in 46 B.C. as a Roman colony, upon the ruins of an ancient town. Within 100 years it had grown to a great cosmopolitan seaport, and eventually attained a population of possibly 500,000 inhabitants, many thousands of whom were slaves.

The location of Corinth on a narrow isthmus gave it both access to the sea from a port on either side, and a pleasant climate. It was a favourite site of the Roman emperors, who frequently endowed the city until it became the richest and finest in Greece. [2] It was deemed the capital of southern Greece, although it was only 80km west of Athens. It was a major centre of travel and trade, and also of philosophy (1:18-31; 15:12). The Isthmian Games held in Corinth every two years rivalled the Olympic contests in splendour and importance.

The chief pride of Corinth was the great hill-top temple of Aphrodite, with its 1000 temple courtesans. The licentious worship of Aphrodite, (along with numerous other deities from many nations), mixed with the varied cultures of many ethnic groups, led to a moral laxity that was scandalous even to the decadent Romans. The expression *"to live like a*

---

(2)    Indeed, life in Corinth became so opulent and expensive that a proverb grew out of it: "Not everyone can go to Corinth" (Horace, Letters Bk I, Ep. 17, Line 36); that is, only the most fortunate could obtain whatever benefit the proverb was being applied to.

*Corinthian"* entered the Greek language as an epithet for drunken or debauched behaviour. (3)

Paul's work at Corinth was mostly among the lower classes, with only a handful of disciples from the upper echelons of society (1 Co 1:26-31). His converts would have been mostly working class people, slaves and freedmen, artisans, clerks, shop-keepers, dock hands, sailors, housewives, school teachers, and the like.

The church in Corinth had its roots in the arrival of Priscilla and Aquila (Ac 18:2, c. 49 A.D.). Paul arrived about a year later, on his second missionary journey, and remained there 18 months (Ac 18:1-11, 18a). His letter was written from Ephesus some 2½ years later. In between, Paul wrote another letter, but no trace of it remains (1 Co 5:9). (4)

The occasion of the letter we are examining here was probably the arrival in Ephesus of visitors from the Corinthian church, who brought Paul both a **report** (1:11; 16:7) of conditions there and a **letter** (7:1) that contained a series of questions (1 Co 1:10-11; 16:15-17). Paul's reply therefore did not take the form of a doctrinal treatise (as in *Romans* or *Ephesians*), but is built around a set of practical

---

(3)    In the late 18th century, and during the days of the Regency (early 19th), it also became current in the English language. A dissipated and licentious person was called a "Corinthian", and a group of singularly dissolute young men were called "the Corinthians". However, to deserve the title, a "Corinthian" usually had to be skilled also in one or more sports, and a notable horseman, and perhaps they were not all lax in morals.

(4)    Some scholars argue that *2 Co 6:14-7:1* is a fragment of that letter. Others claim that some parts of *1 Corinthians* and/or other parts of *2 Corinthians* belong to the lost letter. None of the arguments is fully convincing. It is safe enough to accept our present letters as being genuine documents written by Paul to the church at Corinth.

and ethical instructions, and a response to the queries raised by the Corinthian delegates. (5)

It has often been remarked that Paul provides in this letter a more personal testimony of his relationship with Christ than occurs in any of his other writings –

> In no other letter does Paul give so full a picture of what Christ meant to him. It is clear that Jesus was a person who lived in history, for he had brothers (9:5), was a teacher (7:10; 9:14), suffered betrayal (11:23), died on a cross (1:18; 15:3), and was buried. Yet he was not simply an earthly figure. All things had come into existence through him (8:6); he had been the Rock from which the Israelites drank in the wilderness (10:4). We might assume that a pre-existent being would necessarily be eternal, but Paul does not take that for granted. God raised him from the dead (15:4), confirming him as Christ and Lord ... This Christ will soon come (1:7; 4:5), to complete the conquest of the God-opposing powers, for through him the new age of redemption has come. (6)

I hope that I have maintained the spirit of Paul's relationship with Christ in the pages that follow.

In the meantime, *Part One* explains Paul's responses to the *"report"* he had received; and *Part Two* deals with the *"letter"*.

---

(5)   Note the repeated phrase *"now concerning"* in 7:1, 25; 8:1; 12:1; 16:1. This phrase marks at least some of the places where Paul was responding to the questions he had been asked.

(6)   The Interpreter's Bible, Vol. 10, *Corinthians – Introduction*, by C. T. Craig; Abingdon Press, New York, 1953; pg. 9.

But first, Paul has some nice things to say about the Christians in Corinth, and he begins by calling them (and us) *"saints"* –

*ONE*

# CALLED TO BE SAINTS

*To God's church that was made holy by Christ Jesus and called to be God's holy people in the city of Corinth and to people everywhere who call on the name of our Lord Jesus Christ.* (1 Co 1:2; God's Word)

Paul speaks both to the church at Corinth, and to all of us – *"people everywhere who call on the name of our Lord Jesus Christ."* He names us God's "holy people", that is, "saints". At once we confront one of the most vexing problems Christians face – how to understand who they are in Christ. After all, we don't feel like saints, nor do we look like saints. We could call it –

## AN IDENTITY CRISIS

Popularly, a *"saint"* is a holy person who becomes a religious hero, famous for miracles, or for a martyr's death, or both. Such people, of course, are recognised as saints only after their death; moreover, during their life they never spoke of themselves as saints; indeed, anyone who does call himself or herself a "saint" will no longer be thought saintly!

Yet we who believe are all called saints *now*! Indeed, the term is used many times in the NT of all Christians, and it describes us, not as we shall one day be in paradise, but as God sees us *now* in Christ.

Herein lies our problem – we find ourselves each day looking in the mirror at a person who must be numbered among the

## UNSAINTLY SAINTS

The bother is we can't imagine ourselves matching the popular image of a "saint". So much is this true, that it would sound quite peculiar if I addressed you as "St So-And-So"; and it would be even more eccentric for you to announce yourself by that title. How then can we rightly call ourselves and each other *saints*, not in the coming kingdom, but <u>right here and now</u>? We find the answer in

## THE EXAMPLE OF JESUS

The preeminent "saint" is surely Jesus – yet how strange it is that all the NT leaders, and even the people, are called saints, *except* Jesus – yet they were but pale shadows of him!

Likewise, in history, many people have been designated as "saints" (St Aiden; St Christopher; etc.), yet no one ever says St Jesus!

Perhaps that is because in many ways Jesus did not (and does not) match the usual idea of what a "saint" should be – emaciated, unearthly, crowned by a shining halo, a person who is *of* the world but not *in* it, distant from the lives of ordinary people. But those are all just the things Jesus wasn't! On the contrary, just as we are called to be, he was *in* the world, but not *of* it! (Jn 17:16)

Let us then make *Christ* our model, not church tradition nor popular opinion.

Now notice this vital fact: Jesus began life as a <u>natural</u> man, not as a <u>supernatural</u> man. His conception was certainly a miracle (Lu 1:34-35), but thereafter he developed in his mother's womb, was born, and grew day by day as any normal child must do. (7) What does that mean?

## TRULY MAN AND TRULY GOD

The Church has always maintained both the full *humanity* and the full *deity* of Jesus. That is, orthodox doctrine claims that Jesus is

- one person (the Eternal Logos) (8),

- with two natures (human and divine),

- and probably a single will (that of the Logos).

However, during the years of his incarnation he confined himself to those attributes that are proper to human nature. This means, at no time did Jesus employ any attribute that is proper only to the Deity. He never stepped outside the boundaries of a normal human nature; he used only those faculties and skills that properly belong to a man. Indeed, had he, even for a moment, resumed any of the divine attributes that he had put aside (Ph 2:6-9), he would have disqualified himself as our Redeemer (He 2:13-15). Satan knew that, and tempted Jesus to go beyond his human confines and turn stones into bread (Lu 4:1-4). The Master saw through the devilish ruse, and scorned the temptation.

But if Christ acted only as a Man (albeit one without sin), how then did he do his mighty works? *Answer*: by doing exactly as we must. He had first to discover his true identity

---

(7)    Jesus, being free of sin, was wise beyond his years, and spiritually precocious, but not to a supernatural degree (Lu 2:40, 52). See my further comment just below.

(8)    "In the beginning was the Word (Logos), and the Word was with God, and the Word was God" (Jn 1:1).

in God, and then, to fulfil all that the Father had commanded, he had to utilise the resources available to him through scripture and the Spirit.

So then, to fulfil his destiny, Jesus, just as we must, had to break through every barrier by faith. Among other trammels, he had to overcome

## THE BARRIER OF NATURAL PERCEPTION

Nothing in the natural perception Jesus had of himself could give him knowledge of his divine origin; that knowledge dawned in him (by revelation from the Holy Spirit) only as he daily studied scripture and prayed. He had probably reached full manhood before he gained full awareness of his true identity, with the final realisation perhaps coming to him at the time of his baptism by John (Lu 3:22).

Aside from that biblical revelation of his heavenly identity, the daily evidence of his natural senses told him that he was just a man like any other, with the same needs and vulnerabilities. As he worked at the bench alongside his stepfather Joseph, if he banged his knuckles with a hammer, or cut himself with a chisel, he bled and hurt as much as any man. Like any normal person, he truly needed fresh air, water, food, rest, sleep, and play. His humanity was neither a camouflage, nor a pretence, like that of some mythical deity. It was absolutely real. Notice too how his brothers and sisters, his relatives, and his neighbours, never observed anything unusual in his life until he began his ministry (Mt 13:55; Mk 3:20-21; 6:2,3; Lu 4:22). They possibly thought that he was uncommonly good, and perhaps more serious, more devotional than was normal for a boy; but never to such an extent that they imagined he was seriously different. Many a child has shown greater precocity than Jesus of Nazareth ever did, prior to the Holy Spirit coming upon him at the Jordan.

No matter how ordinary he seemed, Jesus tossed aside all that worldly evidence, and absolutely believed everything scripture said about him. That was not easy for him to do (cp. He 5:8). Think about a carpenter's son trying to apply to himself *Isaiah 9:6-7*! Yet that is just what he did do. As he read scripture, the Holy Spirit bore witness with his spirit that *he* was the one about whom the prophets had spoken.

It was upon that foundation of an inner revelation of the word of God that all the subsequent ministry of Jesus was built. He *believed* what the Spirit and the Word were saying to him. He *knew* the witness was true. He embraced this new identity heartily, and set himself to fulfil all that the prophets had spoken.

Likewise, we too have to break through the contrary message of our natural perception, the witness of our physical senses, and believe what the scriptures say about us, no matter how incredible their statements may seem, nor how unrelated to what we observe on earth. Our cry should be (as someone has said), "God said it; I believe it; that settles it!" You are who God says you are. You can be what God says you can be. You can do what God says you can do. Why? Because you are a person in Christ. [9] Never accept anything less than this as true.

## THE BARRIER OF PEER-GROUP PRESSURE

Jesus' family thought he was mad, and several times the crowds tried to stone him to death (Mk 3:21; Lu 4:16-30; etc.).

---

(9)  From a sermon by Dr Robert Schuller, in the Crystal Cathedral, Los Angeles.

Do you suppose it was easy for Jesus to withstand the fearful pressure of those accusations of insanity made by people whom he loved? Of course not! But he allowed nothing, not even the bitterest social pain, to turn him aside from scripture. Indeed, so much was this true, that he chose the most difficult place of all to announce his Messiahship – the synagogue in Nazareth, *"where he had been brought up"* (Lu 4:16). As he stood up to speak, he looked upon a building filled with people he had known all his life – his mother, brothers, sisters, aunts, uncles, cousins, neighbours, schoolmates, friends. He must have known what their reaction would be – bewilderment, amazement, dismay, then wild, murderous anger. Yet still he spoke. He counted the cost of their rejection as small compared with the necessity for him to speak publicly and boldly what he had discovered about himself in scripture!

Likewise, we too must steel ourselves against the face of man and cling to the promises of God with unshakeable confidence. Said Jesus, *"Speak* to that mountain, and it will obey you!"* – so long as you speak in faith, and in harmony with scripture, and in agreement with the purpose of God (Mk 11:22-24).

## THE BARRIER OF SATANIC OPPOSITION

See the story again in *Matthew 4:1-11; Luke 4:1-13.* Notice how Satan used against Christ the same three temptations he thrusts at us – the lust of the eye ("all the kingdoms of this world and their glory"), the lust of the flesh (how hungry he was after 40 days of fasting in the desert!), and the pride of life ("make a great display, and cast yourself from the pinnacle") – *1 John 2:16,* KJV. Nonetheless after spending six weeks in the wilderness without food, and with only dew to drink – filthy, unshaven, ragged from sleeping among rocks, exhausted from evading wild animals (Mk 1:13), and being brought to the very brink of death — still Jesus triumphed! And he did so, not as the Son of God, but as a *man* filled with the Word and the Spirit!

Those same resources are available to us, namely, the testimony of scripture concerning us; prayer; and the revelation and power of the Holy Spirit. So receive and believe the message that comes to you from scripture, no matter how improbable it seems, no matter what opposition you face, and by the Spirit turn that word into a sharp sword, defeating every Satanic attack.

## A WALK OF POWER

Did you notice, not only are we *called* "saints", we are also called to *be* "saints" (1 Co 1:2); that is, actually to *live* as the supernatural people of God. How can ordinary men and women do such an impossible thing? How can we gain access to miracles, heal the sick, cast out devils, do the works of God, live righteously, and so on?

**_First_**, as we have seen, we must follow Christ's example of boldly embracing the identity God has given us in Christ, as revealed in scripture. We need to live with a *"throne-view"* (Ep 2:6), positioning ourselves with Christ in the heavenlies, and there taking authority over every work of the devil. It is wonderful how a change of position changes a person's outlook! (cp. Pr 20:14). An attacking army always prefers to occupy the high ground. Better to stand over an enemy than to lie under him!

**_Second_**, follow the example of Christ by utilising all the resources of the kingdom through the power of the Holy Spirit.

*PART ONE*

# FROM THE "REPORT"

*TWO*

# A QUARRELLING CHURCH

Paul's friends brought him a sad report of a disunited church – it was falling into immorality, engaging in legal disputes, violating the Eucharist, and indulging in heresy. He hastened to correct these matters in a letter. But notice how first he concentrated on whatever good things he could say about the Corinthians; he commended before he criticised –

> *I always thank God for you because Christ Jesus has shown you God's good will. Through Christ Jesus you have become rich in every way-in speech and knowledge of every kind. Our message about Christ has been verified among you. Therefore, you don't lack any gift as you wait eagerly for our Lord Jesus Christ to be revealed. (1:4-7)*

Even more, despite the matters that were troubling the church, he was confident that God was working among them, and that he would bring them safely home to glory –

> *God will give you strength to go all the way, so that you will be found without fault in the day of our Lord Jesus Christ. God is faithful, and has he not called you into the fellowship of his Son, Jesus Christ our Lord? (vs. 8-9)*

Nonetheless, he could not avoid addressing the problems that were troubling the church, beginning with a group of troubling **_factional divisions_** (1:10-17; 3:1-9, 21-23), which Paul well knew would shatter it, if they were not healed. Yet he did not merely rebuke the warring parties. Rather, he offered them several solutions –

# CLING TO THE CROSS

See *1 Corinthians 1:18-25; 2:1-3*, where the key verse is *1:21* –

> *Since God has chosen by his wisdom that this world will never discover him through its own wisdom, he has also resolved that only through the foolishness of preaching will salvation come to those who believe.*

That is one of the most startling statements in the Bible. It explains in one blunt assertion why such confusion exists in the world of human philosophy and speculative religion – God himself has decreed that by thought alone, apart from the revelation he gives of himself in scripture, *no one* will ever discover him! The reasoning of the brightest mind will be lost in folly. The most profound sage will be unable to discover any ultimate truth. No matter how brilliant their intellects, how powerful their thought, how strenuously they labour, God says, "You will not find me!" Nor do they, until, as we all must, they become like a little child, surrender humbly to the gospel call to repent, and yield their lives to the Father's will in Christ (Mt 18:2-3).

Perhaps forty years ago I spent some time studying the various philosophies of the western world. In particular, I devoured Bertrand Russell's extraordinary tome, *A History of Western Philosophy* [10], and then had great delight discussing it with my eldest son, who was then in his early teens. *The History* spans more than 20 centuries of western thought, and examines a vast array of philosophical ideas. My response to it, apart from being mightily impressed by

---

(10)    First published in 1945, it is still in print.

the brilliance of its writing and the depth of Lord Russell's knowledge, is best expressed in a saying I once heard in a sermon –

> All human philosophy is like a blind man with
> no arms in a dark room feeling for a black hat
> that isn't there!

So many different and conflicting ideas! After more than two millennia of rational analysis, of staggering scholarship, and of pure genius, none of the philosophers could agree! All that emerged was chaos, and not a shred of genuine understanding of the human condition, nor any useful answer to the most vital questions about whom we are, why are we here, and what will the end be?

Perhaps, though, in that last sentence, I am doing Professor Russell an injustice. He did have *some* thoughts about the end of all things. He reckoned that the human race is

> the product of causes ... That (man's) origin,
> his growth, his hopes and fears, his loves and
> his beliefs, are but the outcome of accidental
> collocations of atoms; that no fire, no heroism,
> no intensity of thought and feeling, can
> preserve an individual life beyond the grave;
> that all the labours of the ages, all the
> inspiration, all the noonday brightness of
> human genius are destined to extinction in the
> vast death of the solar system; that the whole
> temple of man's achievement must inevitably
> be buried beneath the debris of a universe in
> ruins — all these things, if not quite beyond
> dispute, are so nearly certain, that no

philosophy which rejects them can hope to
stand. [11]

Well, if it is true that no genuine philosophy can arrive at
anything better than utter despair, then I'll take myself off to
the gospel! At least, as a Christian, I can live with hope and
die with joy. And even if my hope should prove to be based
on an empty myth, and my joy on a futile expectation, I'll
never know it! Death, if the atheist should prove to be
correct, will mean instant and total obliteration of all self and
all awareness. But in the meantime, I will have had a
wonderful and meaningful life!

## THE WISDOM OF GOD

Of course, in reality I cannot doubt the absolute truth of the
gospel, that is, the good news that Jesus came, died for me,
rose again for my justification, and is coming again one day
to receive me into Paradise for ever.

Let us heed then the voice of God, who speaks sternly, even
shockingly, when he decrees –

> *"I will destroy the wisdom of the wise. I will
> reject the intelligence of intelligent people."
> Where then (adds Paul) is the wise person?
> Where is the scholar? Where are the clever
> debaters of this age? God has in fact turned
> the wisdom of this world into nonsense! (1 Co
> 1:20)*

Hence Paul warned the Corinthians to avoid the twin snares
of

---

(11)   L. L. Clover, in a thesis, Evil Spirits – Intellectualism and Logic; Louisiana
Missionary Baptist Institute and Seminary; 1974. (Wikipedia)

- "demanding signs"; and of

- "desiring human wisdom" –

> *Jews ask for miraculous signs, and Greeks look for wisdom, but our message is that Christ was crucified ... (and to us) who are called, he is the power of God and the wisdom of God. (vs. 22-24)*

He does not mean that miracles are wrong, nor that seeking wisdom is sinful. Rather, he is saying that the only foundation of our lives, of our hopes, and of our future, must be the gospel. Once that is settled, then, by all means add to it whatever knowledge may be useful to you, and seek whatever divine intervention may be desirable. God does answer prayer, with a miracle if needed; and increased knowledge is almost always a good thing.

But, for us who believe, *"Christ crucified"* (vs. 22-23) is the bedrock of all wisdom, the only unshakeable foundation for life, and the only safe pathway to eternal life.

Yet there are still those among us who remain heedless of the apostle's admonition. There are some among the Pentecostal movement who are prone to the first fault, craving miracles all the time, never truly content with Christ and Christ alone. There are some among the older churches who are prone to the second, boasting of their sophistication and learning, yet moving ever further away from simple faith in the simple gospel.

Those who are truly wise will both allow room for miracles, and commend the quest for truth; but always their highest and best confidence will be in the cross, and their cry will echo Paul –

> *I am willing to throw away everything, so long as I may know Christ, and the power of his resurrection (Ph 3:8-10) ... I cast aside*

*every clever argument, humble every proud idea that exalts itself against the knowledge of God, and make every thought a captive obedient to Christ (2 Co 10:5).*

## THE FOLLY OF PREACHING

Having revealed that no one by wisdom alone can ever discover God, Paul then adds an even more astonishing fact –

*God has decreed that only through the absurdity of preaching will salvation come to those who believe (1 Co 1:21).*

Well, that deflates all us preachers! We can't boast about *our* wisdom any more than the ungodly can about theirs! The Lord declares that in his sight the very wisest and smartest of preachers is no more than an absurd fool trusting in the absurdity of preaching absurd sermons absurdly to bring salvation to lost humanity. Yet it remains the decree of God that nothing other than such folly can build the church and accomplish his divine purpose.

We are prone to feeling smug about how much we know, how wise we are, how clever our sermons, how much God needs us. But we do well to prod ourselves occasionally with scripture –

*The foolishness of God is wiser than men, and the weakness of God is stronger than men. For consider your calling, brothers: not many of you were wise according to worldly standards, not many were powerful, not many were of noble birth. But God chose what is foolish in the world to shame the wise; God chose what is weak in the world to shame the strong; God chose what is low and despised in the world, even things that are not, to bring to nothing things that are, so that no human being might boast in the presence of God (vs. 25-29).*

God leaves no room for human pride. Not even those among us whom the world deems very clever, or highly gifted, or nobly born, are allowed any room for boasting, save in Christ alone (vs. 30-31). Yet we face a fine paradox. On the one hand, scripture deems the preaching office more highly honoured than any other in the land, for it brings salvation to those who believe, builds the church, and prepares it to meet Christ when he comes. But on the other hand, we preachers are all fools, for we trust in our silly sermons to tear down the strongholds of Satan and build the invincible kingdom of God! Yet, says Paul, that is indeed the wisdom of God, and it mocks the wisdom of this world and turns it into nothing (vs. 19-20).

What shall we say then about that class of preachers who strut around as if the world were their oyster, as if they are the great ones who hold the fate of the earth in their hands, who demand adulation and honour, craving fame and riches? They surely compound *their* folly a thousand fold!

Are you a preacher? Then here is my advice. Whether you are renowned or obscure, astoundingly clever or barely literate, remind yourself every day that you are a fool preaching foolish sermons foolishly. It is good medicine for the soul, and will please the Lord, who says that none of us will ever be wise until we first declare ourselves to be fools –

> *If anyone among you thinks that he is wise in this world, let him first become a fool so that he may then become truly wise! (3:18-20).*

## THE POWER OF GOD

See *1 Corinthians 2:1-5*. There is no conflict here with the previous section, because Paul distinguished between the *"signs"* sought by Jews who declined to accept the witness of scripture, and the unobtrusive genuine work of the Holy Spirit. To Paul, the chief miracles of God are not those of *outer healing* but of *inner transformation.* He certainly did not reject the former, for he himself (as shown in *Acts*) had performed some prodigious miracles, but his true joy was found in the *"immeasurably great power of God",* which is continually at work within each believing Christian (Ep 1:19-20). This is the power that has smashed the guilt and strength of sin, made us a new creation in Christ, elevated us to the heavenlies (2:6), and will be the source of our ultimate resurrection from the dead (Ph 3:20-21). Other than this, there is no greater power!

How enraptured Paul was with the Cross! – *"I made up my mind to preach only one message: Jesus Christ, and especially his death on the cross."*

Does that make him a one-sermon preacher?

*No!* – But it does mean that he would allow nothing to diminish the message of the Cross! The same stance is expected of us –

> Nothing in my hand I bring,
>
> Simply to thy cross I cling;
>
> Naked, come to Thee for dress;
>
> Helpless look to Thee for grace;
>
> Foul, I to the fountain fly;
>
> Wash me, Saviour, or I die. [12]

---

(12)   *Rock of Ages*, stanza one; by A.M. Toplady; first appeared in an article in the October number of *The Gospel Magazine*, 1775. (Hymnopedia)

Yet how hard it is to persuade Christians to trust only in the cross! People are too often like the Jews of old (Ro 10:2-3) –

> *No one can doubt that the Jews love God, yet they remain ignorant of the righteousness that comes from God. Instead, they keep on working hard to establish their own righteousness, all the time <u>refusing to submit</u> to God's righteousness.*

Yet what double folly is this! Can anyone really hope to improve upon the work of Christ? Is anyone truly so foolish as to prefer the lesser to the greater righteousness? Rather, let us humbly cast aside all personal righteousness like a dirty rag (Is 64:6), and embrace heartily and only the divine righteousness that the Father so freely offers to all who simply believe in Jesus. (13)

---

(13)  For further reflections on this passage, see ***Excursus One** – A Tale of Two Cities*, which is at the end of *Part One*.

## *THREE*

# LIVE IN THE REALM OF THE SPIRIT

See *1 Corinthians 2:6-16*, and especially *verse 13*, which could be translated as follows –

> *We talk about these things, not using words that human wisdom might have taught us, but rather words that we learned from the Holy Spirit; for it is only by using "the language of the Spirit" that we can properly interpret spiritual matters.* (14)

This entire passage is focussed on the Pentecostal event, that is, upon a glossolalic baptism in the Holy Spirit; therefore the promises in *verses 9-10, 15-16* belong in particular to Spirit-filled believers. I know that some readers will hotly oppose those claims, yet really, the onus is upon them rather than upon me to prove their case. Why? Simply because this letter (1 Corinthians) is set within a framework of the *charismata* – that is, the supernatural gifts of the Holy Spirit (1:7; 12:1-14:40). Irenaeus, (15) for example, agrees, and notes that Paul addresses his words to those he calls *"the mature"* (1 Co 2:6). He writes –

---

(14) "The language of the Spirit" is glossolalia; see 14:2,15-16; Ep 5:18-19; Ju 20; etc.

(15) Irenaeus (*circa* 130-202) was an early church Father, a bishop in Gaul, and a Christian apologist. He was tutored by Polycarp, who was himself a disciple of the Apostle John.

The apostle says, "We speak wisdom among the perfect," [16] and by "the perfect" he means those who had received the Spirit of God, and who spoke in many tongues by the Holy Spirit, as he himself also spoke. [17] Still today we can hear many brethren in the Church who possess prophetic gifts, and who speak in all sorts of languages through the Spirit. Thus they bring to open day the ... mysteries of God. That is why the apostle calls them spiritual, because they partake of the Spirit, and not because their flesh has been stripped off and taken away, nor because they have become purely spiritual. ... But when the spirit here blended with the soul is united to (God's) handiwork, the man is rendered spiritual and perfect because of the outpouring of the Spirit, [18] and this is he who was made in the image and likeness of God. [19]

The word translated above as either "perfect" or "mature" (*teleios*) [20] was also a technical term, used in the ancient Greek world to describe a person who had been initiated into the mystical rites of a religion. We who believe are "perfect", says Paul, because we have been initiated into Christ and the Church, especially by Holy Spirit baptism. So Paul links this

---

(16)   The Greek word is *teleiois,* which can be translated as "perfect", "mature", "initiated", and the like. In our present text, the latter rendering (initiated) is probably the best.

(17)   1 Corinthians 14:18.

(18)   Acts 2:1-4.

(19)   *Against Heresies,* Bk. 5, Ch. 6. Ante-Nicene Fathers; Vol. 4; a 1979 reprint of the original 19th century work; Eerdmans's Pub. Co., Grand Rapids, Michigan; *in loc.*

(20)   The changed ending (or inflection), from *–ois* to *–os,* represents a different grammatical function in the sentence. Both are derived from *telos.*

initiation with the charismatic ministry of the Holy Spirit (vs. 10-12). Even more particularly, he joins *teleios* (vs. 6) with glossolalia (vs. 13-14). Hence, as I have suggested in the translation above, the passage should probably read, *"interpreting spiritual truths in the language of the Spirit"* – that is, in other tongues, which are folly to the unspiritual man, but are "discerned" by those who possess the Holy Spirit. This is our "secret" rite; this is our "mystery" (compare 1 Co 14:2).

This means more than simply talking away in other tongues. It implies such principles as the following –

- the spiritual man discerns the presence and power of God in glossolalia, and is enriched by it;

- revelation comes to the church through tongues/ interpretation, and prophecy (1 Co 14:5, 26-31);

- the person who speaks in tongues is "edified" (vs. 4);

- those who speak to God in other tongues (vs. 2,28), are "blessing God" and "giving thanks well" (vs. 14-17), which is a source of life both to the glossolalists and to the whole church; and so on.

It all means that God will consider you and me "perfect" (in this sense of fully initiated), if we remain filled with the Holy Spirit, constantly building up ourselves and blessing God by singing and praying both *"with our understanding and with our spirit"* (1 Co 14:14, 15; Ju 20).

## ONGOING CHARISMATA

Further, if the claims made by Irenaeus are true (and there is no reason to doubt them), then more than a century after Paul's death the churches were still enjoying glossolalia, and they fully appreciated the significance of "speaking mysteries" in the spirit. This undermines the dogma of those who insist that the charismata (1 Co 12:4-11) ceased with the death of the apostles. Plainly, they were still flourishing in the churches long after the end of the apostolic age. This fact is strengthened by another passage in which Irenaeus tells about the various spiritual gifts and miracles that were happening in his time –

> Wherefore, also, those who are in truth His disciples, receiving grace from Him, do in His name perform [miracles], so as to promote the welfare of other men, according to the gift which each one has received from Him. For some do certainly and truly drive out devils, so that those who have thus been cleansed from evil spirits frequently both believe [in Christ], and join themselves to the Church. Others have foreknowledge of things to come: they see visions, and utter prophetic expressions. Others still, heal the sick by laying their hands upon them, and they are made whole. Yea, moreover, as I have said, the dead even have been raised up, and remained among us for many years. And what shall I more say? It is not possible to name the number of the gifts which the Church, [scattered] throughout the whole world, has received from God. [21]

Here is wisdom, as Paul said; here is perfection and maturity; here is revelation; here is a communion with God that the ungifted cannot know! Here is a joy reserved only for those who have yielded themselves to the Holy Spirit and to his divine gifts!

---

(21)   Ibid. II.32.4.

I do sympathise with readers for whom those ideas are uncomfortable, who find them too overtly Pentecostal. But allow me to ask this question – if the second chapter of *1 Corinthians* does not mean what I suggest above, then what does it mean? Can you doubt that Paul would agree with me? Remember that he himself was a man who rejoiced in the use of glossolalia (1 Co 14:18), and he urged the church at Corinth to use all the charismata wisely and well (12:31; 14:39-40). We should do the same.

## UNITY AND DOCTRINE

See *1 Corinthians 3:1-9*.

Paul, it seems, was at least partly to blame for the parlous condition into which the church at Corinth had fallen. He had fed them only *"milk"*, deeming them not yet ready for *"solid food"* (vs. 2). As a consequence, after Paul was gone from the city [22], they had become susceptible to false teaching, and to factional divisions. In particular, there were two strong groups, one who followed Paul, and another who reckoned Apollos was superior. The result? They were still not ready to digest the tougher truths of the gospel, those that required weightier thought and deeper consideration. They remained immature and quarrelsome, disunited and therefore both spiritually and physically unhealthy (11:30).

Paul endeavoured to pull them away from allegiance to mere men, and urged them to focus attention on Christ. He warned them that nothing any man (or woman) can do will build the church unless the Lord choses to prosper their labours (3:5-7). Far from putting their hope in any man

---

(22)   He stayed there for about 18 months, after founding the church *circa* 51. He visited the church on at least two other occasions.

(even Paul), they should set Christ and Christ alone as the true foundation of their lives (vs. 11).

*FOUR*

# BUILDING FOR GOD

A notable feature of the early chapters of Paul's *First Letter to the Corinthians,* is how intimately he weaves Christ through every idea. Ten times in the first ten verses, Paul refers to Christ, mostly using the expression, *our Lord Jesus Christ.* He wants to leave no doubt that this is a letter about Christ, the Lord of the church, and he is calling the Corinthians to renew their total allegiance to Christ –

> *I appeal to you, dear friends, in the name of our Lord Jesus Christ, that you will agree with each other, that you will get rid of your factions, and that you will strive for unity, thinking in the same way, and working for a common purpose (1:10).*

If they will not do this, says he, the cross of Christ may be robbed of its power among them (vs. 11-17). But when the church is united in love, serving God heartily, working as partners together with God, then it becomes *"God's **field** and God's **building*** (3:8-9).

***The first of those expressions*** complements what has gone before. He had called them partners, or fellow-workers, with God. But he did not want to leave any impression that they were equal with God, so he also called them God's *"field".* That is they were workers with God only in the sense that a farmer must co-operate with the laws of nature if he hopes for a harvest. He must do all that belongs to his task (ploughing, planting, fertilising, and the like), before the falling rain and the warming sun can do their part. So too, God's favour can fall upon a church fruitfully, only if its people are living in harmony with the laws of his spiritual harvest, co-operating with every divine requirement.

***The second of those expressions*** leads the way into his next remarks, about building on the foundation that is Christ –

## BE CAREFUL HOW YOU BUILD

See *1 Corinthians 3:10-15.*

The church at Corinth had been started by a *"master builder"* (Paul), who had laid for it a superb *"foundation"* (Christ), upon which others must now build. Then comes a solemn warning –

*Be careful how you build!* (vs. 10)

This warning no doubt applies to all Christians, but in particular Paul here means it for those who are teachers in the church (4:1-2; Ja 3:1). They above all have a duty, an awesome responsibility, to build upon the foundation of Christ an edifice of sound doctrine that will carry the people on to maturity in Christ, fitted to receive a full inheritance in the coming Kingdom. He contrasts good and bad doctrine with two colourful analogies – good doctrine is like *"gold, silver, and precious gems";* bad doctrine is like *"wood, hay, and stubble"* (1 Co 3:12).

### WHAT KIND OF BUILDING?

Let us here join with Paul in imagining a great city in which all the buildings began with the same kind of foundations, but then quite different superstructures were erected, some flammable, some not. Suddenly, a terrible fire sweeps through the city; what will be the result? Some buildings emerge as smoking ruins, others survive more or less intact – some flammable parts alone were consumed.

Paul primarily has in mind those who teach or preach; but his analogy is also applicable to those who have received and believed error. Here then is a sobering truth. As surely as teachers are responsible for what they teach, and will answer to God for it, so each person is responsible for what he or she believes. We cannot throw the final responsibility upon those who have taught us. Adam's attempt to blame Eve shows what God thinks about *that* ploy. In the end, each of us must seriously strive to recognise truth from error, accepting only what truly conforms to the gospel.

Why is it important to embrace only sound doctrine? Simply because improper doctrine leads to false development, unbalanced character, wrongful service, a failure truly to bring forth the character of Christ.

All those deficiencies will be made manifest through the fire of that day, perhaps leaving only basic salvation for the person who has built upon the foundation of Christ nothing but straw.

In both sanctification and service, *"straw"* doctrines produce a distorted Christianity that will be purged at the Judgment Seat of Christ (2 Co 5:10).

The testing *"fire"* (3:13) of that day will be applied also, one supposes, not just to the teaching and receiving of doctrine, but to every aspect of our *"work"* (3:14-15) – that is, *"to what we have done in the body, whether good or evil* (2 Co 5:10).

To some, the fire of the Judgment Seat of Christ will come as a wrathful expression of God's judgment upon their carnal lives. To others, the same fire will be a brilliant light, guiding them into the splendours of their Lord's reward. To those whose lives produced only dross, that fire will be a dreadful devouring thing (He 12:28-29); but to those whose hearts were already ablaze in the Spirit (Ro 12:11), the flames of the bema will be simply a more glorious experience of the element in which they rejoiced during their earthly pilgrimage!

## A FIERY JUDGMENT

We have seen that the *"foundation"* represents Christ; that the *"work"* primarily represents sound doctrine, but also faithful stewardship, and the development of true Christian character. What about the *"fire"*? What does that mean? It is a symbol of

- God's presence and majesty, devouring all that is antagonistic to his purpose (Ps 50:3-6).

- The purifying of the saints, so that they will be perfected to minister before the throne of God (Mal 3:2-3; Mt 3:11-12).

- The divine jealousy that will expose all that we have loved more than we ought, and will purge out of us that spiritual betrayal (De 4:24).

- The Lord's acceptance of all that we have wrought that is pleasing in his sight (Le 9:24; 2 Ch 7:1).

- The ruthless destruction of all that we have wrought by our own hands, independently of God, so that only what Christ himself has built into us and through us will remain (Jn 15:1-6; He 12:27-29; and cp. also 10:30-31).

## FLAMMABLE AND NON-FLAMMABLE

The *"gold, silver, and precious gems"* (3:12) are symbols of those things in us that are the work and gift of God; while the *"wood, hay, and stubble"* speak of the products of unaided human labour. The former were done to please God; the latter, to please men. The former will abide the fire – indeed, will be purified and enhanced by it; but the latter will vanish without a trace.

Notice also that gems are a gift of God, which men can only dig up; but people cultivate wood and hay. The first are rare, the second bountiful. The first signify works done by faith, the second, the produce of toil and sweat.

We could summarise the fire of that day as –

- the fire that *reveals* (He 4:13; Re 1:14; 2:18,23); and

- the fire that *purifies* (Mal 3:2; 1 Pe 1:7; Ps 12:6; Ez 22:18-22; Zc 13:9).

The real character of each Christian's life and service will be swiftly and irresistibly revealed. One simple test will suffice (2 Co 5:10) – works that are *"good"* will be non-flammable; works that are *"evil"* will be at once consumed. Thus the destructibility and indestructibility of each person's work will instantly reveal either its true worth, or its worthlessness. Surely, then, those who are wise will heed the admonition of the apostle John –

> *Little children, abide in him, so that when he appears we may have confidence and not shrink from him shamefully when he comes.* (1 Jn 2:28, ESV)

## THE CHURCH IS A TEMPLE

See *1 Corinthians 3:16-20*; and also the parallel passage in *2 Corinthians 6: 14-20*.

In both those passages, the *"you"* in Greek is plural; that is, he is speaking to the congregation as a whole, not to individuals. For that reason, some scholars prefer to restrict the idea of the "temple" to a collective meaning, as if the church alone, in its entirety, is intended. Others reckon that its meaning may rightly be extended to include each individual Christian, which seems to me to be the better reading. In that case, both the whole church and each person are temples of the Holy Spirit, and each of us, along with the church, and as part of the church, will have to undergo the Judgment seat of Christ on that Day. [23]

## FOUR RULES

Finally, in this part of his letter, Paul puts to the Corinthians a fourfold *personal appeal* (see 4:1-21) -

- *"Do not pronounce judgment before the time"* (vs. 1-5)

- *"Nothing beyond what is written"* (vs. 6-7)

- *"We are fools for the sake of Christ"* (vs. 8-13)

- *"I appeal to you: be imitators of me!"* (vs. 14-21).

He reckons that application of those rules to everyone in the church will be a good cure for their factional squabbles, and will help to bring them into true unity and fellowship together.

---

[23]  For a more comprehensive study of what that Judgment will mean, see my book *When the Trumpet Sounds*, Chapter Nine, *The Bema*; Vision Publishing, Ramona, CA.

## FIVE

# DEALING WITH INCEST

See *1 Corinthians 5:1-13*.

One of the tragic characters of ancient Rome, a contemporary of the apostle Paul, was the stoic philosopher Seneca. He began his public life as an adviser and tutor to the emperor Nero, but in later life Seneca angered the emperor and was ordered to commit suicide, which he did by cutting open several veins. He died widely famous for his many plays, treatises, and letters, of which a great number still survive. In one of his dramas a young man, Hippolytus, is horrified to discover that his stepmother Phaedra has erotic designs upon him. He cries out -

> Almighty God!
> God of all gods! Canst thou hear things so foul
> And not be moved? Canst see – and not be moved?
> For what cause shall thy sky be rent with thunder
> If no cloud dims it now? Let ruin wreck
> The firmament, and black night hide the day!
> Let stars run back and all their courses turn
> Into confusion. Thou too, king of stars,
> Lord Sun, resplendent ... Wilt thou
> Not veil thy light and flee into darkness?
> Ruler of gods in heaven and men on earth,
> Why is thy hand not armed, will not thy torch
> Of triple fire set all the world ablaze? [24]

---

(24)   Phaedra, *Act Two*; tr. by E. F. Watling; Penguin Books, London, 1970; pg. 125.

We are left in no doubt about the horror the crime of incest aroused among the Romans! We may say then that incest is

## A UNIVERSAL CRIME (5:1-2 )

The man was committing incest with his stepmother, who, since Paul speaks no indictment against her, was probably a pagan. Had she been a Christian she too would have been thrown out of the church, as her Christian lover was. She may have been a young woman, nearly his own age; or perhaps the relationship was based on the craving that older women sometimes have for young men; or perhaps the crime was provoked by the man's hunger for a mother-replacement. Nonetheless, it was repugnant both inside and outside the church.

Few societies have tolerated incest. It was strictly proscribed under Roman law, and also by the Jews (Le 18:8). Hence Paul was angered at the ill reputation the church would gain, if word of the incest reached the outside world (vs. 1). Yet the Corinthians were *"proud"* of this behaviour! (vs. 2). How is it they were not ashamed? Probably, they had a distorted view of Christian liberty, based on adopting some variation of the antinomian heresy, such as Paul had to rebuke also in his letter to the *Romans* (6:1). [25]

---

(25) "Antinomian" means "against law". It describes people who believe that faith in Christ alone, without obedience to any moral law, is sufficient for salvation. In its corrupt form, it left people free to practise sin, while arguing that in this way the grace of God was magnified. Paul allowed that the theory was partly correct – we are indeed freed from the law – but that it failed, because it forgot that anyone who turns to Christ must seek not only *pardon* of sin, but also *freedom* from it. Like Jesus himself, they must *"love righteousness, but hate iniquity"* (He 1:9). One cannot at the same time express faith in Christ for righteousness while eagerly embracing unrighteousness.

Perhaps as many as 10% of families in our own society have some experience of incest. [26] Current theory says there are 5 common causes – [27]

*(1)* Poor relationships and/or emotional support.

*(2)* Poor communications (especially about sex).

- This can be a factor in religious homes, where there may be a strong taboo about discussing such matters, which in turn may cause people to seek sexual satisfaction only within the "safety" of the family, rather than risk the unknown in the outside world.

*(3)* Male chauvinism and/or dominance.

- This too can be found in some Christian homes, where the men may feel that they have a divine right to control the women in the house.

*(4)* A child victim of incest may continue the pattern in his/her own adult life.

*(5)* Emotional immaturity and poor impulse control in the perpetrator.

No matter what the cause, for a Christian, sexual desire must be focussed upon one's spouse, and no other. This is a matter of self-discipline, in the grace of God.

Virgil (1st century B.C.) is universally recognised as the greatest of the Latin poets. In his renowned poetic treatise on rural life he wrote –

> Unless you make unceasing war on weeds,
> And scare the birds, and check the leafy shade,

---

(26)  From a report that I no longer have in my files.

(27)  Again, I have lost the source of this information.

> And duly pray for rain, in vain, alas,
> Will you admire your neighbour's ample store
> And shake the oak your hunger to assuage.
>
> It is a law of fate
> That all things tend to slip back and grow worse;
> As when a man, who hardly rows his skiff
> Against the current, if he once relax,
> Is carried headlong down the stream again. [28]

In the same way, the tendency to sin must be steadily resisted, in the grace and strength of Christ. Those who neglect to cultivate their salvation, to make full use daily of the means of grace the Father has given us, may find themselves facing a severe penalty (He 2:1-3).

What should you do if you encounter a case of incest? Paul's approach may still be valid in the case of the perpetrator – dismiss him or her from the church! But probably caution is demanded. We live in a different world, where laws against defamation, and the like, are strict, and carry heavy penalties. The same is true of the victim(s). Be careful how you handle them. Be wary of offering amateur advice. Probably the wiser course is to refer the matter to an expert.

Few pastors, and even fewer lay people, are equipped to handle such cases, and amateurs (including pastors practising pop-psychology) have sometimes done much harm to the very people they were hoping to help. Public scandal has been caused, and pastors in Australia, New Zealand, the USA, and other countries have been hauled into court to answer charges of negligence or malfeasance in

---

(28)   The Georgics, Book One; tr. by K. R. Mackenzie; Folio Society, London, 1969; pg. 18-19.

connection with failed attempts to handle incest cases without calling upon expert help.

I find it difficult to sympathise with them. They should not have arrogantly supposed themselves able, without sufficient training or expertise, to handle such tangled problems wisely and well.

Remember, too, that in many countries today the law *requires* counsellors to report a case of incest to the relevant government authority when minors are involved. Note also that Paul, as a method of combating incest, did not advocate *counselling*, but *action!* – that is, the first responsibility of the church was to *itself*, to protect its own purity, and only then to search for some way to help the offending parties.

## HANDED OVER TO SATAN (5:3-5)

The phrase *"handed over to Satan"* could refer to the Roman public prosecutor (the word *"satan"* had a wide meaning in Hebrew, referring to any kind of adversary; cp. 2 Sa 19:22). If this is the meaning, then Paul was using a colourful way of telling the church to hand the offenders over to the police, to be tried in court, and punished by the secular authorities.

However, since he was writing to a Greek church (not a Jewish one), it seems more likely that he intended the Greek meaning, which is simply, the devil. In this case, it would imply making the man vulnerable to some kind of satanic attack, probably by removing him from the congregation. Or, to use a more formal term, it was a dramatic way of ordering them to excommunicate him, banning him from their public assemblies.

The purpose, of course, was not crass vengeance, but rather to bring him to repentance. Which raises the question: is the same action possible today? Can we, or should we, *"hand people over to Satan"*, to teach them not to blaspheme, and to walk in holiness? That would depend upon what action is contemplated. If the idea is that one person can actually place another in the devil's hands, to inflict whatever harm he pleases, then I would say, absurd! But if the intended meaning is nothing more than to exclude someone from the church, then of course, if there is sufficient reason, it is still appropriate to do so. Such a person, removed from the spiritual protection the church provides, is inescapably exposed to satanic attack. How far the devil can go, is something only the Lord can decree (Jb 1:12; and cp. Jn 19:11).

Again, because of the possibility of the church being charged with some form of libel or defamation by an angry excommunicate, discretion is needed. Be wary of public statements from the pulpit, or any public dissemination of the affair. Nonetheless, some action *must* be taken to remove incest from the church, for scripture denounces it as a sin that cannot be tolerated.

## CLEANSE THE CHURCH (5:6-13)

Notice that Paul 6 times commands the Corinthians to cast the offender out of the church (vs. 2b, 5a, 7a, 11a, 11c, 13). We tend to major on the *size* of each church; Paul was more concerned about its *holiness*, [29] because only a little

---

(29)  There is here a perplexing tension. It would be foolish to place any limit on the size to which a church can grow, yet it can hardly be denied that the New Testament pictures mostly small churches, and the descriptions it gives of the local church, and the commands it speaks, seem to be fully workable only in such smaller churches. The kinds of disciplines and discipleship required by the New Testament are hardly achievable in a large congregation. Shall we then forbid big churches and permit only small ones? That seems ridiculous. I cannot discuss this problem any further here; but let me say at least this: whether one is dealing with a large congregation or one that is small, the ideal of holiness must still be earnestly striven for.

corruption is enough to spoil a whole loaf (vs. 6,7); which at once brings Paul an opportunity to point to Christ (vs. 7b, 8). How typical this was of the great apostle! No matter what theme he was discussing, always he saw something there that revealed some facet of the gospel, or, better, of Christ himself. For Paul, every situation was an opportunity to preach the riches of Christ!

But, neither can Paul forget that Christ, as our Passover Lamb, was crucified, and therefore demands the highest level of love and loyalty from his people –

> *Let us therefore celebrate the festival, not with the old leaven, the leaven of malice and evil, but with the unleavened bread of sincerity and truth (vs. 7-8).*

And, lest anyone should misunderstand him, he then proscribes a list of sins, including some that would not have been considered morally culpable outside the church (vs. 9-13; and see also 6:9-11, discussed below), for we are called to set the standard of morality that is required by God, not to allow the world to set it for us.

Unfortunately, it is not uncommon to see Christians falling over each other in their rush to ape the fashions of this world, until any separation between the world and the church becomes invisible. Yet, let me add that Christians also need to avoid being foolishly out of step with the surrounding culture. We prove nothing useful by remaining stubbornly old fashioned. So, elsewhere Paul gives two good rules: *Romans 12:18; Philippians 4:5.*

*Illustration.* Once upon a time, just as winter was fixing its chill upon the land, a mouse met a forlorn cat, and, taking a liking for her, invited puss to share her home. The two unusual friends at once started working together to put up a store of food for winter, and after much toil managed to fill a jar with rich, meaty fat. To protect their food from robbers, and perhaps from each other, they decided to hide it inside a church cupboard. But going to church, as the mouse would soon discover, was no remedy for the folly of keeping bad companions.

As the days grew darker and colder, the cat began to crave some of the tasty fat. She told the mouse that she was godmother to a new kitten, and had to go to the church for the christening. Upon arriving at the church, without a scruple of conscience, the cat went straight to the jar and licked off the top layer of fat. Later, when the mouse politely enquired the new kitten's name, puss told her that it had been called *Skin-off*.

Since the scheme had worked so well, the cat repeated it a month later, this time telling her friend that the kitten's name was *Half-gone*. The mouse was suspicious, but dared not say anything, not even when the following month the cat again attended a "christening" and told her friend that the baby was called *All-gone*.

The winter advanced still further, and since their normal food supply was now exhausted, the mouse went herself to the church to retrieve the jar. How grieved she was to find it quite empty! She knew now why the pretended kittens had such strange names, and rushing home she cast aside all caution and began to berate the cat most bitterly. But puss was hungry again, and finding nothing else in the larder she pounced upon the mouse and ate her up instead. [30]

---

(30)  *Cat and Mouse in Partnership*, from The Fairy Tales of the Brothers Grimm. I have shortened the story. Someone borrowed my copy of the book, and failed to return it, so I cannot provide any further details.

So will it happen to all who make the ungodly their companions without discretion, or who invite sin to dwell with them.

I do not mean that Christians can have *no* association with unbelievers, for, as Paul said, that would mean altogether going out of the world (1 Co 5:10). Nonetheless, believers and unbelievers seldom make good partners, and Christians who are wise will as far as possible avoid close partnerships with the ungodly.

*SIX*

# ON GOING TO LAW

The first man in history to have the epithet *"great"* attached to his name was Alexander the Great, of Macedon (B.C. 356-323). The title was linked with his name about a century after his death by the Roman playwright, Plautus. Since then it has been given to hardly more than 100 people across many different lands. Two monarchs who lived before the time of Alexander – Cyrus I, and Darius I – had the honorific added to their names by later writers, and it has also been granted to three women: Gertrude the Great (a nun); Matilda the Great (ruler of Tuscany); and Catherine the Great (empress of Russia). Others have been awarded the title briefly, but it was soon dropped after their death.

Here is some good news! God wants to add such praise to *all* his saints, so that we might be pronounced *"great in the kingdom of God"*, and Paul tells us what kind of people we need to be to gain this honour! His demands are difficult, and I wonder if any of us truly deserve any sort of honorific!

## BE WARY OF THE LAW (6:1-9A)

*"How dare you go to court!"* he cries, in a strong, emphatic, passionate protest at what he considers scandalous behaviour. It does not seem probable that Paul is prohibiting *all* legal action between Christians, since he has already shown (Ch. 5) that the church must act sternly against criminal turpitude. Rather, his protest seems to be primarily against resorting to the law to resolve personal quarrels, or property disputes, or merely to assert some presumed *"right"*.

Paul's grounds for indicting such behaviour are –

- ***We shall judge the world*** (vs. 2) – which was a common teaching among Jewish apocalyptists –

  The souls of the just are in God's hands, and torment shall not touch them … In the moment of God's coming to them they will kindle into flame, like sparks that sweep through stubble; they will be judges and rulers over the nations of the world, and the Lord will be their king for ever and ever. [31]

  When the congregation of the righteous shall appear, sinners shall be judged for their sins, they shall be driven from the face of the earth … (The) wicked ones will be driven from the presence of the righteous and the elect, and from that time, those who possess the earth will neither be rulers nor princes … At that moment, kings and rulers shall perish, (for) they shall be delivered into the hands of the righteous and holy ones … You righteous ones, fear not the sinners! For the Lord will again deliver them into your hands, so that you may carry out against them anything that you desire. [32]

---

(31)  Wisdom 3:8.

(32)  Enoch 38:1, 3-5; 95:3. "Enoch" is an apocalyptic work, dated c. 150 B.C. It is quoted directly by the apostle Jude, and was obviously familiar to most of the other apostles, since its teaching influenced the shape of some of the major doctrines of the New Testament. It was highly regarded by many of the Apostolic and Church Fathers. (Tr. by E. Isaac; "The Old Testament Pseudepigrapha," ed. J. H. Charlesworth; Doubleday & Co, New York; 1983; Vol. One, *in loc.*)

- *We shall judge the angels* (vs. 3) which includes both good and evil heavenly beings; thus showing the extraordinary elevation that will be ours in Christ on that day.

- *Surely there is enough wisdom in the church* to enable justice to be done among its members? Should we not rather trust the godly counsel of Spirit-filled saints, than the worldly knowledge of secular judges? (vs. 4-5)

- *It is outrageous for "brothers"* (who should be bound together in mutual love) to quarrel in front of unbelievers (vs.6).

- *A true Christian would rather be defrauded* than bring any hurt or pain to a fellow believer (vs. 7-8).

- *Their actions were placing their salvation in jeopardy* (vs. 9)

One of the richest men in the USA in the latter part of the 19th century was Russell Sage. He once called upon his lawyer to discuss a law suit. Sage laid the evidence before the barrister, who was delighted: "This case is iron-clad;" he chortled, "we can't possibly lose!" Whereupon Sage replied: "Then we will not go to court, for what I just gave you was my opponent's argument!" (33)

When Christians go to court against each other, merely to defend some personal interest, they place themselves at the mercy of their real enemy, the devil.

---

(33)   The Book of Anecdotes, ed. by Clifton Fadiman; Little, Brown and Co., Boston; 1985; *in loc.*

Someone may be feeling that Paul showed too much pious zeal in his extraordinary demand, *"Why not rather suffer wrong? Why not rather be defrauded?"* (vs. 7) Yet Jesus taught much the same.

There was the time when someone came up to Jesus and demanded, *"Teacher, tell my brother to divide our inheritance with me!"* But Jesus refused to get involved, and instead rebuked the fellow for being greedy!

Or, there was the time when Jesus made an even more arresting statement –

> *Watch yourselves! "If a believer sins, correct him. If he changes the way he thinks and acts, forgive him. Even if he wrongs you seven times in one day and comes back to you seven times and says that he is sorry, forgive him."* (Lu 17:2-4, GW)

Imagine that! Someone comes up and biffs you. While you are still reeling, he begs you to forgive him, saying, "I don't know what came over me!" Being a good Christian, you pull yourself together, squash your resentment, and say that, yes, you do indeed forgive him. An hour later, he biffs you again, without reason or excuse. This time, agreeing to overlook his violence is more difficult. An hour later – wham! It happens again. Now you find it nearly impossible to say with Portia that "the quality of mercy is not strained", for now it is truly strained, and no longer "droppeth as the gentle rain from heaven." [34] Then a fourth time he strikes, and a fifth, sixth, and seventh – every hour on the hour – and each time begging you to pardon his offence. And all in the same day!

---

(34) William Shakespeare, *The Merchant of Venice*, Act IV, scene i.

Of course, since you are a true Christian, I know that if you were the victim, you would freely, heartily, and without hesitation forgive him for every blow.

Or would you? Indeed, can anyone really meet such a demand? Can I reach it? Happily, I've never been put to such a test, and perhaps if I were, the Lord would give grace enough to reach such lofty heights of patience, forbearance, and love.

Jesus did (23:34). [35] And we should all measure our attitudes and behaviour against his example, which we are expected to follow (1 Pe 2:21).

Too often, however, Christians show the same possessive grip on worldly goods, the same grasping self-assertiveness, the same vindictiveness and jealousy, the same rush to defend themselves, as the ungodly do. If any of us have been fouled by such things, we should repent and yield ourselves to the transforming grace of Christ.

---

(35)   It is interesting that Luke, who alone records the saying about forgiving seven times, is also the only evangelist who records Christ asking the Father to pardon those who were nailing him to the cross.

*SEVEN*

# ON BEING CHASTE

See *1Corinthians* 6:9b-20.

Paul begins his remarks here with a description of

## THOSE WHO CANNOT ENTER HEAVEN (6:9B,10)

Note the five categories of sin that will exclude the *"wicked"* from heaven:

- *moral crimes* (sexual immorality; adultery)

- *religious crimes* (idolatry; temple prostitution)

- *property crimes* (theft, fraud)

- social crimes (slander)

- *indulgent crimes* (greed, inebriation)

Paul had apparently gained his greatest success among the lower strata of Corinthian society (vs. 11a; and cp. also 1:26-28). Yet not exclusively, for there were some in the church who were well-off (11:20-22). Some of the people owned their own homes, and were affluent, while others *"had nothing"*; some were slaves, some were free (7:20-21). It was a very cosmopolitan community, and Paul yearned for it to display the beauty of the gospel, and of Christ, by coming together in real love.

Nonetheless, with such a congregation, of which so many born amongst the worst segments of society, and raised in appalling circumstances, we might think, "Here is a counsellor's paradise! Enough work to keep the finest psychiatrist going for years!" Yet surprisingly, Paul gives not a hint that he thought they must have horrible relational and emotional problems that nothing less than months, if not decades, of counselling would be needed to remedy. Rather, he shows an almost careless dismissal of all their paranoias, phobias, fears, enslavements, habits, lusts, traumas, and dysfunctional temperaments. Decisively, he applies one quick remedy to the whole gamut of human hang-ups; he simply tells them –

## WHAT GOD HAS MADE US (6:11)

### *"YOU WERE WASHED"*

This is in the **middle** voice, which in grammar shows human initiative; that is, before they were *"washed"* they themselves had taken action – probably through presenting themselves for baptism.

### *"YOU WERE SANCTIFIED; YOU WERE JUSTIFIED"*

These are in the **passive** voice, which shows the divinely wrought consequences of their earlier decision (to embrace the gospel and to be baptised).

### *SHALL WE THEN SIN? (6:12-14)*

If we are already justified and sanctified, surely sin can no longer affect us? That is the attitude adopted by many, if not all, the people in the church at Corinth (5:2a), and they supported their case by a popular saying, which Paul quotes twice: *"All things are lawful for me!"* (6:12)

There was some truth in that saying; for there is indeed no law confronting us (with a penalty attached) that proscribes any kind of behaviour. After all, we are now treated by God as those who are *"dead"* in Christ, which means that we are, in a sense, free to do anything! But in practice, he says, we dare not fall into that antinomian trap. So he adds three qualifications, based upon -

## RELATIONSHIP

To encourage holiness in life he calls upon our relationship with Christ, which has four different aspects –

- the hope of resurrection (vs. 14)
- the fact of our spiritual union (vs. 17)
- the indwelling Spirit (vs. 19)
- the price that was paid (vs. 20a)

Anyone who has truly experienced the power of his resurrection, been brought into spiritual union with Christ by the new birth, enjoys the renewing grace of his indwelling Spirit, and understands the awful cost of sin, cannot help but hate it, and resolve to be rid of it.

## EXPEDIENCY

Everything may be *lawful*, but not everything is *beneficial*; if it hurts you, it is foolish to do it. Only a madman perseveres in destructive behaviour simply to assert some so-called *"liberty"*. And that is the case of those who plead Christian liberty as an excuse for continued sin. Wilful and ongoing sin gradually deadens the voice of conscience, until all sense of shame vanishes and the sinner supposes that he or she can escape judgment. The emperor Nero, for example, known to history as a monster of depravity and cruelty, void of any moral sense or tenderness, did not begin that way –

> As a further guarantee of his virtuous intentions, he promised to model his rule on the principles laid down by Augustus, and never missed an opportunity of being generous or merciful, or of showing what a good companion he was. He lowered, if he could not abolish, some of the heavier taxes . . . If asked to sign the usual execution order for a felon, he

> would sigh: "Ah, how I wish that I had never learned to write!" He seldom forgot a face, and would greet men of whatever rank by name without a moment's hesitation. Once, when the Senate passed a vote of thanks to him, he answered: "Wait until I deserve them!" . . . (When he attended the gladiatorial shows) no one was allowed to be killed during the combats, not even criminals. [36]

From that high moral ground, how terribly the young Nero fell, plunging into growing debauchery, until every fine emotion was crushed. Eventually the senate and the army rebelled against him, and he was driven off the throne, saving himself from public execution only by commanding his valet to kill him.

His fate should be a warning to all who carelessly think that sin has no consequences.

## FREEDOM

Everything may be lawful, said Paul, but he refused to be the slave of anything; therefore,

- although his body may need *food*, he declined to fall into bondage to gluttony; and

- although his body may need **sex**, he declined to become a compulsive and helpless fornicator.

Surely, it is absurd to lose Christian liberty by becoming enslaved through the very act of using that liberty! Are we

---

[36]   Suetonius, The Twelve Caesars, "Nero"; tr. Robert Graves; Folio Society, London, 1964; pg. 215, 216.

not called to an exercise of strength and courage? (1 Co 15:58; 16:13) -

> It's easy to cry that you're beaten – and die;
> It's easy to crawfish and crawl;
> But to fight and to fight when hope's out of sight –
> Why, that's the best game of them all!
> And though you come out of each gruelling bout
> All broken and beaten and scarred,
> Just have one more try – it's dead easy to die,
> It's the keeping-on-living that's hard! [37]

But that's just what Christians do! They keep on living. They keep on trying. Further, we are called *"more than conquerors"* in Christ! So he concludes that we should **shun all harlotry**, for this wickedly involves Christ himself in sin (vs. 15, 16). The very thought horrifies Paul. He sees it as taking the claim of Christian liberty to a foul extreme. Yet I have heard two or three pastors do just that. They argued that God, because they had urgent and special needs, had given them a special dispensation for adultery. They reckoned they were free to ignore both scripture and God's standard moral law. For such folly they suffered severely.

In the end, there are no excuses, for the same quality of holiness is demanded from everyone in the church, no matter what their office or calling.

So Paul demands that Christians must shun all immorality, for this is an insane crime, not only against God, but against oneself (vs. 18).

Why is that so? Probably, it is because sexual immorality shatters the real nature and purpose of the body more than

---

(37) Robert Service, The Quitter, st. three; The Best of Robert Service; Dodd, Mead & Co., New York; 1953; pg. 78.

any other sin. It ravages the mystery of our construction in the *"image and likeness"* of God. Hence we should in every way honour God, not just in the spirit, but also *"with our bodies"* (vs. 19-20).

One of the great artists of the Italian Renaissance was the Florentine sculptor Donatello (1386-1466). On one occasion he made for a church a wooden Crucifix over which he took extraordinary pains -

> When he had finished it, convinced that he had produced a very rare work, he asked his close friend, Filippo Brunelleschi, for his opinion. But Filippo, in view of what he had already been told by Donatello, was expecting to be shown something far better; and when he saw what it was he merely smiled to himself. At this Donatello begged him for the sake of their friendship to say what he thought of it. So Filippo, being always ready to oblige, answered that it seemed to him that Donatello had put on the cross the body of a peasant, not the body of Jesus Christ, which was most delicate and in every part the most perfect human form ever created. Finding that instead of being praised, as he had hoped, he was being criticised, and more sharply than he could ever have imagined, Donatello retorted: "If it was as easy to make something as it is to criticise, my Christ would really look to you like Christ. So you get some wood and try to make one yourself."

> Without another word, Filippo returned home and secretly started work on a Crucifix, determined to vindicate his own judgment by surpassing Donatello; and after several months he brought it to perfection. Then one morning

he asked Donatello to have dinner with him, and Donatello accepted. On their way to Filippo's house they came to the Old Market, where Filippo bought a few things and gave them to Donatello, saying: "Take these home and wait for me. I shall be along in a moment."

So Donatello went on ahead into the house, and going into the hall he saw, placed in a good light, Filippo's Crucifix. He paused to study it and found it so perfect that he was completely overwhelmed and dropped his hands in astonishment; whereupon his apron fell and the eggs, the cheeses, and the rest of the shopping tumbled to the floor and everything was broken into pieces. He was still standing there in amazement, looking as if he had lost his wits, when Filippo came up and said laughingly:

"What's your design, Donatello? What are we going to eat now that you've broken everything?"

"Myself," Donatello answered, "I've had my share for this morning. If you want yours, you take it. But no more please. Your job is making Christs and mine is making peasants." [38]

What shape is your life taking – that of Christ, or something far less?

---

[38]   Georgio Vasari (1511-1574), Lives of the Artists, *Life of Donatello*; tr. George Bull, Folio Society, London, 1993; Vol. One (of three volumes) pg. 176-177. Brunelleschi's wooden sculpture, carved *circa* 1412, still exists in Florence.

## EIGHT

# MUZZLING AN OX

See *1 Corinthians 9:1-10:13*.

One of the greatest citizens of ancient Corinth was the cynic philosopher Diogenes (died 323 B.C.) He practised extreme self-denial, and contented himself with a large clay tub as his only home. When Alexander the Great had been elected to take his murdered father's place as the Supreme Commander of the Greek League, he went on a tour to receive the well wishes and congratulations of the nation's rulers. He arrived at Corinth and noticed that Diogenes was missing from the parade of dignitaries. So he went looking for the philosopher, and found him lying in the sun beside his barrel. Alexander extended a courteous greeting to Diogenes, and then asked if he could do anything for him. "Yes," replied the still reclining teacher, "please stand aside; you are blocking the sun!" The king's retinue roared with laughter, mocking the foolish man who could have asked for so much, but wanted so little. But Alexander said, "If I were not Alexander, I would choose to be Diogenes!"

There is indeed much to be said for removing anything that stands between you and the blazing sun of the truth that is in Christ! (10:1) Hence Paul continues, in his letter to the church at Corinth, to persuade them to clear away all that might block them from the light of Christ. He does this by pressing on with his debate about the real nature of Christian freedom. He asserts his *rights* and privileges in various areas, but then counterbalances that with the *duty* he has to proclaim Christ. The key verse is *9:19* — *"Although I am free, and call no man master, yet I make myself a slave to all so that I may win some to Christ."*

In the matter of choosing between rights and duties, Paul always elects *duty* over *privilege*. But it is not all *duty*. There is also a reward to gain (9:24-26). If Paul labours, he does so with an eye on the prize offered him by God. It is not his only reason for serving the Lord, but has a high importance. That leads him to a central passage (10:1-13), which he introduces with an interesting phrase: *"I do not want you to be ignorant."* The same expression is found in *12:1; Romans 11:25; 2 Corinthians 1:8;* and *1 Thessalonians 4:13.* In each place the idea is, "this is an important item, yet one that is often overlooked." In our present text, the idea that is often overlooked is that of Israel as a *"type"* of the church (vs. 6, 11), where Paul finds some striking lessons –

## A GLORIOUS PROMISE

How wonderful were God's promises to Israel! See the extravagance of just one passage, *Deuteronomy 28:1-14.* But why such abundant promises? They demonstrate that God's purpose is always to bring his people into *"Canaan"* (Ex 3:7-8a). The same principle is at work in the church today, for *"Canaan"* is a type of living in the kingdom of God.

But first there are enemies to overcome. For Israel, those enemies were Egypt, the wilderness, and the local inhabitants (Ex 3:8b); which for us represent the world, the flesh, the devil. Israel failed to master its foes and to possess the land. What about us? That is the very issue that led Paul to give

# A PASSIONATE WARNING

## *THEY CHOSE DISUNITY INSTEAD OF UNITY*

See *verses 1-5*. Note the three occurrences of the word *"supernatural"* [39], followed by the tragic, *"nevertheless"*. They had the blood, the sea, the cloud, the manna, the stream, the miracles, the Rock – surely they were entitled to think that God was approving them? Instead, God rejected them. Nothing has changed. People still make the mistake of supposing that the presence of miracles is a guarantee of divine favour. They may indeed be such a sign. But in the end, if more important principles are violated, they count for nothing (cp. 13:2).

We may also learn this: God has a *collective*, not just an *individual* purpose. That is, we can be **individually** saved, yet **collectively** rejected; or, **you** may be personally secure in Christ, yet your local **church** may be under the judgment of God. The Lord may be answering **individual** prayers, and granting miracles in response to personal faith, yet still be planning to chastise his **church**.

God wants to bring his **church**, the entire company of his people, into kingdom power. It is not enough just to look after **yourself**; each of us must also have a deep concern for the **Body** (that is, the local church). We dare not remain content just to get our own prayers answered; for if the church falls, we may well fall with it – just as those very Israelites who were enjoying the miracles in the wilderness also died there!

---

(39) The Greek word is *pneumatikos*, which means ethereal, spiritual, supernatural.

## THEY CHOSE COMFORT INSTEAD OF CONFLICT

They decided that feasting and revelry were more appealing than Moses' command to go on and to go in (vs. 7; De 1:19-21).

So they stayed 38 years at *Kadesh-Barnea*, which was an oasis in the Negev desert, fed by perpetual brooks, some 50 miles inland from the Mediterranean Sea. It was called *"Kadesh"* = *"Holy"*, because it was deemed a miracle of God that such an abundant flow should spring out of the seared wilderness, seemingly from no ordinary watery source. Therefore it was a good place to stay, and indeed, God did bless them there – he gave them manna, a sweet spring of water, and preservation (De 8:4; 29:5; Ne 9:21).

Yet in the end, because they were content with an oasis rather than the whole land, they were doomed to perish in that very desert which had seemed to be the source of their supply.

Just like those Israelites, many Christians are content either **(a)** for their church to remain a self-contained oasis, exercising no transforming influence on the surrounding *"desert"*; or, **(b)** to obtain enough of God's favour to meet their basic needs, while stifling any zeal to seize the higher and better promise.

Don't be like they; resolve to have *"Canaan"*! Press on into all the fullness God has appointed us to obtain in Christ!

## THEY CHOSE THE FLESH INSTEAD OF THE SPIRIT

They got out of Egypt; but Egypt did not get out of them (vs. 8).

We never can possess the kingdom until we are extricated from the ways and motives of the world. We are called to be a separated people (2 Co 6:14-18; and notice the glorious promises God offers to those who do *"come out from among them"*).

## THEY CHOSE THE PAST INSTEAD OF THE FUTURE

See *verse 9*, and *Numbers 21:4-6*, and note their yearning for Egypt. We too are prone to cling to the familiar. The unfamiliar, the new, the untried, all are scary, and people would rather stay where they are, and keep on doing what they know. But like an eagle that *"stirs up its nest"* (De 32:11), so the Holy Spirit is always working upon the church, to stir the saints out of their lethargy, to arouse them to higher endeavour, to force them to soar heavenward, instead of hiding safely behind their familiar routines.

We need to get God's new and unique vision, both for our own lives, but more particularly for the church. Notice also in scripture the following principles -

## THE VARIOUS STRATEGIES GOD GAVE ISRAEL

Have you noticed that the Lord seldom if ever repeated a battle plan? Every time Joshua, or David, or any other commander sought God for direction, he gave them a new strategy – the sound of a trumpet; hail stones from heaven; stinging hornets; thunder claps; an ambush laid; a frontal assault; wait for the mulberry leaves to rustle; and so on.

He is a God of infinite variety! Just so, each local church needs to ask God for his particular plan for that church in its own community. Indeed, the Lord may give your church a plan unlike any other he has ever used before! In some ways it is a sad thing to see so many churches that are carbon copies of each other, even though they minister in different places to different groups of people, and within different cultures. There is room, and dire need, for variety, so that what offends some people will reach others. Almost any way of doing church will please some people, while there is no single style of church life that will ever suit everybody.

## THE MEN OF ISSACHAR

When David began to establish himself as king over Israel, many people joined him, including, it is said, 200 chiefs from the tribe of Issachar, all of them men *"who understood the times, and knew what Israel should do"* (1 Ch 12:32). May God give the same *"understanding of our times"* to us, so that we can move wisely in waging war upon the enemy, and in accomplishing the purposes of the Lord. Each local church should seek God for direction about what it should do, and in what manner, even if it takes them in a direction that no other is following.

An important key to doing this successfully lies in the assertion that the men of Issachar knew what Israel should do because they *"understood the times"*. Different times demand different strategies. What works here may not work there. What is successful in one place, may fail dismally in another. Be wise enough to discern the times, trustful enough to hear from God about what you should do, and bold enough to obey!

## THE MESSAGES TO THE SEVEN CHURCHES

When the glorified Christ spoke to the seven churches in the Roman province of Asia, he had a different word for each of them (Re 2:1 ff.). This suggests that today also, for each church in our city he has a special word of rebuke or of counsel, of warning or of promise, and a unique and different strategy for each congregation. We have a duty to discover that divine purpose, and to fulfil it.

# THEY CHOSE SECURITY INSTEAD OF ADVENTURE

The people of Israel grumbled about the enemies that had to be dispossessed; but where there is *"milk and honey"* there must also be *"bulls and bees"*! (vs. 10) So they had to face all those *"ites"* (Ex 3:8; Js 3:10); they could not avoid danger; they were promised no easy path to conquest. Their refusal to accept that reality, their preference for a risk-free, conflict-free life, cost them their promised inheritance. Instead of possessing the land, they perished in the desert.

We too must be prepared for spiritual warfare if we would possess the land of *"milk and honey"*! There is no possession without dispossession! You will enjoy only as much of the promised *"Canaan"* as you are able to wrest from the hands of the enemy.

## NINE

# AT THE TABLE OF THE LORD

See *1 Corinthians 10:14-11:1; 11:17-33.*

At the **Table of the Lord** we can observe -

## CONTINUATION

*"<u>Do this</u> in remembrance of me"* (vs. 24-25)

The testimony of the Church Fathers shows the high importance the early church placed on regularly observing the Eucharist. Without exception, for the first several hundred years, all the extant writings on the matter show the early church celebrating the Eucharist at least *every* Sunday. Here is one example from the middle of the 2nd century, from the writings of *Justin Martyr* (converted *circa* 132, suffered martyrdom *circa* 165, when he was about 65) –

> On the day which is called the day of the sun there is an assembly of all who live in the towns or in the country; and the memoirs of the apostles or the writings of the prophets are read, for as long as time permits. Then the reader ceases, and the president speaks, admonishing us and exhorting us to imitate these excellent examples. Then we arise all together and offer prayers ... both for ourselves and for ... all men everywhere, with all our hearts. ... (Then) we salute each other with a kiss when we have ended the prayers.

> Then is brought to the president of the brethren bread, and a cup of water and wine. And he takes them and offers up praise and glory to the

Father of all things, through the name of his Son and of the Holy Ghost, and gives thanks that we are deemed worthy of these things at his hand. When he has completed the prayers and thanksgiving, all the people present assent by saying *Amen*. ...

When the president has given thanks and all the people have assented, those who are called deacons with us give to those present a portion of the Eucharistic bread and wine and water, and carry it away to those that are absent. ...

We hold our common assembly on the day of the sun, because it is the same day (on which) Jesus Christ our Saviour rose from the dead. [40]

Over the past 200 years some evangelicals have minimised the spiritual value of the Eucharist. Some have virtually eliminated it from their church life; others celebrate it once a month, or once a quarter; others celebrate it only when it is convenient to do so; others make it a mere addendum to a church service, a kind of optional extra; others have replaced it with a different ceremony.

I feel that such practices have led inevitably to spiritual loss in those churches. By contrast, Christ is at the heart of the Eucharist, and a church that truly has the Eucharist at its own heart will be vigorous and fruitful.

---

[40]    Apology, Bk I, ch 65-67; dated c. 150. Taken from Documents of the Christian Church; selected and edited by Henry Bettenson; Oxford University Press, London, 1973; pg. 66, 67.

## CELEBRATION

*"When he had given thanks"* (vs. 24)

Note that Matthew, Mark, and Luke all draw particular attention to Jesus *"giving thanks"* when he celebrated the Passover with his disciples. The Greek verb is *eucharisteo*, and in its noun form it has been used in the church from the earliest times to describe the weekly celebration of the *Lord's Supper*. This indeed is one of the proofs of the resurrection of Christ, for nothing less than an unshakeable certainty that Jesus had conquered death could have enabled the first Christians to take hold of a ceremony that spoke of *death* and turn it into a celebration of *life*! The very Table that should have made them shudder with horror, because it spoke of the dreaded cross, instead filled them with boundless *joy*!

Thus, when we break bread, we too should celebrate –

- our union with Christ in his death and resurrection

- our union with each other in unbreakable love

- the triumph of the church over every foe (vs. 26)

## COMMEMORATION

*"Do this <u>in remembrance</u> of me"* (vs. 24, 25)

Protestants usually see the communion service as an act of *remembrance*; but Roman Catholics (and some others) see it as an actual crucifying of Christ afresh. So the question arises: is this a *table* (of remembrance), or an *altar* (of sacrifice)?

The 16th century Protestant Reformers began calling it the *Table of the Lord*, *The Lord's* Supper, or *Holy Communion*, because they objected to the sacrificial aspects of a *mass* celebrated at an *altar*. [41] Since then, their terminology has been widely adopted by the various Protestant churches especially among evangelicals..

Indeed, even among Roman Catholics, the idea of a *"sacrifice"* did not develop until the 10th century, when the suggestion was first made (and gradually adopted by the Roman Catholic church) that the elements of bread and wine were turned by the priest into the real body and blood of Christ. This became the doctrine of *transubstantiation*, which holds that the elements keep the *appearance* of bread and wine, but take on the *substance* of flesh and blood. Thus, when the bread is broken and the wine drunk, the communicant is presumed to partake of Christ's actual flesh and blood – it becomes both "a sacrifice and a meal", which requires an innate repetition of Calvary at each mass.

Surely though, such claims defy

- **reason**: for they require that every priest in every Catholic church who performs the mass must work an astonishing miracle;

- **natural perception**: for the bread and the wine still carry their natural look, feel, and taste;

- **scripture**: which says that Christ has died *once* for all people, and will never die again; and the clear

---

(41)   "Mass" comes from a Latin word meaning "send" or "dismiss", which was used at the close of the Eucharist, to end the service, and to send ("dismiss") the people home. In the medieval Roman Catholic church, the term "mass" had already replaced the more ancient (and more biblical) term "Eucharist", and it was already closely associated with the idea of the priest making a sacrificial offering at the church altar.

- ***traditions*** of the apostolic church; for not one of the Fathers ever suggested anything other than that the bread and wine are simply symbols of the body and blood of Jesus.

I think we should avoid such unnecessary ideas and keep to the plain teaching of scripture. I think also, that we should follow the example of the early church, and observe the Eucharist regularly (that is, weekly), with all dignity and yet with utmost joy. [42]

## COMMUNICATION

Nonetheless, *"remembrance"* does mean more than merely calling to mind a past event. In Hebrew idiom, it meant *"remember with a view to action"* (Ps 25:6-7, plus many other examples). That is, the Eucharist must be accompanied by either some ***divine*** or ***human*** action or response, or both. We say that **both** are required. But **how** does God act in the Eucharist? And how should **we** act? In the case of the worshipper, scripture looks for a response of trust, joy, obedience, surrender, renewal of vows, reconciliation with God and neighbour, repentance, and faith. But what does God do?

Yet again, we face controversy –

- do the bread and the wine really turn into the flesh and blood of Christ (as *Rome* teaches); [43] or

---

(42)   I use the word "think" here, not because there is any doubt in my mind about the truth of my opinion, but simply because I respect those who hold to a different set of dogmas about the Eucharist.

(43)   The doctrine is called transubstantiation – from two Latin words that mean "changing one substance into another".

- do they convey to us the actual flesh and blood of Christ, while remaining unchanged themselves (as *Luther* taught); [44] or

- do they simply convey to the believer all that the flesh and blood of Christ signify (as *Calvin* argued); or

- are they merely symbols, mementoes of the Cross, but conveying nothing (as *Baptists* and others maintain)?

I think the scriptures require us to reject –

- The magical propositions of Rome.

- Luther's view that the body and blood of Christ are conveyed to us within the bread and cup.

- Calvin's view that only the values of the body and the blood are conveyed to us.

- The mere ritual of the <u>baptistic</u> position.

What then shall we say?

The truth seems rather to be somewhere between the *Lutheran* and *Calvinist* positions; which means that the eucharist is a <u>sacrament</u> – that is, a channel through which the grace of God flows to the believer. Therefore, I see the bread and the wine as symbols of the real presence and power of Christ, who acts through them to fill the believing recipient with himself.

This grace can be found in other ways, but it is particularly and powerfully available through the bread and the cup of

---

(44)   This doctrine is called consubstantiation, from two Latin words that mean "together" and "substance" – hence the doctrine that, after the consecration of the bread and wine at the Eucharist, the substance of those elements dwells side by side with the substance of the body and blood of Christ.

the Eucharist. So I have no objection to calling the Eucharist a "sacrament", because, in my opinion, scripture teaches that every person who breaks bread and drinks the cup in repentant faith will receive a communication of divine grace. This contrasts with those who prefer the term "ordinance", because to them the Eucharist is no more than a celebration in memory of the passion of Christ. They do not expect any flow of grace into those who share the Lord's Table.

Let us take up this idea of a *sacrament* –.

## A SACRAMENT

"Sacrament" comes from the Latin translation of the Greek word *musterion*, a "mystery", which meant something that is secret until it is revealed to an initiate. In the religious world, *musterion* meant a revealed secret that would bring a person into an intimate union with some god or goddess.

This was usually accomplished by participation in some secret rite or ceremony, and it was often linked with concepts of death, resurrection, and a hope of gaining immortality.

So *musterion* lent itself readily to use in the gospel, and occurs in the NT at least 30 times, with diverse connections. Always, however, there is an underlying idea that when the mystery of Christ is revealed to a believing heart, the immediate result will be an inflow of the grace and power of God.

So it is not surprising that very early in church history it became increasingly connected to the Eucharist. This was especially true after *musterion* came into Latin as *sacramentum*.

Now *sacramentum* had more the sense of a "sacred oath" of loyalty. But that made it even better fitted for the Eucharist, for there, at the Lord's Table, we encounter, and partake of the "sacred" life of Christ and proclaim him Lord.

So *sacramentum* came into English as "sacrament", and is used to describe both the Eucharist and water baptism, which are channels of divine grace to the believer.

Yet there are times in the NT when *musterion* does have more the sense of the English word "mystery" – that is, something that cannot be explained and that baffles our understanding. Indeed, the original meaning of the Greek word was "shut your mouth"! Thus Paul says in one place, *"Beyond all question, the mystery of our religion is great, that God appeared in a human body ..."* (1 Ti 3:16). Likewise, we cannot penetrate the "mystery" of how we partake of Christ through the bread and the cup – but we can believe it!

How do we know that there is such a release of life and power in the Eucharist? We can infer it from the warning to *"examine"* ourselves carefully before we eat and drink (see vs. 28). But why must we so carefully examine ourselves before we dare to take the bread and the cup? Because here, at the Lord's Table there is –

## CONFRONTATION

Paul warns communicants, before they take the bread and the wine, to *"examine themselves"* (vs. 28). Why is this self-scrutiny so important? See *verses 27, 29, 30-32*. There is the answer! At the Lord's Table we confront either *life* or *death!* Paul makes the astonishing assertion that there is power in this table to **kill** a careless communicant! But if so, then there is abundantly more power to make **alive!** This means, at this table, there is a marvellous quality of **life** waiting to be seized by the hand of faith. Let us then boldly believe, heartily receive, and be fully made whole in the grace and power of Christ our all-conquering Lord!

If this power of death, and of life, is not apparent in the church, if people are neither dying nor living because of the

Eucharist, then it reflects the weakness of the church, not the ineffectiveness of the table. Surely, in preference to a powerless table, we should like our church to know the energy of the early church (see Ac 5:12-13), even if that means terrifying acts of divine judgment (Ac 5:5-11). Whatever its faults may have been, the church in Jerusalem was at least holy enough to provoke the Lord to defend its purity!

## COLLABORATION

So far, I hope I have established three things –

- The Eucharist is more than a mere memorial service.

- Yet it is also less than a repetition of the crucifixion of Christ.

What then?

- It is a powerful means by which the grace of God is communicated – it is a sacrament, built around a commemoration of the Last Supper and of the Passion of Christ.

But now two other questions arise –

- Is the Eucharist affected by the **administrant**?

That is, can we accept the RC position that a sinful priest has no affect upon the efficacy of the Eucharist? To some extent we _must_ do so, because there is no such thing as an altogether pure and faultless priest or pastor. Yet in the end, we Protestants do demand a high standard from all who claim a right to minister to us and among us. Still, one would have to say that even if the administrant were quite wicked, the bread and the wine would remain effective for anyone who receives them with sincerity, humility, and faith.

- Is the Eucharist affected by the **communicant**?

That is, can we accept the RC position that the condition of the communicant has no affect upon the efficacy of the Eucharist? The claim is made that the bread and the wine convey their saving benefits to those who receive them, whatever the state of the recipients, whether wicked or holy. The elements do this, says the Roman church, because of an inherent power that sacraments possess. Again, to some extent we are obliged to agree with this, for if receiving the grace of God depended upon human perfection none of us would ever get even a sip of it!

Yet in the end we cannot allow that grace must be imparted by some law of necessity. There must, at the least, be present in the communicant a genuine measure of repentance and faith.

Catholics sometimes countermand this by pointing to the woman who touched the hem of Jesus' robe, and was healed. They say that just because she touched him, virtue flowed into her, and the same is true of the bread and the wine in the Eucharist.

Yet that claim ignores the many others who touched Jesus and remained unaffected, and it ignores the clear statement in the gospel that the woman came humbly to Jesus, and with earnest expectation of a miracle (Lu 8:42-47).

So, we rightly demand, with the apostle, that those who come to the Table of Christ must do so in two ways –

## WITH GENUINE FAITH

*Without faith, it is impossible to please God!* (He 11:6)

Yet faith must have a focus, and here too, opinions differ.

Some say that the bread and the cup are important only as an aid to remembering the cross and that faith must be directed, not at *them*, but at *Christ* himself and the power of the Spirit.

Without disparaging the value of such faith, we say that the scriptures demand more. Surely Eucharistic faith should focus on the bread and the cup themselves and see in them not merely <u>passive symbols</u> but <u>active channels</u> of the grace and life of Christ. If this is not so, then it is hard to see how they possess any value at all, except as a piece of ritual, which is inconsistent with the way the apostles speak about them.

So we expect to find healing, pardon, freedom, and other treasures of grace as we eat and drink, and to find them in a way that is unique to the Eucharist, because we expect also to partake of Christ himself in the bread and the cup – *"I speak as to sensible people; judge for yourselves what I say. The cup of blessing that we bless, <u>is it not a participation in the blood of Christ</u>? The bread that we break, <u>is it not a participation in the body of Christ</u>?"* (1 Co 10:16, ESV)

Notice here –

*"The cup of blessing that we bless"* – we give thanks for the cup that brings us the blessing of God; and through the cup and the bread, we "participate in the blood and body of Christ". That is, we partake of Christ himself, imbibing his life and grace. But again we stress that this is true only when one eats and drinks with repentance, humility, and, above all, <u>*with faith*</u>.

But note this again — this participation in Christ does not depend upon some magical transformation wrought by a priest, but, in response to each believer's faith; it is wrought by the immanent presence of the Holy spirit, and by the empowering presence of the Word of God.

## IN A WORTHY MANNER

The Eucharist calls for a response of trust, obedience, surrender, and renewal of vows, reconciliation with God and neighbour, and repentance. It should be collaboration between the celebrant and the congregation. It should be a time, as very word means, of **_celebration_** and **_boundless joy_** !

# CONGREGATION

## A PEOPLE EULOGISING

Paul talks about *"the cup of BLESSING that we BLESS"* (10:16). In both places the Greek word is *eulogeo*, from which come our words "eulogy" and "eulogise". The English verb means simply to say nice things about someone. But the Greek verb has a much stronger meaning – not just to praise someone, but to speak so as to *impart* a blessing, as in –

> *Blessed be the God and Father of our Lord Jesus Christ, who hath blessed us with all spiritual blessings in heavenly places in Christ. (Ep 1:3, KJV)*

Thus, *"the cup of blessing that we bless"* is the cup that conveys blessing to us from God as we speak blessing upon it by faith.

## A PEOPLE PARTAKING

Through the cup and the bread we *"participate in the blood and body of Christ."*

How many furious debates there have been about what this means!

The Greek word is *koinonia*, which means fellowship, communion, sharing, partaking, distributing, contributing, and the like. But what does it mean here? It seems to me that Paul himself provides the answer –

> *Do I mean then that a sacrifice offered to an idol is anything, or that an idol is anything?*

*No, but the sacrifices of pagans are offered to demons. (vs. 19-20)*

In the background of Paul's comment lies the pagan belief that when they ate part of an animal that had been sacrificed in a temple, the god entered into that meat and became part of the body and soul of each worshipper. Of course, that was nonsense, because the idols were nothing – yet behind every idol was a demon, so, says Paul, those worshippers really did come into union with a spiritual power!

Hence he warns Christians never to share in those meals –

> *I do not want you to be participants with demons. You cannot drink the cup of the Lord and the cup of demons too; you cannot have a part in both the Lord's table and the table of demons. (vs. 20-21)*

Therefore, as surely as a pagan worshipper was bound to a demon when meat from a sacrifice was eaten, even more so should we come into a mystic union with Christ through the bread and the cup. Thus our text once again –

> *I speak as to sensible people; judge for yourselves what I say. The cup of blessing that we bless, is it not a <u>participation</u> in the blood of Christ? The bread that we break, is it not a <u>participation</u> in the body of Christ?"*

But again, this can be true only when one eats and drinks in faith – just as the water of baptism is ineffective apart from faith, or the printed page of the Bible, or the bricks and mortar of the church.

## A WORTHY PEOPLE

> *Anyone who eats and drinks unworthily eats and drinks judgment upon himself* (1 Co 11:29 lit.)

But what does that mean?

- Anyone who has another god (1 Co 10:14, *"Therefore my dear friends flee from idolatry."*)

- Anyone who has another loaf (vs. 17; 11:17-19)

- Anyone who has another focus (1 Co 11:20-22)

- Anyone who has another perception (vs. 28-32)

Contrary to the popular idea ("if going to church does you no good, at least it won't do you any harm"), Paul warned the Corinthians: *"your meetings do you more harm than good"* (11:17; also see vs. 18-22). What a sad state of affairs: they were worse for going to church than if they had stayed home!

Let us therefore make sure that we do sincerely *"discern the Lord's body"* (vs. 29), and that we always come together for better, not worse, and leave the service richer not poorer, stronger not weaker, healthier not sicker.

The best way to achieve that admirable aim is to add one more dimension to our celebration of the Eucharist –

## CORONATION

Here, as everywhere, Christ must be, and will be Lord!

## *TEN*

# HAIR AND HATS

See *1 Corinthians 11:2-16*.

The key text is *verse 10*, which highlights the fact that there is nothing so ludicrous, nor so sad, as a church that has lost its sense of the supernatural – that is, a church locked within natural wisdom and skills. Rather, says Paul, we should live *"in the presence of angels"*; that is, in a supernatural dimension, in touch with the heavenly realm, with all the resources of God's mighty warriors as close as the breath in our lungs!

From this he draws two powerful lessons -

## SEPARATE FROM THE WORLD IN LIFESTYLE

See verses 4-6, 13-16.

Paul uses a strange argument in those verses. It is confusing, because

- in the <u>Greek</u> world, both sexes worshipped uncovered.

- in the <u>Jewish</u> and <u>Roman</u> worlds, both sexes worshipped covered.

- among male <u>philosophers</u> long hair was common, and revered as a mark of distinction.

- among women, long hair was in some places the sign of a harlot.

Why then does Paul present his rather tortured argument, insisting that Christian custom required men to have relatively short hair, and to worship with an uncovered head; while the women should have relatively long hair, and worship with a covered head? No one is quite sure, and even Paul seems a little unsure of his ground! (11:16, and perhaps also vs. 11-12).

However, one idea does seem dominant, that Paul was reaching for a distinctive Christian lifestyle. This was the real issue, not *hair* or *hats*; he wanted every Christian to be clearly marked in society; he wanted them not only to be different on the inside, but to look different on the outside, to be separate from all the surrounding cultures, whether Jewish, Greek, or Roman. And indeed, there should be no confusion between us and the world. Yet neither should we press Paul's words to an opposite extreme, as some do, who suppose that they should trumpet their Christian identity by wearing gaudy gospel buttons, or by looking frowzy. Rather let our difference be deeply found in a supernatural quality of love and faithfulness in all our dealings with each other. Which becomes Paul's second theme –

## SEPARATE FROM THE WORLD IN RELATIONSHIP

Where do you look for your pattern of human relationships? All too many Christians allow their manners, their attitudes, their standards, to be shaped by TV, popular magazines, secular movies and books, and the like. Scripture alone should be our guide and rule. So in this passage Paul has two great goals –

- to put the family into divine order (vs. 3, 7-9)

- to give equal power to both sexes (vs. 11-12).

He achieves his aims by establishing the principle that both male and female are under authority; neither has final rule over the other; they both have their rightful place; they are both under the dominion of Christ. Notice also, how he talks throughout the passage about *"men and women"*, not just *"husband and wife"*; so he has in mind a broad view, not only of the home, but also of the church as the family of God.

## THE WOMAN IS UNDER AUTHORITY (VS. 10)

During the Revolutionary War that the Americans waged against the British in the late 18th century, much harm was done to the British cause by various guerrilla bands. One of them was headed by Ethan Allen, who gained renown as the leader of a group of warriors known as the "Green Mountain Boys". Allen had the misfortune to be married to a woman who was notorious for her bad temper and foul attitudes, a truly bitter shrew. When she died, Allen was asked who should be invited to carry the coffin. He replied, "Ask any of my neighbours. There is not a man in this town who would not be glad to carry her away!" [45]

A Christian wife should yield leadership to her husband, supporting him, encouraging his pastoral role, promoting his goals. She should do this even when he is undeserving, for it is nothing to meet virtue with virtue, nor to match love with love. The time may come when a violent, or unreasonable, or tyrannical, or unfaithful, or drunken, or befouling spouse must be abandoned; but don't give up too soon!

Some of you ladies are gardeners, and how patiently you till the stubborn soil and war against weeds, pests, and disease. Would you do less for a man?

The American film star Robert Mitchum enjoyed a long and happy marriage across 57 years, which ended only with his death in 1997 – perhaps unusual for Hollywood. After living for 30 years with his wife Dorothy, he was asked, when so many other marriages had collapsed, what he thought had

---

(45)  Fadiman, op. cit., in loc.

made his last so well. He replied: "Mutual forbearance. My wife keeps on believing that I will do better tomorrow." [46]

Mr. Mitchum's definition of "mutual forbearance" is rather quirky, but the idea is right. Each spouse must show the Christian graces of *"patience, goodness, kindness, and gentleness"* toward each other (Ga 5:22-23). While these days a woman may be a powerful executive or leader in the secular world, in the home she should still acknowledge the headship of her husband. But "headship" is not "tyranny" because scripture insists also that-

## THE MAN IS UNDER AUTHORITY (VS. 10)

When Margaret Thatcher became prime minister of Great Britain, she and her husband Denis naturally moved into Number 10 Downing Street. On the day of the move a reporter asked Denis who would wear the pants in their new house? He said, "I will. And I will also wash them and iron them!"

The question, of course, was absurd, for husbandly authority (as Denis realised) cannot be translated to mean rule or control. Yet here we encounter a delightful ambiguity! The same Greek phrase (*"a veil over her head"*) may mean (and is elsewhere translated) *"possessing authority"* = "an environment of authority". That is, the veil is a mark of *her* authority, which she wears in the presence of angels, and which she alone has the right to wear in such exalted company.

In this startling way, Paul prevents the male from arrogantly assuming dominance over his wife. His *"headship"* is not one of power, nor that of bully or boss. Rather, his role is that of

---

(46)    Ibid. , op. cit., in loc.

the *protector* and *enabler* of his wife; guarding her from harm, and creating a context in which she can flourish and fulfil all her potential as wife, mother, woman, and Christian. Thus Matthew Henry wrote, in his commentary on Genesis (2:21-22) –

> (Adam was made) last of (all) the creatures, as the last and most excellent of all, (but) Eve's being made after Adam, and out of him, puts an honour upon that sex as the glory of the man (1 Co 11:7). If man is the head, she is the crown, a crown to her husband, the crown of the visible creation. The man was dust refined, but the woman was dust double-refined, once removed further from the earth ...

> (Observe how) the woman was *"made of a rib out of the side of Adam"*; not out of his head to rule over him, nor out of his feet to be trampled upon by him, but out of his side to be equal with him, and under his arm to be protected, and near his heart to be beloved. (47)

The husband's example is Christ, who gained the right to be Head of the Church by his loving sacrifice, and now Christ expresses his authority (just as the man should do for his wife) by *protecting* and *enabling* the church, not by acting the despot over her.

Robert Browning captured both those ideas in his striking poem, *A Woman's Last Word* (a poem that was no doubt born out of the remarkable love and sympathy that existed between him and his wife, Elizabeth Barrett) –

---

(47)   Commentary on the Whole Bible, *Vol. One;* a 1953 re-print of the original early 18th century work, by Marshall, Morgan, and Scott, London, UK.

Be a god and hold me
With a charm!
Be a man and fold me
With thine arm. [48]

Teach me, only teach, Love!
As I ought
I will speak thy speech, Love,
Think thy thought – [49]

Meet, if thou require it,
Both demands,
Laying flesh and spirit
In thy hands. [50]

But a husband might ask, what if she is

## INSOLENT?

Well, she is the weaker vessel, and you the stronger, so that you might bear with her, and nurture her, which in the end is to your own advantage. Someone once asked Socrates (B.C. 469-399) why he had married Xantippe, who was a shrew, and a brawler, and why he remained with her. He replied: "That I might have within my own house a school of philosophy, and thereby be disciplined every day, and trained in meekness!" [51]

---

(48)　Protector.

(49)　Enabler.

(50)　She fully yields herself to him.

(51)　I have lost the source of this story, although it is well known, and dates back to before the time of Christ. It also may be unfair to Xantippe, for other ancient sources portray her as a good wife and loving mother of the three sons she bore for Socrates. Nonetheless, she remains in the

..........continued on the next page.

## INCOMPETENT?

Was she not the same when you married her? So then, pray, and teach, and be patient. Perhaps, too, she is only meeting your expectations of her? When the Cunard Line built the *Queen Mary*, they intended to call it the *Queen Victoria*. But an executive told George V that the ship was to be named after "the greatest of all English queens", and the king replied at once, "Oh, my wife *will* be pleased!" [52]

A man (even a king) who reckons his wife to be "the greatest of all queens" is bound to have a happy marriage!

## INSURGENT?

Then do not command, but persuade with love, as Christ does for his Church! Long ago, John Chrysostom preached on wifely obedience and husbandly love –

> You have seen the measure of obedience (a wife owes her husband), hear also the measure of love (a husband owes his wife). Would you have your wife obedient unto you, as the Church is to Christ? Take then yourself the same provident care for her, as Christ takes for the Church. Yes, even if it shall be needful for you to give your life for her, yes, and to be cut into pieces ten thousand times, yes, and to endure and undergo any suffering whatever — refuse it not. Though you should undergo all this, yet will you not, no, not even then, have done anything

---

*..........continued from previous page.*

popular mind as the archetype of a shrew, and Socrates as the exemplar of a patient husband.

(52)    Fadiman, op. cit., in loc.

like Christ. For you indeed are doing it for one to whom you are already knit; but He for one who turned her back on Him and hated Him. In the same way then as He laid at His feet her who turned her back on Him, who hated, and spurned, and disdained Him, not by menaces, nor by violence, nor by terror, nor by anything else of the kind, but by his unwearied affection; so also should you behave yourself toward your wife. Yes, though you see her looking down upon you, and disdaining, and scorning you, yet by your great thoughtfulness for her, by affection, by kindness, you will be able to lay her at your feet. For there is nothing more powerful to sway than these bonds, and especially for husband and wife. A servant, indeed, one will be able, perhaps, to bind down by fear; nay not even him, for he will soon start away and be gone. But the partner of one's life, the mother of one's children, the foundation of one's every joy, one ought never to chain down by fear and menaces, but with love and good temper. For what sort of union is that, where the wife trembles at her husband? And what sort of pleasure will the husband himself enjoy, if he dwells with his wife as with a slave, and not as with a free-woman? [53]

And what is true of the man and the woman is equally true in reverse.

---

[53] The Nicene and Post-Nicene Fathers, ed. by Philip Schaff; *First Series, Vol. 13, Chrysostom, Homily Twenty. on Ephesians 5:22-24.* Eerdmans Pub. Co, Michigan; 1979 re-print of the 1889 edition.

Shortly after their marriage in 1840, Queen Victoria and Prince Albert had a bitter quarrel –

> Albert stalked out of the room and locked himself in his private apartments. Victoria hammered furiously upon the door. "Who's there?" called Albert. "The Queen of England, and she demands to be admitted!" There was no response, and the door remained locked. Victoria hammered at the door again. "Who's there?" The reply was still, "The Queen of England," and still the door remained shut. More fruitless and furious knocking was followed by a pause. Then there was a gentle tap. "Who's there?" The Queen replied, "Your wife, Albert." The Prince at once opened the door. [54]

They enjoyed great love and happiness for twenty-one years, until he died of typhoid fever in 1851, aged only 42 years. The Queen never married again and wore mourning for the rest of her long life. Mutual respect, unfeigned love, patient endurance, and unshakable goodwill, one toward the other, these are some of the ways that marriages truly become "made in heaven"!

### CONCLUSION

Rid yourself of the idea that life should be fair, and that you are absolutely entitled to a beautiful, happy, loving, home. Why do you suppose the 10th Commandment says, *"thou shalt not covet thy neighbour's wife, goods, land,"* and the like? It is there because life does not always work out the way

---

(54) Fladiman, op. cit., in loc.

we think it will. After a few years of marriage, you may discover that you could have made a wiser choice for a spouse; or you may meet someone whom you think could make you happier. But that is not a sufficient reason to discard your present spouse, and so violate solemn vows made in the presence of God.

The reality of life is the same for all of us. Careers may not blossom as we had supposed; or events may conspire to keep us from the best of our dreams; and so on; but they cannot excuse lapsing into jealousy, or envy, or bitterness.

Kahlil Gibran, in his remarkable work of poetic philosophy, *The Prophet*, wrote about the pleasures and the pain of love —

> When love beckons to you, follow him,
> Though his ways are hard and steep.
> And when his wings enfold you, yield to him,
> Tho' the sword hidden among his pinions
> may wound you.
>
> And when he speaks to you, believe him,
> Though his voice may shatter your dreams as the
> north wind lays waste a garden ...
>
> But if in your fears you would seek only love's peace
> and love's pleasure,
> Then it is better for you that you cover your nakedness
> and pass out of love's threshing floor
> Into the seasonless world where you shall laugh
> but not all of your laughter, and weep,
> but not all of your tears. [55]

---

[55]    Alfred A. Knopf, New York, 1968; pg. 11, 12.

We are indeed called to live in a higher dimension, where we truly discover the sweetest happiness – but in Christ, and in the love of Christ, not in material things.

We live, said Paul (1 Co 11:10), in the presence of angels; so let us walk meekly, gently, lovingly, faithfully, as those who worship Christ and hope above all things to inherit the kingdom of God!

*EXCURSUS*

# A TALE OF TWO CITIES

See *1 Corinthians 2:1-5.*

When Charles Dickens wrote his stirring novel about the French Revolution he called it *A Tale of Two Cities*, and began with the famous words, *"It was the best of times, it was the worst of times."*

Paul might have said the same about another two cities: **Athens** (the worst of times); and **Corinth** (the best of times).

## PAUL AT CORINTH — *THE BEST OF TIMES*

### THE SUPERNATURAL CHURCH

Paul was committed to a ministry of miracles (vs. 4-5). See also *Romans 15:17-19; 1 Thessalonians 1:4-5;* and cp. *Hebrews 2:3-4; etc.* Indeed, in the reckoning of the entire early church, the gospel could not be *fully* preached without the presence of the supernatural. Yet how soon they fell away from that exciting dimension! Early in the post-apostolic era, supernatural occurrences became ever more sporadic, and eventually faded away almost entirely. A resurgence of miracles was aroused during the Montanist revivals in the 5th century, but they too eventually vanished. Across the centuries occasional miracles are recorded, but only the outbreak of the Pentecostal revival at the beginning of the 20th century restored the full panoply of the charismata to the church.

But then, after a few decades, the incidence of miracles once again began to decline. Now we are in the second century of the movement, and while signs and wonders still occur from time to time in diverse places, they seem to be steadily diminishing in number and power.

Why is this so, and can we reverse it? There are, I suppose, several reasons for the decline of the supernatural in our churches, but perhaps the main one arises because the church inescapably functions in –

# THE NATURAL WORLD

The church exists in a natural environment in which it faces two relentless foes —

## SATAN HATES THE SUPERNATURAL

Miracles strike at the heart of his own supernatural kingdom, so the devil strives to lock the church into the natural world, where it will remain largely ineffective. It is surely absurd to suppose that a metaphysical realm can be overcome by one that is merely physical, or a supernatural dimension by one that is mostly natural. A lesser miracle can be defeated only by one that is greater (Mt 12:27-29). But by the grace of God, and through the supernatural gifts of the Holy Spirit (1 Co 12:7-11), we are equipped with more than enough divine energy to overthrow the powers of darkness.

## THE WORLD HATES THE SUPERNATURAL

### MIRACLES STRIKE AT ITS NATURAL WISDOM

How this world loves its own wisdom! Thus, the 12th century Persian poet and philosopher, Omar Khayyam, called his family around his death-bed to hear his last wishes and final prayer. And he said, "Oh Lord, I have known You according to the sum of my ability. Pardon me, since verily my knowledge is my recommendation to You." (56)

His knowledge was his only claim to grace, as it is of many proud people today. Because they have wide learning, and are wise in the eyes of their contemporaries, they little doubt that the Almighty is equally impressed. I am reminded of a joke I heard somewhere. A group of scientists decided that anything God had done, they could equal. So they approached the Lord, and challenged him. He politely asked if they could make a living man out of dust, as he had done. "Of course we can," they cried, reaching down for a handful of dirt. "Oh! No," the Lord protested, "You must first make your own dirt!" When they could build a planet out of nothing, then they might have something to boast about!

But of course, wonderful as human knowledge is, even the cleverest person cannot ever do more than think God's thoughts after him. And even then, the highest of human knowledge falls far, far short of the wisdom and knowledge of the Creator of the far-flung universe (Is 55:8-9). In any case, the Lord has no interest in debating the matter. He simply does a miracle or two, which makes the debate irrelevant!

Thus miracles of

- <u>healing</u> defies the physician's wisdom, when he says there is no hope. (57)

---

(56)  Omar died in 1131. The story comes from his biographer Ali ibn Azidu'l-Baihaqi. In his lifetime, Omar was mostly renowned as a mathematician and astronomer, in the employ of the Sultan Malik Shah. See The Ruba'iyat of Omar Khayyam, tr. by Peter Avery & John Heath-Stubbs, Penguin Classics, 1983, pg. 33.

(57)  After the birth of our second child, my wife was twice told by leading medical specialists that it would be impossible for her to bear another child. But twice more we prayed, trusted the promise of God, and each

..........continued on the next page.

- <u>supply</u> defies the banker's wisdom, when he says there is no money. [58]

- <u>intervention</u> defies the scientist's wisdom, when he says God is impotent.

- <u>revelation</u> defies the philosopher's wisdom, when he declares that God does not exist (1 Co 1:19-21).

I do not mean to disparage physicians, scientists, bankers, or any other profession. The skill, wisdom, and knowledge amassed by these clever people have brought multiplied benefits to us all, for which I am deeply grateful. But when some of them vaunt their knowledge against God, or claim that it makes them wiser than the Lord, or even wipes the Almighty out of the universe, then they indeed become objects of mockery. It then becomes true of them what scripture says, *"It takes a fool to say, 'There is no God'"* (Ps 53:1).

### MIRACLES STRIKE AT ITS NATURAL PRIDE

Think about W. E. Henley (1849-1903), crippled by a diseased leg, suffering constant pain, lying in hospital and writing his great yet ultimately absurd poem *Invictus* —

> Out of the night that covers me,
> Black as the pit from pole to pole,
> I thank whatever gods may be
> For my unconquerable soul.

---

*..........continued from previous page.*

time she conceived and gave birth to a healthy child (our younger sons, Eric and Baden)!

(58)   After a lifetime of ministry, I can echo David, "I have been young, and now am old, but I have yet to see the righteous forsaken or their children begging for bread!" (Ps 37:25).

> It matters not how straight the gate,
> How charged with punishment the scroll,
> I am the master of my fate,
> I am the captain of my soul. (59)

His words are brave. They are defiant. He shakes his fist at heaven. But it is nonsense, for he is dead, his pretensions void, and his vanity a meal for worms. Now he awaits the Day of Judgment, as we all must.

Ultimately, the only people who are truly free are those who have surrendered to the Lord. As the ancient *Collect for Peace* says, "In his service (alone) there is perfect freedom." (60)

But God long ago revealed his opinion of human hubris – *"He who is enthroned in heaven laughs; the Lord holds them all in derision!"* (Ps 2:4). And each miracle of answered prayer (of which I have seen many) shows that man is not the master of his world.

Yet secular society continually presses the church to purchase respectability at the cost of the supernatural. The price is too high. We dare not abandon the call to remain a supernatural people serving a supernatural God. We believe, and must believe, in miracles!

---

(59)  First and last of 4 stanzas. *Invictus* first appeared in 1875, in a volume called Book of Verses; published by D. Nutt, London.

(60)  From the 16th century *Book of Common Prayer*, written by Archbishop Thomas Cranmer, who was burnt to death by command of the Catholic Queen Mary in 1556. At one point during the imprisonment and torture he had endured, Cranmer wrote a retraction of his Protestant views. Because of that temporary lapse, he announced in advance that when he was burnt he would thrust his right hand first into the flames, as an act of contrition and penitence, which he did, until it was consumed.

However, there was a time when Paul yielded to that worldly pressure —

# PAUL AT ATHENS — THE WORST OF TIMES

## PAUL THE PLAUSIBLE

*When I first came to you, brothers, I didn't preach about the mystery of God with high-flying words or lofty wisdom ... Indeed, I was with you in weakness and in fear and much trembling. (1 Co 2:1, 3)*

Paul, weak, fearful, trembling? How much out of character those words seem! Elsewhere in Acts and in his own letters, Paul is displayed in terms more reminiscent of the ascription Taylor Caldwell gave him in her eponymous novel, *Great Lion of God*. It seems almost impossible to visualize a trembling, weak, and fearful Paul!

Perhaps he was simply suggesting Christian grace and humility (as some have suggested), while in reality he remained his usual forceful and abrasive self? But it seems unlikely. The language he uses is that of real anxiety (cp. 2 Co 7:15; Ep 6:5; Ph 2:12). So, how do we explain this quivering and worried apostle?

Note that Paul came to Corinth from Athens (Ac 18:1). Perhaps something happened at Athens that robbed Paul of his bold confidence?

A clue lies in the extraordinary sermon that Paul reached in Athens, at a public assembly at the Areopagus (Ac 17:19-34), also known as Mars' Hill, just below the glorious Parthenon. It was a marvellous sermon, which has ever since been cited as a superb example of the orator's art. I doubt if any book on Christian homiletics has ever been printed that has failed to urge its readers to learn from Paul's Areopagus sermon.

But there is one problem – the sermon *failed*! (see vs. 32-34; and cp. Ac 22:16-18; Mk 16:15-20).

Now I would be delighted if any sermon of mine resulted in *"some men joining the church, along with a high-ranking aristocrat, a prominent lady, and a few other people"* (Ac 17:34). I have sometimes had even better results, and also worse! But what is suitable for me, was hardly enough for Paul. I'm primarily a teacher and writer.

But Paul was an *apostle*!

He was called to, and gifted for, a vastly different ministry – to preach Christ, to plant and build churches, to work mighty signs, wonders, and miracles (cp. Ro 15:18-20a; 2 Co 12:12). But after his Areopagus sermon, he realised that he had tried to be too clever. He cleverly tried to appeal to the world-weary, cultured, sophisticated Greek audience, and used all the arts of public speaking he had learned at college. But those Athenians had heard many an orator smarter than Paul, and they were unimpressed. He looked on the scant response to his masterpiece, and knew that he had altogether missed the plot.

So he quickly left Athens, never to return.

Yet what an opportunity was lost! Athens was the capital of world culture. As went Athens, so went the world. The Greek language, far more than Latin, was universal. Greek civilisation, art, literature, music, was everywhere admired and emulated. A great church, a powerful spiritual revival in Athens, would have had a world-wide impact, far more than a similar move in any other city, even great Rome.

But it was not to be. The chance was gone for ever. For Paul, Athens was the place of his humiliation; he could never bring himself to go back there. He travelled east and south and west of Athens, but there is no record that he ever again set foot in that city.

But as he trudged from Athens down to Corinth, God dealt with him. He arrived at Corinth deeply resolving never again to commit the folly of trying to appeal to the world on its own terms. He was done with fine words, secular wisdom, and clever oratory. From now on, he cried, *"I am determined to know nothing among you except Christ and him crucified!"* (1 Co 2:2). So despite arriving in Corinth exhausted, nervous about failing again, and trembling, perhaps feeling that in Athens he had angered God, he became

## PAUL THE POWERFUL

By the time he reached Corinth, Paul was a changed man — see 1 Co 2:4-5. There he raised up a great church, in which there were almost *too many* miracles! Paul made so sure that they would not lack any supernatural gift of the Holy Spirit (1:7), nor miss any aspect of the power of God (2:4-5), that he failed to instruct them properly on how to use the gifts. Hence his letter to them, telling them how to use prophecy, tongues, interpretation, and the whole gamut of charismatic endowments.

And he raised up in Corinth the great church that he probably should have built in Athens – yet no church in Corinth could ever shine with the worldwide radiance that one in Athens might have achieved.

## CONCLUSION

If my argument is correct, then something was irretrievably lost at Athens. Let us learn that while we should value all natural skills, we dare not depend upon them alone. In the end, real faith must rest, not upon human wisdom, plausible words, clever wit, but upon the power of God. We Christians are constantly called to live in a dimension beyond ourselves, being carried from glory to glory by the indwelling Spirit of God. (2 Co 3:18)

***"Athens"*** or ***"Corinth"*** — Natural Wisdom or Pentecostal Power – the worst or the best: *which will you choose?*

# PART TWO

# FROM THE *"LETTER"*

## SECTION ONE

## DIVORCE AND RE-MARRIAGE

## ELEVEN

# WHAT ARE WE TALKING ABOUT?

See *1 Corinthians 7:1-40*.

Paul is often criticised for this passage, as if he had reduced marriage to the lowest level of physical gratification; but see *Ephesians 5:22-23*, where he expresses one of the noblest concepts of marriage that has ever been penned. His motivation in the letter to the Corinthians was different. Here, he was simply answering some questions, which apparently were –

- is celibacy better than marriage? (1-2, 6-9)
- what are the duties of each spouse? (3-5)
- is divorce permissible for a Christian? (10-11)
- what about an unbelieving spouse? (12-16)
- what about those who are unmarried? (25-38)
- can a woman marry after her husband dies? (39-40).

I will attempt an answer to those questions, with a special focus on the issue of divorce and re-marriage.

## GRACE OR LAW?

Tertullian, a renowned third-century Christian lawyer and philosopher, wrote a treatise on the Christian doctrine of marriage. In it he laments the lowered standards of his day, and the ease with which many people were changing spouses. He says that such careless divorce and remarriage were never part of God's law nor even true to the best aspirations of the pagan Roman world. Then he makes this remarkable statement –

> So true, moreover, is it that divorce "was not from the beginning" (Matthew 19:8; Mark 10:5), that among the Romans it is not till after the six hundredth year from the building of the city that this kind of "hard-heartedness" is set down as having been committed." [61]

Six hundred years without a divorce! Is that true? Who can tell? But it certainly shows that the stern early Roman republic held a high view of the sanctity of marriage. However, by the time of Tertullian Rome had been mistress of a vast empire for three hundred years, and a moral collapse had become endemic. This decay of virtue greatly alarmed thoughtful people, who saw in it the first signs that Roman hegemony was doomed.

The same kind of moral decline is again becoming epidemic in our own time, which is marked by a steadily increasing divorce rate. What is worse, the divorce rate among church-goers is now nearly equal to that in the outside world. Both secular man and Christian saint have abandoned the old standards.

How should a Christian respond to the rampant wrong, the collapse of the family, which is unravelling the fabric of our society and undermining the ethical integrity of the church? Different people will answer that question differently; but my own response is to strive to establish a balance between two attitudes –

---

(61)   On <u>Monogamy</u>, ch. 9.

- <u>stern adherence</u> to the highest standards of marriage; and

- <u>compassionate yielding</u> to the desperate pain of divorce.

Therefore this study will try to establish the following things –

- that the divine ideal for marriage is its sacred inviolability and permanence;

- that divorce should ordinarily be allowed on two grounds alone:

  - *porneia* (Matthew 19:9); and

  - the *Pauline Privilege* (1 Co 7:15); [62]

- that where divorce is allowed, re-marriage must also be allowed as a necessary and humane corollary;

- that re-marriage, if divorce occurs on any grounds other than the two stated above, is ordinarily not permitted.

But how should those two grounds be interpreted? Plainly, people choose to read them in different ways. But how do I read them? My choice is to define them broadly rather than narrowly. Do I mean that personal opinion is more important than scripture in solving these problems? Of course not! But scripture does have to be interpreted – that is, a decision has to be made about what its words mean, and how they should be applied to life in our time. Every reader has his or her own way of making that decision. So, before

---

[62]  Both of those grounds are explained more fully below.

presenting you with my conclusions, it is fair that you should know how I reached them.

## PRINCIPLES OF INTERPRETATION

No one can approach the task of interpreting any document with a truly neutral attitude. Each interpreter is predisposed to read things in a certain way, and every reader is inclined to emphasise some ideas above others. We are all conditioned by temperament, culture, education, and by life experiences, to adopt certain presuppositions, to look at the world through a particular pair of eyes. The inevitable result is that, consciously or unconsciously, we interpret any piece of writing within an established framework; we are already inclined to construe in a personal way whatever evidence is presented to us.

Whether wittingly or not, therefore, people must (and do) make certain choices before they begin reading any piece of literature; and those choices establish the way they understand and apply what they are studying. That is true for anybody reading anything.

So, dear reader, you and I alike are already pre-conditioned, by who we are and where we have come from in life, to interpret things in a certain way, to view them against a particular background, to respond to them according to our own inner necessity. This means that some readers will be profoundly convinced by the arguments contained in these pages, while others will remain unmoved, adamant that my conclusions are less than sure, if not utterly wrong!

Of course, the preliminary choices we make are not always subconscious. Sometimes the interpreter will be at least partly aware of what he is doing. If so, he has examined the options, and has openly decided to adopt a certain approach to his task. This is what I have done in the following study.

Let me then tell you honestly the choices I have made, and why.

## THREE NECESSARY CHOICES

One thousand years ago a godly abbot ruled the great monastery at Cluny in France. His name was Odilo, and he became famous for his extraordinary ability to match strong leadership with cheerful generosity, and to link a deep piety with much sympathy for the struggling people around him. His most noted saying was: "I would rather be damned for being too merciful than for being too severe!"

That seems to me to be an admirable philosophy. But it does highlight the fact that several options are available to those who seek to understand what the Bible teaches about human behaviour. In the main, there are three choices –

## A STRICT OR A FLEXIBLE INTERPRETATION?

You can choose to follow either a strict interpretation, or one that is generous and flexible.(63)

Life will certainly be easier for the pastor or teacher who generally says "No!" to divorce and absolutely rejects re-marriage. He is spared the distress, the ethical dilemma, of struggling to decide what is right in each case. He can just quote (say) *Matthew 5:31-32,* (64) and for him that ends the

---

(63)  Of course, it is always taken for granted that scripture itself is the ultimate authority, and that flexibility is possible only when the biblical text permits it. I mean, there are many places where the Bible itself uses expressions that are open to diverse interpretation, emphasis, or application. And where such choices are permissible, I usually lean toward the kinder rather than the harsher view.

(64)  "I tell you," said Jesus, "that any man who divorces his wife, except for immorality, makes her an adulteress; and any man who marries a divorced woman is committing adultery."

matter. But I am suspicious of such a rigid approach. I want to ask those stern moralists, "Why do you not follow the same strict rule when you interpret other sayings of Christ – especially those that occur right alongside his comments on divorce?" For example, consider Jesus' plain instruction in *Matthew 5:29-30*,

> *If your right eye causes you to sin, tear it out and throw it away ... If your right hand causes you to sin, cut it off and throw it away!*

That command, like his rule about divorce, is part of Jesus' *Sermon on the Mount*. Yet how many people (including the harshest interpreters) do you know who have literally obeyed it? I do not observe many one-eyed or one-handed teachers in the church! But are we not all drawn into sin by eye and hand? How is it we do not heed the Master's doctrine, and chop off these offending limbs? "Absurd!" you say, and I agree with you. But if softening one pungent saying is warranted by common sense, who can rightly prevent us from softening another? Do you remain unconvinced? Look then at *verses 40-42* –

> *If someone wants to take your coat, give him your shirt as well, and if he forces you to carry a load for one mile, offer to carry it for two miles! Give to everyone who begs from you, and don't turn aside anyone who wants to borrow from you.*

Even the dourest teachers find ways to avoid taking those uncomfortable injunctions too literally! Yet it is surely arbitrary and unfair to read some of Christ's sayings with adamant strictness, while modifying other sayings to suit either a more rational interpretation, or modern cultural mores. Either be inflexible or flexible; but at least let the interpreter be consistent! Perhaps also those severe moralists should be asked why they are so determined to read narrowly scriptures that readily admit a broader, more compassionate message? Why do they not have more of the gentle heart of Abbott Odilo – or better, the gracious compassion of Jesus himself?

It seems to me that fear more than faith motivates such people. They are governed by law rather than by grace. Disliking the daring liberty God has given us in Christ, they yearn to bring the church under the command of unyielding rules. Perhaps they trust neither the integrity of the people of God nor the personal guidance of the Holy Spirit. They seem to be under some necessity to turn ethical principles into imprisoning chains. If that is an unfair judgment, then I apologise. But I remain puzzled about the motivation of those who impose harsh yokes upon others. Ordinary people who are struggling to restore their shattered hopes and happiness need something more than a cruel rod flailing their shoulders; they cry for generous and compassionate counsel. Which brings us to the **second** choice the interpreter must make –

You can choose to be true to the gospel in one of two ways; either

- by refusing re-marriage on the ground of upholding a high standard of love and fidelity in marriage (and thus risk a charge of legalism that denies the grace of Christ); or,

- by allowing re-marriage on the grounds of mercy and grace (and thus risk a charge of sentimentality and compromise).

If I have to bear my opponent accusing me either of holding too much law or too much grace, then, like Odilo, my own choice will usually be to carry the latter stigma. Grace is always a happier burden to shoulder than law! Indeed, I say this boldly – in my opinion, the only thoroughly biblical approach to the question of divorce and re-marriage is one that *is* compassionate and therefore flexible. The legalistic, unyielding rigidity displayed by some moralists seems far removed from the spirit of the New Testament. I think the gospel allows much freedom of choice within general ethical guidelines.

Then a **third** choice must be made –

You can choose to respond to the secular environment either

- by standing firm against "the world", resisting all its influence, deaf to all its wisdom; or,

- by recognising that God sometimes speaks to the church through "the world".

The history of Christian ethics unhappily shows there have been times when the world has surpassed the church in comprehending (without realising it) the mind of God. We must always remain sensitive to what the Spirit may be saying to the church through events and trends in secular society.

So those are the three choices you can make.

Which one should you choose?

You will have to answer that question for yourself; but my own response is this –

## THE PRINCIPLE GOVERNING THIS STUDY

Whenever a passage of scripture is open to different interpretations, I have adopted the alternative that seems to me more humane and more consistent with the compassion of Christ.

Where scripture permits a choice, I always prefer to be generous rather than strict. Legalistic interpretations arouse in me suspicion. To paraphrase the Master: *"The Bible was made for man, not man for the Bible."* Scripture should be read in a way that offers solutions to human need, not in a way that builds intolerable burdens. [65] Nonetheless, the diversity of opinions among sincere and godly people practically compels each searcher to strike in his own fashion the ore from the mother-lode of scripture. As William Blake once wrote –

> The vision of Christ that thou dost see
> Is my vision's greatest enemy . . .
> Both read the Bible day and night,
> But thou read'st black where I read white! [66]

You will have to judge for yourself whether or not, in this study, I have written "black" or "white"!

Then, added to the above, the following ideas also have shaped my conclusions –

## FURTHER GUIDELINES

### THE ROMAN CATHOLIC VIEW

The Roman Catholic Church allows no divorce at all. But Catholics have adopted a special interpretation of *porneia* (Mt 5:32) and of the *Pauline Privilege* (1 Co 7:15), which enables the Church to declare a marriage "defective" and to annul it. The parties are then reckoned never to have married, and of course are free to enter into marriage with another partner. That is a practice based more on the traditions of the Church than on scripture.

---

(65)   Think about Jesus' fierce indictment of the Jewish legalists, *Matthew 23:1-4; Luke 11:45-46*.

(66)   English poet and artist (1757-1827); from his poem, *The Everlasting Gospel* (4.50.1, 13).

## THE STRICT PROTESTANT VIEW

The strict Protestant view is that *porneia* and the *Pauline Privilege* permit divorce but deny any right of re-marriage. Some severe ethicists modify that stern rule a little: they do allow re-marriage by the "innocent" party when the divorce was solely on the grounds of *porneia*, but not otherwise. But who will determine who is innocent of any fault when, because of infidelity, a marriage collapses? It may sometimes be true that the offended spouse is wholly free of blame; but the straying spouse often has some cause for complaint – which of course does not justify adultery, but it does muddy the issue of innocence.

## A MORE NATURAL VIEW

### A FALSE ASSUMPTION

A false premise undergirds rigorous views on divorce. Those who want to make firm rules on these matters tend to assume that the New Testament contains all the ethical guidance needed to form their policy. Their unyielding rules imply that scripture contains an exhaustive treatment of the subject of failed marriages. In fact, discussion of the ethics of marriage is minimal. The New Testament nowhere presents a formal or comprehensive Christian approach to divorce and re-marriage. When the subject occurs at all it does so in response to actual situations, as, for example, when *"the Pharisees came to Jesus and tested him by asking . . ."* (Mt 19:3).

Jesus adroitly stepped out of their trap. Nonetheless, his comments must be limited by that setting. Likewise, Paul did not volunteer any teaching on the matter, but replied to a question: *"and now, concerning the matters you wrote about . . ."* (1 Co 7:1). The answers given are appropriate to the questions asked, but they do leave other questions unanswered, whose solution must be sought elsewhere – whether in scripture, or in the larger world, or both.

## *THE ERROR OF CASUISTRY*

"Casuistry" is the pejorative term used to describe the kind of moralising that strives to reduce all human behaviour to a set of rules. The word was coined in the 18th century, initially to describe people who yearn to close every gap in an argument. A casuist, it was said, is a person who cannot bear to leave any question unanswered. Later, the word came to include those who make every decision according to a pre-determined system, who insist that every choice must fall under a regulation, who cannot bear to leave any ethical dilemma unresolved.

Since casuists have a prescriptive rule to cover whatever problem people face, individual action, and freedom of personal decision, are inevitably severely limited.

Alexander Pope, that biting satirist, had no patience with such legalism –

> See skulking Truth to her old cavern fled,
> Mountains of casuistry heap'd o'er her head! [67]

Here is the great fault of casuists: they bury the truth under mountains of suffocating law, they cause her to hide her head in shame. I cannot find the heart of Christ in such hair-splitting legalities. In a similar vein, the great 19th century novelist, George Eliot, wrote –

> The great problem of the shifting relation between passion and duty is clear to no man who is capable of apprehending it: the question

---

[67]    *The Dunciad,* 1.641, written in 1728.

whether the moment has come in which a man has fallen below the possibility of a renunciation that will carry any efficacy, and must accept the sway of a passion against which he had struggled as a trespass, is one for which we have no master-key that will fit all cases.

The casuists have become a byword of reproach; but their perverted spirit of minute discrimination was the shadow of a truth to which eyes and hearts are too often fatally sealed – the truth, that moral judgments must remain false and hollow, unless they are checked and enlightened by a perpetual reference to the special circumstances that mark the individual lot.

All people of broad, strong sense have an instinctive repugnance to the men of maxims; because such people early discern that the mysterious complexity of our life is not to be embraced by maxims, and that to lace ourselves up in formulas of that sort is to repress all the divine promptings and inspirations that spring from growing insight and sympathy. And the man of maxims is the popular representative of the minds that are guided in their moral judgment solely by general rules, thinking that these will lead them to justice by a ready-made patent method, without the trouble of exerting patience, discrimination, impartiality – without any care to assure themselves whether they have the insight that comes from a hardly-earned estimate of temptation, or from a life vivid and intense enough to have created a wide fellowship with all that is human." [68]

I like to think that I am one of those "people of broad, strong sense, (who) have an instinctive repugnance to the men of maxims." I look for a better way of solving the moral dilemmas of life, and of interpreting scripture. Join with me now as we search for that way in the following pages.

[68]   The Mill on the Floss, Book VII, the closing paragraphs of Chapter Two. "George Eliot" was actually a woman, Mary Ann Evans (1819-1880). She is reckoned to be among the half dozen greatest of all English writers.

## *TWELVE*

# WEDDED FOR LIFE

> Jesus was sitting in Moses' chair.
> They brought the trembling woman there.
> Moses commanded she be stoned to death.
> What was the sound of Jesus' breath?
> He laid his hand on Moses' law;
> The ancient Heavens, in silent awe,
> Writ with curses from pole to pole,
> All away began to roll. [69]

The compassionate grace of the gospel is lacking from the cold rules, the forced conformity, the unbending precepts of the casuist. See how Jesus, confronted by the trembling adulteress, did not pronounce against her Moses' fierce sentence of death, but spoke a compassionate word of pardon (Jn 8:3-11).

Why then are some Christian teachers eager to interpret scripture narrowly and harshly? Why are they reluctant to permit a broader and more generous reading of the sacred text? What motivates them so unfeelingly to impose crushing burdens upon people who are already desperately hurting? Why are they so thirsty for law and so angry at grace? They love God, they are zealous for scripture, but they seem to me to pluck out of the earth of God's word not flowers but weeds, not medicine but poison, not an easy yoke but galling chains. [70]

---

(69)   William Blake, op. cit.

(70)   How differently Jesus spoke! See *Matthew 11:28-30*.

The gospel is more directed toward general principles than to implacable maxims. It is ruled by grace, not law, by love, not rigid rules. Certainly, there are *some* commands that must be obeyed, but they are not many, and even then, always some room is left for grace to intervene. Mark how Paul, copying the way of Christ (Mt 19:11-12, *"let those who are able to receive this teaching, do so!"*), allowed room for people to be different – *1 Corinthians 7:5-6, 17, 26-28, 36-40* –

## EACH CASE IS DIFFERENT

Before trying to determine what the Bible says about divorce and remarriage, the reader must first ask what problem each passage is addressing. As we saw in the previous chapter, this issue is never discussed in an abstract way, but only in response to a particular need, or to a specific question. The author records the solution to the problem, but other aspects of the matter are usually ignored. Scholars call this a "situational context", and it means that a wise reader will not jump to hasty conclusions based on inadequate evidence. You need to know what the question was before you hang too much weight on the answer.

In the same way, just as different questions called forth sensitive and different responses from the biblical authors, so in our time the background and circumstances of each couple must be carefully considered before one can fix on a godly remedy for their pain. I think that ethicists who hold a very strict view of divorce are unrealistic in their handling of the complex situations that arise. How different are the circumstances, the hurts, the needs, that surround each struggling couple!

Furthermore, a doctrinaire approach fails to take proper account of the new insights into marriage and divorce provided by modern medicine, psychology, and sociology; nor does it give due recognition to the comparative paucity of scripture data; nor does it allow sufficient credence to alternative views. The biblical data do not comprise a box that contains all the pieces of the jigsaw puzzle, so that a complete and lovely picture can be made. On the contrary, it is more like a puzzle that has a number of missing pieces. Enough can be put together to give a good sense of what the picture should be; but the entire picture cannot be seen.

These ideas are given more space below; but first, look at

## THE OLD TESTAMENT VIEW

The absence from the New Testament of any formal statement that deals with the issues created by an unhappy marriage may seem surprising. But it shows that the apostles accepted the teaching of the Old Testament on the subject. They apparently thought that the ethics of the prophets were still generally applicable to the church. They added to those ethics some specifically Christian dimensions, but otherwise left them unchanged.

What then did the prophets teach?

### ACCOMMODATING HUMAN FRAILTY

The Old Testament forcefully argues for a high view of marriage as a divine institution; yet it looks also with compassion upon human frailty. The impression conveyed is that the sanctity, beauty, and joy of marriage are hardly preserved by compelling an unhappy couple to remain together in hostility. Corrosive human tension, ugly conflict, incessant pain, bring neither glory to God nor honour to the institution –

> *Eating a dry crust alone and in peace is better than sharing a feast in a house that is full of conflict ... A quarrelsome spouse is more aggravating than a tap you can't turn off ... Life on top of the roof is more pleasant than*

*staying inside with a nagging spouse ... Living alone in the desert is better than sharing a house with a complaining and quarrelsome spouse ... Why stay inside the house and be nagged to death? You would be happier living on the roof! ... Like rain that never stops, so is an endlessly nagging spouse.* [71]

Several hundred years later, similar sentiments were expressed by the aged and shrewd Rabbi Sirach –

Cage me up with a lion or a dragon rather than house me with a malicious woman. Her rancour eats away her beauty; she grows worse than a bad-tempered bear. Listen to the bitter sighs of her husband whenever he can escape to a neighbour's house! ... Ask an old man to climb a sand dune! Ask a quiet man to endure a railing wife! ... Deep depression, a gloomy countenance, a broken heart, these are all wounds inflicted by a mean-spirited wife. Show me a man whose wife fails to bring him happiness, and I will show you one whose hands are weak and whose knees tremble. ... Would you put up with a constantly dripping tap? Then why do you allow a garrulous woman to say whatever she likes? If she will not accept your correction, then bring the marriage to an end!

But how happy is the husband of a good wife! She will prolong his years upon the earth. Standing always at his side, she is his greatest

(71)   Proverbs 17:1; 19:13; 21:9, 19; 25:24; 27:15.

asset, and he dwells each day with her in peace. How great a blessing is a good wife! What a splendid gift from the Lord she is to her husband! Riches or poverty make no difference to him, for nothing can cloud the smile on his face, and his heart is content." (Sir 25:16-26:4). [72]

The issues of divorce and re-marriage never touch the latter fortunate spouse; but what about others, whose marriages have plunged from heaven to hell? Have they no escape? Must they abandon all hope of happiness?

Consider the passages quoted above from *Proverbs*. They offer no suggestion that divorce provides an immediate and easy escape from an unhappy union. The nagging wife and her spousal victim are still wedded, even if he has fled to the rooftop, or run away into the desert! But they leave no doubt that a marriage, where love has failed, has been stripped of most of the benefits that should result from the conjugal state. An impression is left that while no marriage should be too readily dissolved, a level of distress can be reached that leaves no rational choice except to dissolve the union.

Sirach was more forthright than Solomon, for he plainly counsels the tormented man to bring his marriage to an end. Sirach was a devout rabbi who could not have given such

---

(72) I apologize for the unabashed chauvinism of the old rabbi. What he says about the benefit a man receives from a good wife, I would say equally for a woman with a good husband. Notice also his confident claim that a happily married man will enjoy a long, healthy life. Remarkably, modern research has demonstrated the truth of that assertion. Many surveys in recent times have shown that happily married men have an average lifespan considerably longer than men who are single. Indeed, even those who are unhappily married tend to live longer than men who have never married. Divorced men (especially when the divorce was bitter) have the lowest average of them all. And the same is probably true of women.

advice without believing that the laws of Moses sanctioned it. The question we must ask is, "Did Sirach rightly interpret Moses?"

## FULFILLING MARITAL DUTIES

Moses declared that every wife was entitled to expect from her husband three things: *"food, clothing, and marital rights."* If he failed to provide these, she was free to leave him without penalty or restraint (Exodus 21:10-11). In other words, each spouse had certain responsibilities to the other, and if those duties were not done, then no marriage remained that was worth the name.

Moses also forbade any man or woman to allow their marriage vows to hinder their service of God; on the contrary, *"the one who seeks to entice you away from the Lord your God must be taken out and stoned to death!"* (De 13:6-10).

Further, a man who had taken a slave girl into his bed as his wife, but then wearied of her, was not permitted to reduce her again to slavery. He was bound by law to release her *"to go wherever she may choose"* (21:14).

All those injunctions, and others like them, show that marriage had a relative importance in the mind of the great Lawgiver. It was not the ultimate expression of virtue; other strictures had a higher moral claim upon the people, and if observance of those loftier principles meant the dissolution of a marriage, then so be it.

Modern research endorses that Old Testament view –

> It is common knowledge with psychologists that a bad marriage is psychologically destructive. It creates bitter, hostile, and unforgiving attitudes in the couple. It may work all sorts of psychological damage on the

children. To maintain a destructive marriage on the basis of being loyal to a Christian ethic of no divorce is hardly justifiable.

Love, justice, mercy, and redemption are ground underfoot to preserve a moralistic view. [73]

## DIVORCE SHOULD NOT BE EASY

I am not saying that an unhappy or difficult marriage should be quickly dissolved. Divorce always exacts a heavy toll upon families that suffer its trauma. Parents and children together will be long hurt by divorce – especially children. While some children may benefit from a divorce, others remain hurt for years to come.

Research suggests that many children from broken homes experience fierce anger, especially against the father, which takes deep root, continuing for many years, and often for life. Loneliness, resentment, depression, a withdrawal into fantasy, strike in varying degrees at children from broken homes. Their ability to form firm relationships in adult life, especially with the opposite sex, is often harmed. Despite appearances, divorce is neither easy nor cheap. The cost is always high.

However, in other cases, children of divorced parents may show less trauma, less ill effect mentally, emotionally, socially than children forced to live in a conflict-ridden home. They may fare better living with one parent, free of tension or abuse, than they would if they had to share the quarrels of two. This is especially so when the separated

---

(73)    Bernard Ramm. I have lost the source of this passage.

parents explain what is happening, and when they exonerate the child from all blame or guilt for the divorce, and affirm their continued love and care for the child. Once again, I find it unreasonable to lay down a hard rule and pronounce it true for every family.

## THE DIVINE IDEAL

Let me emphatically state: it is the duty of every Christian couple to struggle earnestly to fulfil God's ideal for their union. Absolutely nothing in scripture supports a careless attitude toward divorce or re-marriage; yet the evidence begins to accumulate that there are circumstances in which divorce, though not demanded, becomes the more sensible option. And, where *divorce* is permitted, *re-marriage* must also be allowed. More on this later.

## THIRTEEN

# "ONE FLESH"

God intends marriage to be a life-time union, in which the couple become *"one flesh"* physically, emotionally, spiritually, and socially. [74] Therefore, no Christian should ever enter marriage with anything less than the deepest commitment to complete fusion with his or her spouse.

## A DIVINE "MYSTERY"

Marriage must be more than a legal way in which to gain sexual gratification and a housekeeper/provider. It is a divine *"mystery"* (Ep 5:21-32). A Christian couple should strive to achieve and maintain a God-wrought spiritual quality in their union. They should never allow the supernatural (the heavenly) aspects of their union to become submerged under its physical and material components. Those who treat marriage casually, who do wilful violence to

---

(74)    Note however, that marital unity does not necessarily include becoming *one flesh* culturally, intellectually, or personally. Attempts to compel conformity of one spouse to the other in those areas have brought many marriages to ruin. Within the closest marriage each partner should still be able to maintain his or her own individuality and uniqueness. There is no necessity for them to enjoy exactly the same music, or read the same books, or pursue the same hobbies, and so on. No man has the right to squash the personal interests and desires of his wife, to subjugate her to his whims and pleasures; nor should a woman do so to her husband. The very expression "one flesh" precludes any thought of the woman being inferior to or subject to the man. They stand equal together in the sight of God (Ga 3:28).

its mystery, usually pay a high price. According to David Larsen, a senior researcher for the US Federal Government –

> Religiously committed people not only have much lower rates of divorce, but their level of satisfaction and enjoyment of marriage is quite high. It's not as though religion keeps people married who would really rather be divorced. On the other hand, divorce leads to all kinds of problems. "No-fault" divorce is an oxymoron. Children of divorced parents have higher rates of school dropout, delinquency, psychiatric disorders, physical diseases, suicide, and drug abuse ... Divorced males and females have significantly higher levels of psychiatric disorders. The list of social and economic costs could go on and on. Males tend to think that if they divorce they will be better off financially and free from the responsibility of raising the children. Cancer rates for divorced males, however, increase dramatically ... Divorced men are going to die younger than their friends who stay married. [75]

## A PERMANENT UNION

Are you about to enter marriage? You should do so intending a permanent, lifelong union of yourself with your spouse. Christians should not marry thinking they have an option of breaking their vows if the union should prove difficult or inconvenient. God hates divorce! (Ma 2:14-16). As I write these words, my first and only wife Alison and I have been

---

[75] From an interview in *Christianity Today* magazine, November 23, 1992.

married nearly 60 years (since March 6, 1954). Divorce was unthinkable to us when we first stood together in church and swore to be bound together until death alone came to separate us. And divorce has remained unthinkable throughout all the intervening years. It is still unthinkable for us today.

Let me state this firmly – anyone who reckons this study encourages a casual approach to marriage, or an indifferent attitude to divorce, or to remarriage, is misrepresenting both me and the scriptures! Neither easy marriage, nor easy divorce, nor easy remarriage are proper Christian responses to the demands of scripture and of holy living! Alison and I pledged ourselves to each other for life by the most solemn vows made in the presence of Almighty God. Nothing less than a truly catastrophic collapse could change either her commitment or mine to the permanence of our marriage. We believe passionately in life-long marriages that reflect the integrity, selfless love, and steadfast faithfulness of the Lord himself.

Short relationships are shallow ones. How is that? Let me answer by asking, "How old are you?" As I write these lines I am approaching my 80[th.] year, yet I am still learning about myself. A lifetime is scarcely sufficient for anyone to begin truly and fully to know even himself! How much more difficult it is then to discover the hidden depths in another person! Permanent marriage alone provides the degree of intimacy and the constancy of association that are required to experience the wonder, the joy, of exploring the mysteries and of revealing the beauty that lies in one's spouse –

> If marriage is not considered a permanent trust for life, it is in permanent crisis. If the "freedom" to leave is regarded as a real option, it becomes a spectre which haunts the marriage. Consequently, there is not the

requisite freedom to develop an authentic relationship. [76]

# NOT PLEASURE, BUT HOLINESS

Has your marriage become painful or difficult? That by itself is no reason to dissolve it. Despite the self-indulgent yearning for unsullied happiness, total personal gratification, and unfettered freedom, which characterises this generation, there remains an important place for suffering. Patience under pain is an integral element in the development of Christian character, and in preparing the Christian to inherit the kingdom of God. A petulant envy of the apparent happiness of other couples is not an adequate reason for a Christian to try to escape a burdensome union. The goal of our lives is not pleasure, but holiness –

> Every time I stand before a couple and recite the words, "for better, for worse, for richer, for poorer, in sickness and in health," I declare the outrageous proposition that happiness is neither the goal nor the promise of marriage. Both Christianity and marriage teach us that life cannot be chiefly about happiness. If life is learning how to tell the truth and how to receive strangers, then how on earth can life be about happiness? For neither truth nor hospitality occur without some pain." [77]

(76)   Baker's Dictionary of Christian Ethics, ed. by Carl F. H. Henry; Baker Book House, Grand Rapids; 1973; article *Marriage*, pg. 407,408.

(77)   William H. Willimon, in an article in *The Christian Century*, June 4-11, 1986, pg. 544.

Indeed, Clement of Alexandria, writing *circa* 200, declared that it required more grace to remain true to Christ in marriage than in celibacy –

> It is not he who merely controls his passions that is called a content man, but he who has also achieved the mastery over good things ... (One) is not really shown to be a man in the choice of a single life; but he surpasses men, who, disciplined by marriage, procreation of children, and care for the house, without pleasure or pain, in his solicitude for the house, has been inseparable from God's love, and withstood all temptations arising through children, and wife, and domestics, and possessions. But he that has no family is in a great degree free of temptation. Caring, then, for himself alone, he is surpassed by him who is inferior as far as his own salvation is concerned, but who is superior in the conduct of life, preserving certainly, in his care for the truth, a minute image. [78]

## THE WRONG SPOUSE?

Most people discover eventually that they have married the "wrong" person! The thought (even if it soon passes) seizes them, "I have made a terrible mistake!" Three things commonly cause this feeling –

- they meet a new person whose virtues alone are visible, who seems more desirable, more compatible

---

[78]   *Miscellanies*, Bk 7, ch 12; The Ante-Nicene Fathers, Vol 2, pg. 543; Eerdman's Pub. Co; 1979 reprint.

than the spouse whose faults and blemishes have become all too plain.

Men in particular are often surprised to discover that they, like Solomon, are quite capable of *"loving many women"* (1 Kg 11:1). Nonetheless, the law of God requires that we (both men and women) should choose one spouse, and strive to be faithful to that choice for so long as our first partner lives.

- they come to the dismaying realisation that the image of themselves, built with such care to impress their partner when they were courting, has now been exposed for the sham it always was.

Some people cannot bear to have their camouflage removed, their disguises torn away, their self-delusions exposed. The knowledge that a spouse has come to know them as they really are, is too painful to be endured. They seek another whom they can once again deceive.

- they discover that their spouse constantly interferes with the crazed goals of our present culture: personal autonomy, unrestrained consumerism, unhindered self-fulfilment, and un-darkened happiness.

Incredibly, many people enter marriage, which is the antithesis of those goals, in order to achieve them! They take a spouse to escape parental control. They view marriage as an expression of adult freedom instead of responsibility. They treat their vows as the purchase price of untrammelled sexual enjoyment; their spouse is simply another consumer item they have paid for. They expect their spouse to be the means of making them happy, and of fulfilling their personal dreams. Such pitiful illusions deserve to be, and quickly will be, shattered. Rather, let us be Christians indeed, seeing in marriage a proving ground of real holiness, where the love of God is mirrored in an unfailing love for each other. Here the security of the kingdom of God is reflected in the absolute trust the Christian man and woman show toward each other;

the gates of hell cannot prevail over their mutual vows. Here they find what happiness really means as they work and play, laugh and cry, worship and pray together. Here they discover the best opportunity to learn the grace of Christ as they forgive each other, cling together in hope, rejoice in the darkest night, and master the virtues of patience, kindness, tolerance, and gentleness.

Then, to the three reasons given above, we may add another –

- sometimes the fading of outward beauty causes people to feel that they married the wrong spouse.

That is a shallow folly which has often been rebuked by wiser minds over the centuries –

> O Beauty, but a dubious boon
> Art thou to man, brief gift of little stay,
> Lent for a while and all too soon passing away . . .
> Passing . . . as the field's spring glory
> Fades in the summer heat, when fiercely
> Burns the high sun at noon, when night's
> Wheels roll too rapidly. As lilies
> Languish and their leaves grow pale,
> The head must lose its glory of hair,
> The glowing cheek of youth
> Be ravaged by the hand of time.
> Each day that passes takes its toll
> Of body's beauty. Beauty cannot stay;
> Would any wise man trust so frail a thing? [79]

Marriage possesses a great bourn of happiness; but there is a price to be paid of integrity and discipline, of fortitude and

---

[79]  Seneca, in his play Phaedra, Act Two; tr. by E. F. Watling; Penguin Books, London, 1970; pg. 128, 129.

perseverance, of patience and tolerance. Yet the rewards, both now and in eternity, are immense! Can you doubt that I strongly favour lifetime unions between people who are totally committed to each other in Christ?

Yet having said that, I must now add that scripture does recognise human frailty, and so provides for those situations where even the most earnest saint cannot achieve the ideal. I have been singularly blessed with a devoted and utterly faithful wife. Others are not so fortunate. For some men and women, marriage turns into a living hell. Is there no relief? That question is taken up in the next chapter.

## FOURTEEN

# WHAT JESUS SAID

The major passage is *Matthew 19:3-12*; see also *Matthew 5:31-32; Mark 10:2-12; Luke 16:18.*

The primary teaching of Christ is simply this: divorce, and re-marriage after divorce, are both forbidden. That was a harsh statement, and it caught the Pharisees (also the disciples, *Matthew 19:10*) quite by surprise. They all had expected either a cautiously ambiguous statement, or else a much laxer standard.

Why was the Master so stern? He was responding to the two schools of thought that were dominant among the Jews of that time –

- there was the liberal school of **_Rabbi Hillel_**, which permitted divorce for almost any reason;

- and there was the conservative school of **_Rabbi Shammai_**, which permitted divorce only for infidelity.

The Pharisees (in Mt 19:3) were pressuring Jesus to declare whose side he was on, Hillel's or Shammai's? It was a trap. Whichever answer he gave would anger many hearers.

Jesus knew that both schools based their arguments on certain rules Moses had given Israel, which the Pharisees had referred to in their question: *"Why then did Moses ... etc."* (Mt 19:7). He realised that they were *"testing"* him by trying to force him either to favour one school, thus antagonising the other; or to make enemies of both by countermanding Moses altogether. So they said (echoing

Hillel), *"Is it lawful for a man to divorce his wife on any and every ground?"*

Would Jesus agree with Hillel's broad and loose reading of Moses, or would he choose the sterner rule of Shammai?

Christ artfully avoided the trap simply by going back to a still earlier authority: the record of Genesis! There the scripture shows –

## GOD'S ORIGINAL STANDARD

In the beginning the Creator made the human race male and female, and revealed his ordinary intention that they should live together as man and wife. This union is so complete, and the attraction that leads to it so strong, that a man will leave the social group in which he has spent all his previous life and unite himself to a woman he has but recently met. The bond of family is deep; but the bond between a man and his wife is deeper.

### ONE MAN, ONE WOMAN

God gave Adam but one wife, and Eve but one husband, which indicts both polygamy and polyandry. God reckons one mate is sufficient, and he wants the man and his wife to apply themselves to the vocation of finding satisfaction only with each other, and of living only with each other, for life.

### JOINED BY GOD

The deeper reason for this exclusive union is given in the words *"they shall be one flesh"* (Ge 2:24). By his emphatic repetition of that quotation, Christ showed its crucial importance (Mt 19:5-6). And then he added also the solemn injunction, *"What God has joined together, do not allow anyone to separate."*

## HOW ARE THEY JOINED?

A problem arises: what is the significance of the phrase *"one flesh"*; and just when are a couple actually *"joined together"* by God?

Some say that both declarations become true on the first occasion of sexual intercourse, whether or not the two people are married, and that any subsequent union with another partner (even with a spouse) is adulterous. Others say only a marriage where both partners are God-fearing is wrought by God, and only in such a union do the couple truly become *"one flesh"*.

The third view, and the one favoured in this study, argues that this is –

## NOT A CASUAL RELATIONSHIP

Outside of marriage, how can a casual relationship, or even an extended one, fulfil the requirements of the statements in *Genesis*? There the couple become *"one flesh"* only on the basis of the man leaving his former home and *"being made one with his wife"*; or, in the words of the old version, *"cleaving to his wife"*. The words *"cleave"* (to glue, to cling, to adhere) and *"wife"* imply a union that is lawful, exclusive, and permanent. No adulterous or illicit relationship can fit those terms.

Someone may ask, "What about *1 Corinthians 6:15-16*?" I do not think that passage disturbs what I am saying. Although Paul does use *Genesis 2:24* to make an ardent protest against harlotry, he is engaging in a kind of special pleading. He is plucking a single idea out of the passage and using it in a very restricted sense. A harlot is not a wife. No holy covenant exists when a man has intercourse with a whore. It is unthinkable that such a union should be made indissoluble.

A prostitute and her lecher become *"one flesh"* only in a limited and corrupted sense. [80]

## A PRIMEVAL LAW

The statement *"what God has joined together"* is a commentary by Christ on the meaning of *"one flesh"*. The couple are *"joined"* (literally, "yoked") and become *"one flesh"* only in the sense that God intends their commitment to each other to be permanent and exclusive. Married couples are *"joined together by God"*, not by personal divine intervention in each marriage, but because the primeval law of God stands behind every wedding. That law mandates, for the entire human family, that a man should cleave to his wife and to her alone, for the remainder of his life. The law expects the same fidelity from the wife.

Thus the ancient law of marriage goes beyond the bounds of the church, and embraces the whole of humanity. It declares that any couple who vow to live together as man and wife, and who wed according to the laws and customs of their own social group, are *"God-joined"* because they are acting in harmony with his universal law. In his sight they become *"one flesh"*.

## GOD HATES DIVORCE

A further ground for the inviolability of marriage, and a further revelation of the purpose God has ordained for marriage, is given in *Malachi 2:14-16 –*

---

(80)   Note also the several references in the early books of the Bible to men visiting a prostitute (e.g. Ge 38:15-18). There is never any suggestion that intercourse with a harlot had any significance beyond a temporary satisfying of sexual desire.

*The Lord was watching when you and your young wife made your vows to each other. But now you have been unfaithful to her, although she is your companion and your wife by a holy promise. Have you forgotten that God made you both into one? Is not the same Spirit of life in you both? Was it not God's purpose that you should bring godly children into the world? So beware! Control your behaviour. Let none of you be unfaithful to the wife of your youth. This is what the Lord God says, "__I hate divorce!__" And the Lord of Hosts demands, "Why are you so cruel to each other?" So bring your passions under control, and be done with all this treachery!*

God hates divorce! Why? Because

- it involves breaking solemn oaths and covenants; and

- it hinders the creation of godly homes where parents can raise their children in love and security (compare Ep 6:1-4);

- it is a source of cruelty, violence, and sin.

Christ himself drew attention to this third reason: *"If a man divorces his wife ... he drives her into adultery"* (Mt 5:31-32). In those days that was often literally true. There were no government pensions, nor any alimony. A discarded wife might well have to resort to prostitution to sustain life. Also, perhaps Jesus meant that re-marriage, where the grounds of divorce were insufficient, would fall under God's judgment as an act of harlotry; or, the divorce might cause her neighbours to believe she had been guilty of adultery. In any case, divorce is hateful to God.

# RE-MARRIAGE PROHIBITED?

> *If you divorce your wife and marry another woman, you commit adultery; and anyone who marries a woman divorced from her husband is also committing adultery (Luke 16:18).*

That passage further enforces the prohibition against divorce. The Lord God refuses to permit people casually to destroy his law about the inviolate nature of marriage. No human decree can by itself countermand a divine fiat – *"What God has joined together, let no man put asunder"* (Mt 19:6). A couple may divorce, but in the reckoning of God they are still bound to each other, and any subsequent marriage is therefore adulterous. That is the basic law of God. Any later exceptions or amendments to that law do not remove the law itself. It remains the divine standard for every marriage.

When the Pharisees heard Jesus state that austere rule, they at once pounced on him – *"Why then did Moses command a man to give a certificate of divorce, and to put his wife away?"* (Mt 19:7).

The Master's reply completely silenced them –

> *Because of your hardness of heart Moses allowed you to divorce your wives, but from the beginning it was not so (vs. 8).*

People often think that Christ reproached Moses for passing an inferior law. That is not true. Rather, Jesus neither commended nor condemned Moses' rule, as the following comments will show –

## A DECAYED IDEAL

The original ideal of marriage, which had sadly decayed long before the time of Moses, was largely restored by him. So wise are the Mosaic statutes that they still form the basis of the marriage codes of the whole Western world. Those statutes allowed both divorce and re-marriage. But what did Jesus think about them?

## COMMANDED OR PERMITTED?

Christ did not abrogate the Mosaic statutes; but he did countermand the distorted teaching of the Pharisees. This is shown by the difference between the words of Christ and those of the Pharisees. They said, *"Moses commanded us ..."* But Christ countered, *"Moses permitted you ..."*

The passage they were quoting is *Deuteronomy 24:1-4*. Some of the older translations do not fairly render the original Hebrew text. Moses was not instructing the man to divorce his wife, as some versions seem to say, and as the Pharisees taught. Christ properly interpreted the passage to mean that while Moses may have allowed divorce, his real purpose was to regulate that unhappy practice, and to prevent promiscuity.

Hence most modern translations rightly give the passage the following sense –

> *If a man takes a wife, and if she then falls into disgrace in his eyes ... and if he chooses to divorce her ... and if she goes off and marries another man ... and if the latter husband divorces her ... or if the latter husband dies ... then her former husband may not take her again to be his wife.*

The *"ifs"* all refer to existing practices, which Moses, because of the hardness of their hearts, was prepared to *"suffer"*. But to find the actual *command* of Moses you must look in the last clause – a divorced woman who has married another, may not return to her former husband. That command is apparently still valid, and is a strong rebuttal of those who claim that divorced people who have married again should break up and return to their original partners.

## THE RULE CHRIST GAVE

Moses allowed a man to divorce his wife if *"she found no favour in his eyes because he had discovered something shameful in her."*

The school of Hillel gave those words such a broad meaning that a man could dismiss his wife for almost any cause, including such trivial things as a badly cooked meal, or gossip, or talking too loudly. The school of Shammai insisted that Moses was referring exclusively to unchastity.

Which school would Jesus endorse?

He ignored both of them! He made no attempt to explain the words of Moses. He cited only two authorities: the primeval law (Ge 2:24); and his own command: *"And I say to you, whoever divorces his wife, except for unchastity, and marries another, commits adultery."*

That is surprising, for at first sight, Shammai's view might appear to be the same as Christ's. But it was not. Shammai interpreted Moses too strictly, Hillel interpreted him too loosely. Christ declined to approve either of them. He allowed Moses' words to stand, and left their interpretation an open question (although, as I shall show in a moment, he did give a further explanation to his disciples in private, *vs. 10-12*).

Then, on his own authority, and confirmed by the primeval law (Ge 2:24), Jesus asserted that divorce was not permissible except on the ground of *"unchastity"* (*porneia*). By this emphatic statement he tried to ennoble the discussion, to call his hearers back to a high view of marriage as a holy estate, and to fortify the sacredness of its obligations. But did Jesus want his words to be turned into an absolute ethical rule? Was he asserting an inflexible, undeviating moral law, one that must be imposed upon every married couple regardless of their circumstances? I think the answer must be, "No!"

Note again how Jesus sidestepped the immediate demand made by the Pharisees (to choose between Hillel and Shammai). Note also that he did not actually countermand Moses' rule. He avoided both an explanation of what Moses meant and any suggestion that Moses was at fault. He simply called them back to the pure state of things *"in the beginning"*, and set that before them as God's highest goal.

Yet in the face of human frailty how severe this demand seems! Did Jesus really mean to be so harsh? His disciples at first took him literally, for in a later private discussion they reacted with some heat – *"If that is the rule for a man with his wife, then it would be better never to marry!"*

Why were they so upset? Simply because they knew (as we do) that many things can smash the dream of a happy marriage –

- one of the spouses may have a serious neurosis, or an impossible obsession that was hidden during courtship;
- one of them may prove to be sexually deviate;
- one of them may become hopelessly alcoholic, or become involved in crime, or addicted to drugs; and so on.

Must an unoffending partner be condemned to remain in a house that has become hell? If so, then we may well agree with the disciples: it is wiser to remain unmarried! The risk is too fearful.

Jesus' reply was surprising, and showed a compassionate relaxation of the dour austerity of his earlier public statement. In public, confronted by the hypocritical Pharisees and their friends, he allowed no easing of the severest possible standard. Into the crass slackness of their selfish view of marriage he threw the unyielding demand, *"There shall be neither divorce nor remarriage!"* But in private, confronted by an inquiry from men who sincerely desired to do the will of God, he allowed, *"Not everyone can receive this precept, but only those to whom it is given"* (vs. 10-12).

Here is a definite softening of his earlier demand. Yet still, Christ does not satisfy our quest for more detail, nor does he offer any further comment on the grounds that Moses allowed for divorce (that is, a *"shameful"* act by a spouse). Both the meaning of Moses' rule, and the explanation of who can *"receive"* Christ's own strict precept, remain open questions.

So we come to a reasonable conclusion: the ethicists in each generation must remain free to apply the broad principles given by Moses and Christ to their own contemporary societies. Sometimes that will require them to call people back to *"the beginning"*; sometimes it will require them to accommodate human *"hardness of heart"*. But always a balance must be struck between upholding the loftiest ideals of marriage – one man and one woman in a lifetime union of love – and the sometimes harsh realities of daily experience. It is a choice between inflexible law and fitting grace. It recognizes that not everyone can embrace the highest standards, that people differ enormously in their emotional capacity and spiritual strength, and that each case must be assessed on its own merits.

## *FIFTEEN*

# A GROUND FOR DIVORCE

Let us now go back to *Deuteronomy 24:1-4*. Notice that Moses allowed divorce if a wife no longer pleased her husband because he had discovered in her *"erwath dabhar"*. Translators offer various renderings of that phrase – *"scandalous behaviour, indecency, something improper, unchastity, lacking favour, a shameful thing, something displeasing"* – and so on. Hillel emphasised the idea *"found no favour"*, and permitted divorce for the most flippant reasons; Shammai emphasised the idea of *"scandalous behaviour"*, and understood it to mean only adultery. The one was too loose, the other too narrow.

Today we can safely assume that Moses was referring to divorce for reasons other than adultery. Why? Because under his law the death penalty, not divorce, was the proper response to gross immorality (Le 19:20-22; 20:10-12; 21:9; etc.). But just as clearly, *"erwath dabhar"* means something more serious than careless housekeeping, or slovenly dress, and the like.

The problem with the Pharisees was that,

> they were always emphasising the Mosaic concession, whereas Jesus constantly emphasised a greater principle: that husband and wife are, and must remain, one." [81]

---

(81)   Hendriksen, in loc.

That is the main effect of *Deuteronomy 24:1-4*. It is a law, not about easy divorce, but about the sanctity of marriage. Moses accepted the destruction of the first union, but he was anxious to enhance the sacredness of the second. This new marriage, he said, is just as binding and as inviolate as the first. The husband has lost all claim upon his former wife. The wife has lost all claim upon her former husband. If they have married another person after divorce, they must devote all zeal to making the new union successful. Further, this law protected wives from being treated like chattels. They could not be passed randomly from man to man. Thus Moses enhanced the social status of women.

Men also were affected by the law. It made a first husband pause before he casually dismissed his wife; for once he had sent her away, and she had married another, he could never bring her lawfully back to his bed.

## DEFINITION OF "PORNEIA"

Christ allowed divorce on the ground of *porneia*. Out of the controversy about the meaning of this word, three common interpretations have arisen –

### PRE-MARITAL UNCHASTITY

Some limit *porneia* to unchaste behaviour before marriage that had remained undiscovered until after the marriage had taken place. But the death penalty, not divorce, was the prescribed OT method of handling that offence (De 22:13-21). After which, of course, the surviving spouse was free to marry again.

No doubt serious hidden pre-marital unchastity still provides adequate grounds for divorce, since the death penalty is happily no longer applicable. However, there do not seem to be any strong reasons for limiting *porneia* to such a narrow meaning. One might also object that giving *porneia* such specific definition provides too easy a means of dissolving too many marriages – for there are few unions in which both partners are wholly free from pre-marital moral blemish.

## CONSANGUINITY

Some scholars argue that *porneia* was the technical word for a sexual union that violated one of the forbidden degrees of relationship (cp. Le 18:6-18). Jesus used *porneia*, they say, in this narrow sense. Therefore he allowed divorce only when a couple, after the wedding, discovered their union was illicit because they were closely related.

But how often would people find themselves in that plight? Rarely enough to make it improbable that Jesus would give it special attention. Anyhow, the proper solution to a consanguineous marriage is not divorce, but annulment, which is a legal assertion that there never was a true marriage. In that case, the now separated couple are surely each free to take a valid spouse. Why would Jesus forbid them to do so? Why would he speak about divorce instead of annulment?

The evidence that *porneia* should be restricted to a forbidden blood relationship remains forced and unconvincing. So we are left with a third choice –

## ADULTERY AND/OR FORNICATION

I can easily show that the New Testament uses *porneia* to describe a wide variety of sexual immorality, perversion, deviation, and fornication – see *Mark 7:21; Romans 1:29; 1 Corinthians 7:2; Galatians 5:19; 1 Thessalonians 4:3; Revelations 14:8;* etc.

The several lexicons I have consulted all agree that the Greeks (and the apostles) used *porneia* to describe *"every kind of unlawful sexual intercourse or immoral behaviour"*.

Likewise, in the Greek version of the Old Testament, *porneia* has a wide meaning; thus we find it in *Genesis 38:24* ("prostitution"); in *Numbers 14:33* ("fornication"); in *Isaiah 47:10* ("harlotry"); *57:9* ("whoredom"); and likewise in *Ezekiel 16:15,22,25,33-36,41*; and in more than a score of other places.

Several of those passages link *porneia* with both pre-marital and post-marital immorality, and with various kinds of fornication. A Greek-speaking Jew would therefore have used *porneia* to describe not only the behaviour forbidden in *Leviticus 18:6-15*, but also in *16-23; 20:10-21*; etc. See also the following verses, which use the closely related word *porneuo* (to practise prostitution, or sexual immorality in general) – *Deuteronomy 23:17-18; Psalm 106:39; Ezekiel 6:9*; etc.

Thus the Greeks applied *porneia* to: pre-marital immorality that remained hidden until after the marriage; infidelity after marriage; sexually deviant behaviour in general; and to forbidden consanguinity. It is surely unreasonable to limit *porneia* either to pre-marital unchastity, or even to adultery, when it plainly includes a wide range of corrupt or condemned sexual behaviour.

## A GROUND FOR DIVORCE

Where such *porneia* exists, said Jesus, divorce becomes the right of the offended spouse. He did not command it in such cases; but it is certainly permitted. A wronged partner may have good reasons to overlook an offence and to welcome back the erring spouse. However, there is no compulsion to do so.

However, a Christian spouse does have an obligation to forgive any and every fault, and never to waver in offering the love of Christ. But forgiveness does not necessarily require the restoration of the wrongdoer to a position of trust, nor to a level of partnership. We must all earn those privileges.

## AN ETHICAL PROBLEM

We now encounter a problem similar to the one we faced above: _an ethical fuzziness_. Scripture uses _porneia_ so broadly that opinions will always differ about its application to a given marital problem. The narrowest view would limit it to adultery; the broadest would apply it to any violation of marital trust, whether moral, fiscal, physical, mental, social, and so on. The truth probably lies in the conservative centre.

Godly ethicists therefore have the task of defining _porneia_ for each new set of social conditions, and for each new spousal conflict. In other words, what level of _porneia_ becomes an adequate ground for divorce must be separately determined by and for each couple, with the proviso that the pressure of scripture is always toward saving a marriage rather than too easily destroying it.

## THE BURDEN OF THE LEGALIST

If you are a rigorous moralist, I suppose that the prospect of allowing one couple to divorce for a given act of _porneia_, but not another, will seem appalling. People who find it necessary to structure life around stern rules tend to value their rules above the needs of individuals. They insist that every family must be governed by the same canon. No variation or exception can be allowed. To them, the moral and ethical discretion scripture so daringly allows each Christian is scandalous. They are sure that people will always corrupt such liberty into licence that moral chaos will inescapably result from an ethic based on broad principles rather than fixed decrees.

But of course that has always been one of the great tensions in the gospel. God has indeed given us a startling freedom in Christ. Each of us has liberty to conform ourselves to our own unique vision of Christ (for we all see him differently). Sadly, the reaction of the church to that remarkable, almost frightening, freedom has always been to go either to one extreme or the other; that is, either to legalism, or to licentiousness. Paul's letters are full of this tension. He found himself continually obliged to withstand either the one side or the other, that is, to contend against both legalists and libertines.

## PAUL AND THE CASUISTS

Despite the possibility that some profligates might turn Christian liberty into an excuse for casting off all moral restraint, Paul refused to adopt the expedient of law. The casuistic spirit was anathema to him. He could not permit sophists to reduce dynamic Christian life to a list of deadening regulations. He constantly urged people to be filled with the beauty of Christ, to have the mind of Christ, to allow the Holy Spirit to be their personal guide, and thus to live truly as the free-born children of God (Ga 4:28-5:1).

Does that lead to weak marriages and easy divorce? Only to those who want to mock the grace of God (cp. Ro 6:1-2). But if Jesus (and not merely some dictum) truly is Lord in a home, then marriage will thrive in holiness, integrity, faithfulness, trust, and love.

## TWO OTHER PRECLUSIONS

It is worth noting that there were two other situations where Moses strictly outlawed divorce –

- when a man had falsely accused his wife of pre-marital unchastity (De 22:13-19); and

- when a man had intercourse with a woman and was forced to marry her (22:28-29).

The prohibition in those cases, of course, was only against the man dismissing his wife against her will; although, I suppose, if she became guilty of post-marital infidelity, he would then be free to divorce her.

\*\*\*\*\*\*\*\*\*\*\*\*\*\*\*\*\*\*\*\*\*\*\*\*\*\*\*\*\*\*\*\*\*\*\*\*\*\*\*\*\*\*\*\*\*\*\*\*\*\*\*\*\*\*

## INTERIM CONCLUSIONS

Let me summarise what I have shown you thus far –

- Christ established a basic opposition to all divorce and remarriage, and there can be no doubt that those who desire to please him will strive mightily to conform to his will in this matter.

- Christ allowed a specific exception to that basic rule – divorce may be allowed on the ground of *porneia*. However, there is such breadth in the definition of *porneia* that a separate ethical decision concerning its meaning and its application must be made in each case.

- By default, in that he did not specifically countermand it, Christ apparently intended the Mosaic law, and the general teaching of the OT on marriage, to remain effective, or at least, to be used as a valid guide toward establishing a Christian marital ethic.

\*\*\*\*\*\*\*\*\*\*\*\*\*\*\*\*\*\*\*\*\*\*\*\*\*\*\*\*\*\*\*\*\*\*\*\*\*\*\*\*\*\*\*\*\*\*\*\*\*\*\*\*\*\*

## IS RE-MARRIAGE PERMITTED?

When a divorce was lawful, Moses said that the woman could go and *"become the wife of another man"* (De 24:2). I take it that Christ accepted this rule. In other words, the exception stated by Christ (*"for any cause other than porneia"*) is applicable not only to divorce but also to re-marriage. Thus Henry Alford argues that the structure of the Greek text in *Matthew 19:9* requires the reading, *"He who marries a woman thus divorced* (that is, for a cause other than unchastity) *commits adultery."* [82]

In other words, when a Christian has divorced a spouse on lawful grounds (that is, because of *porneia*), that Christian is free to remarry. The only exception lies in the *Pauline Privilege,* which is considered below.

The Jews of Christ's day unanimously agreed that the scriptures allowed re-marriage after a lawful divorce. They squabbled about what constituted a lawful divorce, but they never doubted that Moses allowed a couple to re-marry after their marriage had been legitimately dissolved. [83] On that point there was no quarrel.

Christ appears to have approved that principle, except for placing a definite limitation on what constitutes a lawful divorce. Subject only to this restriction, the Lord apparently agreed that a divorced couple were free to re-marry.

But someone may protest: "Surely Christ specifically forbids ALL re-marriage in *Mark 10:11-12* and *Luke 16:18*!" I can only reply that you must read those passages in the light of the exception found in *Matthew 5:32* and *19:9*. Since Christ based that exception on a reference to *Deuteronomy 24:1-4*, I cannot avoid applying it not only to divorce but also to re-

---

(82)   The Greek Testament, Vol 1, page 194; Guardian Press, Grand Rapids,1976 reprint of the 1844 original.

(83)   Notice, for example, how Moses precludes a priest from marrying a divorced woman, but by that very rule implies that other men may do so (Le 21:7).

marriage. Hence, a lawfully divorced couple are free to re-marry. (84)

Note the subtle way in which Mark differs from Matthew in his account of this debate between Jesus and the rabbis. According to Mark, Jesus asked them, *"What did Moses command you?"* (Mk 10:3) But the rabbis replied, *"Moses allowed . . ."* (vs. 4) At once Jesus re-joined that Moses did not merely *"allow"*, but rather *"commanded"* (vs. 5) them to write a certificate of divorce. (85)

Why? Because only then (as Moses taught), would the woman be free to re-marry. I think Jesus heartily endorsed the need to offer protection to the vulnerable spouse, and he recognised that divorce and re-marriage might be the lesser evil. Nonetheless, he steadfastly stressed that God's original and unchanged purpose was toward a lifelong union (Mk 10:6-9).

## THE INNOCENT SPOUSE?

Because Moses (Le 20:10; etc.) decreed the death penalty for persons guilty of adultery, and of other forms of immorality, some have taught that only the innocent party is free to re-marry; they refuse remarriage to the guilty party. Others say the guilty party should be allowed to marry only if the innocent party marries again.

---

(84)  By "lawful", I am referring to biblical, not secular, law. Also, the concept that divorce automatically conveys a right to re-marry seems to be taken for granted in the legal codes of all civilized communities.

(85)  The changes between *Matthew* and *Mark* in their use of "allow" and "command" in this debate, show how important context and intention are in the matter of understanding what the Bible is teaching. The gospel writers use the same incident in the life of Christ, but draw subtly different meanings from it, or give it a subtly different thrust.

We may ask, though, is any party in a divorce case wholly innocent or wholly guilty? It may be so occasionally, but usually there will be at least some blame on both sides. In any case, Christ confirmed the substitution of divorce for the death penalty (which the Jews were no longer inflicting for adultery), nor is there any suggestion in his words that the privilege of re-marriage should be restricted to the innocent party.

## A LAWFUL DIVORCE DISSOLVES A MARRIAGE

So it seems that a lawful [86] divorce completely dissolves a marriage. The former partners then become as though they had never married. They are therefore free to proceed as single persons, except for whatever restraints or obligations the laws and customs of their own society may place upon them. As single persons they are wholly released from their former bond, and are free to marry whomever they choose – except that Christians are instructed to marry only *"in the Lord"* (1 Co 7:39) – that is, a fellow Christian.

This complete dissolution of the former marriage bond is confirmed by the prohibition (mentioned above) against a divorced couple re-marrying each other. They are to be to each other as though they did not exist (that is, providing at least one of them has in the meantime contracted another marriage, De 24:4.)

## JESUS ON CELIBACY

Christ's words in *Matthew 19:11-12* show his awareness that for many people an unmarried state is fraught with grave

---

(86)   Once again, I mean "lawful" in biblical, not secular, terms.

difficulties. He freely allowed that a demand for celibacy is within the grasp only of those who are gifted for such continence. This being so, it is not consistent to suppose he would allow divorce without also allowing re-marriage. The one seems to be an unavoidable consequence of the other.

The same ideas occur in *1 Corinthians 7:1-2, 5, 9; 1 Timothy 5:14*, upon which further comment is given below. In the meantime, notice again that this principle is applicable only to a divorce on scriptural grounds. If people choose to remain unmarried, or to divorce on grounds other than scripture allows, then they must determine to live in celibacy and chastity.

## *SIXTEEN*

# THE TEACHING OF PAUL

At first sight there is a passage where Paul appears to teach that no one can re-marry while a former partner is alive – *Romans 7:1-3*. However, Paul is not dealing there with the subject of divorce, but with two simple facts –

- that a married couple are ordinarily bound to each other for as long as they live; and

- that death automatically dissolves a marriage.

Paul makes those ordinary facts an illustration of our relationship with the law and the gospel.

Since the issue of a broken marriage was not in the apostle's mind when he wrote to the Romans, it is not valid to use too eagerly his comments there to establish a position on divorce and re-marriage. Rather we should turn to a passage where the apostle does deal specifically with the matter of a ruined relationship – *1 Corinthians 7:1-10*.

Once again we find, not a formal statement of all the problems caused by marital infidelity, but a response to particular questions. Hence we must supplement the teaching in this passage with that found in other places in the scripture.

I have already mentioned that Paul is often criticised for this passage, as if he had reduced marriage to the lowest level of physical gratification. He is scorned for presenting marriage merely as a device for the lawful fulfilment of sexual desire. But, again, the statements he makes here, in response to certain enquirers, must be measured against his words elsewhere, which define marriage in the highest and noblest terms as akin to the union between Christ and the Church (Ep 5:21-33; etc.). But in his letter to the Corinthians he was simply answering several questions that had been put to him in a letter. As we have seen, those questions appear to have been –

- is celibacy better than marriage? (1-2, 6-9)

- what are the duties of each spouse? (3-5)

- is divorce permissible for a Christian? (10-11)

- what about an unbelieving spouse? (12-16)

- what about those who are unmarried? (25-38)

- can a woman marry again, after her husband dies? (39-40) [87]

Paul had a firm answer for each of those questions –

## THE QUESTION OF CELIBACY

See verses 1-2, 6-9, 25-38. Celibacy was much admired in antiquity. The ancients reckoned it a higher state than marriage. So it is not surprising that in the church at Corinth there were some forceful advocates of celibacy. Since Paul himself was a bachelor (vs. 7) they no doubt thought they had apostolic authority for their position. Actually, Paul takes great care to strike a fair balance between the connubial and celibate states; he points out the weaknesses and the advantages of each –

---

[87]  Note: scholars are divided about whether vs. 36-38 refer to a father giving his daughter in marriage, or to a betrothed couple. In either case the meaning is clear: Paul suggests that a couple should delay marriage until the time of trouble has passed; yet there is nothing wrong in going ahead with the marriage.

## CELIBACY IS GOOD

*"It is a good thing for a man to have nothing to do with women"* (vs. 1).

Notice, *"good"* is not the same as *"better"*. There are benefits in celibacy, but the single state is not necessarily superior to the married. Within marriage also there is much "good" – compare *Ephesians 5:22-33; 1 Timothy 3:1-4; 5:14*; etc.

However, when Paul wrote to the Corinthians, they were facing a period of persecution (*"in a time of trouble like the present"* – vs. 26), and for this reason he recommended they should all remain as they were: *"It is best for a man to stay as he is. Have you contracted a marriage? Then do not cast your wife aside. Are you unmarried? Then do not seek a wife"* (vs. 27). He said this, not to advocate celibacy, but only to spare them sorrow – *"Those who marry will suffer pain because of the present conditions, and my aim is to spare you"* (vs. 28-35).

Paul was careful to say that his advice did not stem from any direct command of God, but was his own opinion – *"On the question of celibacy, I have no instructions from the Lord, but here is my opinion, which comes from one who by God's mercy is fit to be trusted"* (vs. 25). So he added, despite his anxiety about persecution, that they were free to marry if other considerations made it advisable to do so – *"If however you do marry there is nothing wrong in it"* (vs. 28; and see also vs. 36-38).

## MARRIAGE IS GOOD

Despite the value of celibacy, and despite the problem of worldly distractions (vs. 29-35), the rule for most people is plainly stated –

> *Because there is so much immorality, let each man have his own wife, and each woman her own husband (vs. 2).*

And again –

> *I say this by way of concession, not command. I would prefer you all to be as I am myself; but everyone has the gift God has granted him, one this gift, and another that (vs. 6-7).*

Here is the weakness of celibacy – it opens the celibate to severe temptation (compare also vs. 5) and to the suspicion of being unchaste. This leads Paul to make a vital statement – *continence and conjugality both require, and both are, a gift of God.* The grace of God at work in some will draw them to celibacy. That same grace at work in others will draw them to marriage. Both equally depend upon a divine inflow. Neither state can be lived as God wants it lived, without his help, or indeed, his special call and gift. Hence it would seem to be against scripture to impose a lifetime of celibacy upon a reluctant man or woman.

I understand fully that life circumstances, quite apart from any biblical injunction, sometimes prevent people from marrying, even when they very much wish to do so. Reluctantly or not, if they wish to remain righteous they must also remain chaste. But plainly, the normal, and desirable state for most people, is marriage. Paul recognizes that, and his teaching embraces it. He has no desire to impose celibacy upon people for whom it would be an unhappy state, fraught with tension, making them susceptible to temptations that may be too strong for them.

## THREE GROUPS OF CELIBATES

According to Christ, only three groups of people can accept celibacy – see *Matthew 19:10-12*. He said this because the disciples had exclaimed, *"It is better not to marry!"* But

Christ replied, *"You cannot expect everyone to accept that. It belongs only to those who have received a gift from God."* He then went on to point out that continence was usually limited to those who

- are *"incapable of marriage because they were born that way"* (that is, they were born either with a physical disability or with a celibate nature);
- are incapable of marriage because they *"were made that way by men"* (by surgery or accident);
- have *"renounced marriage for the sake of the kingdom of Heaven."*

Then he concluded – *"Let those accept it who can!"*

For those who can *"accept it"*, celibacy is the proper calling. But for the remainder of mankind marriage is the ordinary and expected state, and should be embraced gladly as the will of God. [88]

## MARRY IF YOU CAN

With all that in mind, Paul writes –

> *To those who are unmarried, and to widows, this is my advice: it is good for you to remain single, as I am myself. But if you cannot control yourselves, then you should marry. It is better to marry than to be on fire with passion (vs. 8-9).*

---

[88]    Note: the renunciation of marriage "for the sake of the kingdom of Heaven" does not sanction any form of self-mutilation, which is strictly forbidden – *Leviticus 19:28; Deuteronomy 23:1-2.* The reference here is to those who, like Paul, have received from God the special gift (Greek "charism", a spiritual endowment) that enables them to sustain a single state with joy.

Did you notice that the words *"you should marry"* are a command? Paul does not support the idea that there is something meritorious in suppressing sexual desire. It is more virtuous to marry than to struggle constantly against passion. Hence the words of both Christ and Paul show that Christian people should normally control sexual desire through the proper use of marriage.

Martin Luther embraced the same good sense. In his commentary on *Galatians 5:16*, he cites the example of even the holiest of saints who suffered agonies of temptation, and he insists that part of the meaning of *"walking in the Spirit"* (Ga 5:16) is to govern the flesh by getting married! –

> Jerome [89] ... who was a marvellous lover and defender of chastity, doth plainly confess – "O (saith he) how often have I thought myself to be in the midst of the vain delights and pleasures of Rome, even when I was in the wild wilderness ... I, who for fear of hell had condemned myself to such a prison, thought myself oftentimes to be dancing among young women, when I had no other company but scorpions and wild beasts. My face was pale with fasting, but my mind was inflamed with desires in my cold body, and although my flesh was half dead already, yet the flames of fleshly lust boiled within me."

> If Jerome felt in himself such flames of fleshly lust, who lived in the barren wilderness with bread and water, what do our holy belly-gods the clergymen feel, think ye, who so stuff and

---

(89) A 5<sup>th</sup> century ascetic, scholar, preacher, most renowned for his Latin translation of the Bible, known as The Vulgate.

stretch out themselves with all kinds of dainty fare, that it is a marvel their bellies burst not? [90] Wherefore these things are written ... to the universal Church of Christ and to all the faithful: whom Paul exhorteth to walk in the Spirit, that they fulfil not the lust of the flesh; that is to say, not only to bridle the gross motions of the flesh, as carnal lust, wrath, impatiency, and such-like; but also the spiritual motions, as doubting, blasphemy, idolatry, contempt and hatred of God. ...

Therefore if the flesh begin to wax wanton, repress and bridle it by the Spirit. If it will not be, marry a wife, *"for it is better to marry than to burn."* Thus doing thou walkest in the Spirit: that is, thou followest God's word and doest his will. [91]

Do notice in particular that last paragraph above. I think it well represents Paul's approach to these matters.

## FIND WHAT IS RIGHT FOR YOU

Paul concludes – *"All this I say by way of concession, not command."* (1 Co 7:6, 12, 25, 35, 40. That is, he is not instructing them either to marry or to remain single, but is giving permission for either state. Neither is superior to the

---

(90)    Luther is drawing attention here to the scandalous licentiousness of many of the priests of that time (16th century), who were supposed to remain unmarried and celibate.

(91)    A Commentary on St Paul's Epistle to the Galatians; Martin Luther; based on lectures delivered in Latin at the University of Wittenberg in 1531; first published in English in 1575; James Clarke & Co. Ltd., London, 1956; pg. 500-501.

other. As Paul says, *"We all have our own gift from God; you may have one gift, but someone else will have another"* (vs. 7).

Only one thing is finally right for each of us: *find the will of God, and do it.*

## SEVENTEEN

# A BUNDLE OF QUESTIONS

This chapter continues with more of the questions that Paul was apparently asked by the church at Corinth, beginning with –

## THE QUESTION OF MARITAL DUTY

See *1 Corinthians 7:3-5* –

> *The husband must give the wife what is due to her, and the wife equally must give the husband his due.*

The word *"due"* could be translated as *"their debt to each other"*. It shows that each party owes to the other, equally and habitually, certain conjugal rights. The husband must give full satisfaction to his wife, and likewise the wife to her husband. They are to concentrate, not on getting their *due*, but on giving their *duty*. They should each seek their partner's pleasure above their own.

So pressing is this debt that Paul says a couple should withhold it from each other only for the most compelling reasons, and then only by mutual consent –

> *Do not deny yourselves to one another, except when you agree upon a temporary abstinence in order to devote yourselves to prayer ... otherwise, for lack of self-control, you may be tempted by Satan (vs. 5).*

Husband and wife belong to each other so fully that the withholding of the body is (in the stronger word of the old version) an act of *"fraud"* and therefore reprehensible in the sight of God.

The reason for this rule is stated – the marriage covenant involves a surrender of the right to sole control over one's own body –

> *The wife cannot claim her body as her own; it belongs to her husband. Equally, the husband cannot claim his body as his own; it belongs to his wife (vs. 4).*

But the question to be raised here is this – does a "marriage" consist only of two people observing legal forms and thus being pronounced man and wife? Or is there an inescapable presumption that a man is no true husband, nor is a woman a true wife, unless they each honourably fulfil their marital duties toward each other?

Should a man still be called "husband" if he incessantly abuses his wife (whether physically, verbally, or emotionally), and denies her his duty of care, protection, love, intimacy, and fellowship? Should a woman still be called "wife" if she refuses to honour and love her man, and withholds from him intimacy, partnership, and joy?

Can a marriage that deserves the name be built upon continuing *"fraud"*? (the same Greek word is used in 1 Co 6:7). Is it the business of the church to preserve unions that have become "marriages" in name only, without any of the qualities that are embraced in the very terms "marriage", "husband", and "wife"? Or do we have a higher Christian duty to create marriages that exist, not just on a record in the government registrar's office, but also in heaven? What is a marriage? A legal form alone, or a loving relationship alone? Surely it is both, and if either dimension is missing then can it still be said that the marriage exists?

# THE QUESTION OF DIVORCE AND RE-MARRIAGE

See *1 Corinthians 7:10-16, 39-40*.

## WHERE BOTH PARTNERS ARE CHRISTIANS

The rule is strong, for Christ himself has spoken on this matter (Mt 5:31,32; etc.). So Paul writes –

> *For married couples, this is my rule (which is not mine but the Lord's): a wife must not separate from her husband, and if she does, she must either remain unmarried or be reconciled to her husband; and the husband must not divorce his wife" (vs. 10-11).*

If you and your spouse are both Christians, what do those words mean?

Paul's application of the words of Christ to a Christian couple, but not to a couple of which one or both are unbelievers, suggests he held to the view I have suggested above: that Christ directed his prohibition against divorce and re-marriage more toward the godly than the ungodly.

The godly are expected to strive for the highest standards; the ungodly are known to be hard of heart and probably unable to keep the laws of God.

So Christians ought not to divorce nor separate; rather, they should seek the help of God to reconcile their differences.

If they find it impossible to become reconciled, and they do separate, they should remain unmarried, and continue their search for reconciliation.

The above rules presume that both parties are committed Christians, and that the source of their discontent is entirely personal grievance, for which they should find a solution in the grace of Christ. However, if the source of their marital breakdown is *porneia* (Mt 5:32) or something truly *"scandalous"* (De 24:1) then divorce presumably becomes a lawful option, with re-marriage permitted as a necessary consequence.

But within the church (as I have already stated), the pressure is strongly towards the maintenance of a marriage, and people should contemplate divorce only when the most serious reasons exist. Divorced Christians, if they re-marry, risk committing adultery in the sight of God, thus are incurring his wrath (cp. 1 Co 6:9-10; He 13:4). However, if one of the Christian spouses without consent divorces the other, and goes off and re-marries, then the deserted spouse is presumably free to marry another. The same rule might apply even where there has been no divorce – that is, where one of the spouses has been wilfully deserted by the other. The deserted spouse, if there is no hope of reconciliation, might be reckoned free to sue for divorce, and then to marry another.

There are other cases even more difficult to resolve that present a troubling ethical problem for those who yearn to see God's highest ideals fulfilled in marriage. Compassionate pastors, confronted with a collapse of human love and a cruel violation of Christian standards, know that no easy answers can be found – neither in simplistic law, nor in sentimental pity. The mind of God will have to be discovered in each case, which may require a genuine spiritual struggle. Perhaps much prayer will be needed, along with a careful study of the biblical ethical principles.

## WHERE ONE PARTNER IS AN UNBELIEVER

If one partner in a marriage is an unbeliever, how does that affect the marriage, and what attitude should the Christian spouse have? That brings us to

# THE QUESTION OF MIXED MARRIAGES

Paul begins his answer with the words, *"Concerning the rest I would say this (and this is my personal view, not the word of the Lord), . . . "* (vs. 12). By *"the rest"* he means marriages where one spouse is an unbeliever. Unlike the former case, where he was able to quote a direct pronouncement of Christ, Paul is here not able to cite any precedent. Nonetheless he does not hesitate to express his opinion, as one who can rightly claim divine authority (vs. 40).

Paul's wording shows his belief that the saying of Christ (Mt 5:32; 19:9; etc.) is applicable primarily to marriages where both partners fear God and desire to serve him. In other cases, where one spouse either is not a Christian or has ceased to behave in a Christian manner, a different set of rules come into operation.

Furthermore, when Christ spoke about marriage and divorce to the Jews the church had not been founded, hence the problem of mixed marriages had not yet arisen. Paul reminds the Corinthians of this in order to clear the way for him to make some new rules on the matter that are applicable only to the Church. He is says in effect –

> *Although the Lord did not speak on this matter, I am now able to do so as an apostle speaking by the Spirit of God, and I add this new rule to the law of Christ.*

## THE PAULINE PRIVILEGE

Paul's first new rule is this – no Christian should leave an unbelieving partner, nor refuse to cohabit with that partner, solely on the ground of his or her unbelief. The marriage is still sanctified in the sight of God, the union is *"honourable"* (He 13:4), and its duties are unchanged. The offspring of the marriage are legitimate; and, at least until they reach an age of personal accountability, hold the same relationship to God as do children of a wholly Christian marriage. Thus Paul writes –

> *If a Christian man has an unbelieving wife, and she is happy to live with him, he must not divorce her. Or if a Christian woman has an unbelieving husband, and he is happy to live with her, she must not divorce him. For an unbelieving husband is reckoned holy by God because of his Christian wife, and an unbelieving wife is reckoned holy by God, because of her Christian husband. Otherwise your children would be unholy, but now they too are holy" (vs.12-14).*

But what if an unbelieving spouse has lost all joy in the marriage, and is no longer willing to make any effort to sustain it in love?

That is our next theme.

# EIGHTEEN

# WHEN LOVE FAILS

Suppose an unbelieving partner is not willing to live peaceably with a Christian spouse, what then? Paul answers –

> *If an unsaved partner insists upon a separation, then let him/her have it" (vs. 15).*

That is, the Christian spouse is not to hinder the unbeliever from going.

Two reasons are given (vs. 15, 16) –

## A CALL TO PEACE

*"God has called us to live in peace"*

In other words, to cling to a marriage that the other partner is determined to end, leads only to disturbance and unhappiness. But God desires a peaceful life for his children, so that they may freely serve him.

This raises another question. Does Paul's rule apply only, or strictly, to an "unsaved" partner – that is, one who was never a Christian? Or may it be applied also to a "Christian" spouse who has begun behaving more like a sinner than a saint? Here is a Christian woman, for example, who could rightly walk out of her marriage if her "unsaved" spouse treated her with hatred and abuse. But suppose he claims to be "saved"? Is she then obliged to accept vile treatment patiently? Does a mere profession of faith, without the substance of it, preclude her from divorcing a violent "Christian" husband? My own opinion is that people who insist upon behaving like "unbelievers", whatever their former profession of faith may have been, should be accorded the status they deserve. He who persistently acts like a sinner should be treated like a sinner.

## A CALL TO COMMON SENSE

*"How do you know that you will be able
to save your spouse?"* (92)

There is no guarantee that clinging to a marriage will lead to the salvation of an unbeliever, so it is better to allow the unbeliever to go. Paul is not in favour of marriage being viewed as a missionary institution. He does not approve of a Christian aggressively taking advantage of the intimacy of marriage to bombard a spouse with the gospel. Within marriage, the believer's witness should be more that of a beautiful life than a verbal assault (cp. 1 Pe 3:1-4).

## A GROUND FOR DIVORCE

Says Paul, *"In such cases a Christian husband or wife is no longer bound by the marriage vows"* (vs. 15). That is, when an unbelieving spouse (93) wishes to "depart", the Christian is released from his/her commitment to the marriage.

The word *"bound"* probably refers back to the clause in vs. 12, *"he must not divorce her;"* which means that the rule

---

(92)   I am aware of the ambiguity of the Greek text, which leads some translators to render the text as suggesting that patience by the Christian spouse might be rewarded by the salvation of the unbelieving spouse. Other versions suggest, as I do above, that such a hope is probably futile, and is not enough to demand that the believer should struggle to maintain a miserable marriage.

(93)   Which includes, as I have mentioned just above, supposedly "Christian" spouses who insist upon behaving like unbelievers.

against a Christian divorcing an unbeliever is effective only if the unbeliever *"is happy* (that is, willing) *to live with"* the Christian. But if the unbeliever wants to separate, then the Christian is no longer *"bound"* by this rule, and may take any steps necessary, including divorce, to secure his or her property, rights, and well-being.

The word *"bound"* may also refer to the marriage "bond". If so, then Paul is saying that the departure of the unbeliever releases the Christian from all obligations to the marriage. The Christian is then free to turn that moral release into a legal one by divorce, which must then include a right to re-marry.

Notice that the clause *"in such a case the Christian is not bound"* cannot mean only that the believer is free to be deserted, for that would be absurd. If an unbeliever is determined to go, what can the Christian spouse do to prevent it? Therefore, Paul must mean that the Christian is no longer bound to the deserting partner, nor to the marriage vows they had both formerly taken.

## SEPARATION UNDER ANOTHER NAME?

So the apostle has given us an additional ground for divorce. But if so, then a Christian who has divorced a deserting partner must also be free to re-marry, for divorce without permission to re-marry is an exercise in futility – it is just separation under another name. Notice Paul's statement again –

> In such cases, the Christian husband or wife no longer has any (marital) obligations. Remember that God has called us to live in peace.

Those words strongly imply that desertion has severed all ties with the defaulting unbeliever, and if the Christian can find peace in a new marriage then he or she is free to do so.

If you still doubt that Paul's use of the word *"separate"* or *"depart"* in verse 15 means divorce, with its corollary right of re-marriage, then look at Paul's use of the same word in verse 10. There he talks about a Christian wife *"departing"* from her Christian husband, and says she may not marry another. But unless such a departure includes divorce, she would not be free to re-marry in any case. The inference is clear. When Paul permits departure, he also permits divorce, and hence re-marriage.

The Greek word translated *"bound"* literally means enslaved. It suggests that nothing in the gospel endorses the idea that a marriage fallen into a condition of slavery for either spouse deserves to be continued.

## WHAT DOES "DEPART" MEAN?

What constitutes *"separation"* or *"departure"* by an unbelieving spouse?

Some teachers limit the meaning of Paul to actual desertion, a complete physical *"departure"* from the conjugal home. But I feel obliged to include also moral and social default. An unbelieving husband, for example, may decide to remain in the house with his wife. But why? Perhaps for no other reason than to torment her. He may also fail to give what is her due as his wife, and so *"defraud"* her, denying her the rightful claim she has upon him. If so, then he has, in effect, shown himself not *"willing to live with her"* as man and wife. To me, that is desertion in principle, if not in fact. (I am assuming the default has occurred solely because the wife is a Christian, and that she has not been lax in fulfilling her own obligations.) Where the husband is the Christian partner the reverse would be true.

I am not saying that a Christian must leave, or sue for divorce, under such circumstances, only that he or she has liberty to do so. There may be other reasons (e.g. the welfare of children) that make it more desirable for a Christian to continue living with a defaulting unbeliever.

Christians who choose to remain with an aggravating unbeliever, may find comfort in a more positive translation of vs. 16. Most translations (like the one cited above) give the verse a negative cast, but others make it positive –

> *Think of this – as a wife, you may be your husband's salvation; as a husband, you may be your wife's salvation!"*

But, in reality, that hopeful rendering seems to me to run counter to the general thrust of Paul's discussion, which is practical, shrewd, and focussed on making the best out of an unhappy situation. Still, I cannot doubt that a godly spouse, patient, serene, lovely in the beauty of Christ, may indeed be able to win the wickedest sinner to repentance and faith!

## THE QUESTION OF THE PRESENT CRISIS

See *1 Corinthians 7:25-28*. I have mentioned this passage above, in connection with celibacy, but it also has something to say about divorce. The gist of Paul's teaching is clear. He saw that a time of trouble was about to fall upon the church, and therefore advised the Corinthians to remain as they were (whether married or unmarried) until more peaceful days had returned. But in the process, Paul unconsciously alluded to some ideas that are important for this study. Notice verses 27-28, to which several versions give a meaning like the following –

> *Are you married? Then do not seek a divorce. Are you unmarried? Then do not look for a spouse. Nonetheless, you will not be doing anything wrong if you choose to marry; and if a virgin decides to marry she will not be committing a sin.*

Notice two things –

**First,** Paul distinguishes between *"virgins"* and the *"unmarried"*, who therefore must have been previously married. But why are they now unmarried? Were they widowed, or divorced? Plainly, they were divorced, because Paul uses the same Greek word (*luso* = to loose) in both places. The passage reads literally –

> Are you married? Do not seek to be <u>loosed</u>. Are
> you <u>loosed</u>? Do not seek a wife.

**Second,** there is no reason (apart from prejudice) to agree with those who translate *luso* as "divorced" in the first place, but as "unmarried" in the second. [94] Therefore, the verse may be correctly translated –

> Are you married? Do not seek a divorce. Are
> you divorced? Do not look for a wife. But if you
> do marry, you have not sinned.

So, having told the *"virgins"* and the *"divorced"* not to marry/remarry because of *"the present crisis"*, Paul still says to both groups, *"But if you do marry you have not sinned."* (There is, of course, an unspoken proviso that those who were divorced had dissolved their marriages on lawful grounds.) I cannot avoid the conclusion that Paul did permit at least some divorced people to remarry.

## THE QUESTION OF A SECOND MARRIAGE

See *1 Corinthians 7:39-40*. This is the last of the questions on marriage that the Corinthians submitted to Paul. It

---

(94)  The gospels use a related verb (*apoluo*) to describe divorce in *Matthew 5:31-32* (three times); *19:3-9* (five times); *Mark 10:2-12* (four times); *Luke 16:18* (twice).

concerns the matter of marrying after a former spouse has died. Paul gives two rules, which I will be content simply to mention here, since discussion of them really belongs in another study –

- you can marry again after your spouse dies, but only *"in the Lord"* – that is, only to a Christian.

- you can marry *"whom you will"* – which suggests that specific divine guidance in relation to choosing a spouse is not ordinarily available. God expects us to use the normal resources of asking questions, of intelligent courtship, of responsible measurement of temperament and character, as we search for a suitable partner.

## CONCLUSIONS

(1) Under certain circumstances the Bible allows both divorce and re-marriage. Nonetheless it everywhere urges the highest possible view of marriage, and therefore presents a general ban against both divorce and re-marriage, except where a former partner has died (1 Co 7:39). A Christian approach to the matter will reflect that biblical stance: that is, the major focus will be upon the preservation of marriage, not its dissolution; yet allowance will be made for human failure, including the need for divorce and the freedom to marry again. My remaining conclusions below, spell this out in more detail.

(2) However, Christ taught that *porneia* so destroys the unity of marriage, and so violates the divine purpose for marriage, that divorce can be permitted on this ground. Yet it is not commanded, and the expectation is that reconciliation will be attempted, and that divorce will follow only if the *porneia* has caused an irrevocable collapse of the marriage. Whether that

collapse has in fact occurred is something that must be determined separately in each case.

(3) Christ preferred not to offer any other ground for divorce; yet he allowed that human frailty and hardness of heart made it necessary for the Mosaic principle to remain effective. Beyond that, Christ expected his own people to grasp the higher, not the lower, standard.

(4) Paul gave permission for a Christian to divorce an unbeliever who wished to separate (or who had destroyed the marriage by default.) We might also construe this to include a "Christian" spouse who has so denied the faith as to abandon any pretence of fulfilling his or her marital obligations.

(5) Where divorce is permitted, re-marriage is also necessarily permitted; but re-marriage following an unlawful divorce may involve the partners in adultery. The scripture allows separation on grounds other than the two just mentioned, but generally not divorce – for in scripture the sanction of divorce involves also the sanction of re-marriage. Christian couples, however, are discouraged from separating (and even more from divorcing), since they should be able to reconcile their differences in the grace of the Lord (1 Co 7:10-11). However, nothing in scripture obliges a Christian spouse to endure a situation fraught with abuse, violence, incessant conflict, infidelity, drunkenness, and the like. Spouses who so behave have effectively *"departed"* from the marriage, and may be treated as if they were "unbelievers".

(6) Christians who have never married, or who are lawfully released from a former marriage, are free to marry *"whom they wish, except that it must be in the Lord"* (1 Co 7:39). That is, Christians are forbidden to

contract marriage with an unbeliever, but they may marry any other Christian they deem would make a suitable partner. While one would trust in God for guidance in meeting and choosing the right spouse, the responsibility is actually more ours' than his. "Marry whomever you please," says scripture, "so long as it is in Christ." The Lord expects his people to behave intelligently, wisely, prudently, and practically in this, as in all matters. Don't blame God if you rush into marriage, or yield to passion alone, and later find you have made an awful mistake!

(7) When a Christian is already married to an unbeliever, the Christian should continue to fulfil with love and devotion all the obligations of marriage. Scripture insists that a spiritually divided home can still be a happy one, and that Christian spouses should apply neither social nor spiritual pressure upon their unbelieving partners. Sadly, in contrast with Paul, nowadays it is often the Christian spouse who is not *"content"* with the union, rather than the reverse. That is not an acceptable attitude for a Christian to hold.

(8) In all marriages, husband and wife are to acknowledge and to fulfil their mutual responsibilities in cohabitation and devoted care of each other.

(9) The Bible contains ethical guidelines on the issues of marriage, divorce, and re-marriage, but it does *not* present a comprehensive and definitive set of rules which provide a clear and easy solution to every problem. Many issues are not discussed at all. Ethicists who draw a handful of absolute rules from scripture, and compel every couple to conform to them, are guilty of legalism and of failing to treat fairly all the data the Bible does give.

Given the lack of final definition in what the scriptures say, it is clear the Spirit did not intend to give glib answers to deeply complex human tragedies, but rather to provide a foundation upon which each generation, and each person, may build sound ethical judgments. These judgments cannot be forged easily, nor by formulating inflexible rules, but rather by prayer and by an earnest endeavour to isolate the real needs of each couple. Then from such revelation as the Bible does give, the counsellor must seek a solution that will best glorify God, honour marriage, and bring healing to those who are hurting.

(10) The pastor who allows re-marriage should first look for the following in the couple that are being counselled –

- Repentance of whatever fault may have been theirs in the failure of their previous marriage(s).

To this repentance there should be added a sense of the offence against divine righteousness that all divorce represents, and of the hurt that divorce does, to the church, to Christian standards, and, most of all, to the people involved. It mars the image of God in them. No Christian can glibly tolerate divorce, as though it were a matter of small consequence. On the contrary, its harvest is bitter, and lifelong, and reaches even into eternity. Divorce should be reluctantly allowed only when it has become the least destructive of the available options.

- A desire to identify the reasons for the previous marital breakdown.

To this there must be added definite steps toward self-improvement, so that former faults will not be repeated.

- A readiness to forgive the offences of the former spouse(s), with a sense of their own need of the forgiveness of Christ.

- A true appreciation of how God views marriage and a commitment to do all that is humanly possible in the new marriage to fulfil the divine standard.

- A willingness to accept the place of suffering in Christian life.

Too many marriages founder on the shoals of sheer selfishness, torn apart by a crazy notion that people have a right to go through life easily and comfortably, free from conflict, tension, or pain. In an article on this subject, Barry Chant writes –

> The true value of suffering is often missed. In today's comfortable world, we are often led to believe that suffering is always wrong, and therefore always to be avoided. However, it is written even of the Lord Jesus Christ that *"he learned obedience by the things that he suffered"* (He 2:10; 5:8). And to Timothy, Paul wrote: *"Take your share of suffering"* (2 Ti 2:3). Sometimes the lessons learned through a difficult marriage are of greater value than the pleasures we all look for.

> I do not wish to be misunderstood here. I believe with all my heart that God's plan for marriage is for it to be blissfully joyful and deeply and truly satisfying. When two people build on God's principles, their marriage cannot help but be the most exciting, and rewarding relationship on earth. However, if for some reason it does not work out this way, even the suffering may be for good (Ro 8:28). It is not necessarily right to look for an easy way out, especially if it is contrary to God's word.

# FINAL COMMENT

The rate of divorce in our society has reached a tragic level. It has been truly said that holy wedlock has become unholy deadlock. Yet the rigid stance that the church has often taken on the issue of divorce and remarriage has not enhanced its moral authority. It may well be true that under pressure of changes in society, and of the better understanding of scripture we now have, the church should re-appraise its ethic on marriage. The aim must never be to weaken what scripture says, but rather to understand what it says, and to apply better its healing balm to the countless broken homes and broken lives that surround us.

Marriage is an honourable and sacred estate (He 13:4; Ep 5:22-33; Cl 3:18-20: Pr 18:22, 19:14; etc.) It should not be entered lightly; nor should it be broken except in dire circumstances. Married people have an obligation not only to themselves but also to the Lord God.

Let those who contemplate marriage do so in the fear of the Lord, seeking a partner of God's choosing.

Let those who are married give no thought to dissolving the union, unless they are compelled by circumstances beyond their control.

Let those who have become separated or divorced seek to be reconciled to their former partners. If that is impossible, they must not marry another except within the limits laid down by the scripture.

Thus will our homes be established in the strength and blessing of the Lord, and a godly seed will rise up to praise his glorious name.

# ADDENDA

## THE MODERN DILEMMA

After writing the above notes, I came across the following passage, in which Colin Brown comments on the inadequacy of the biblical data to cover every marital exigency –

> Remarriage is therefore sanctioned (in the New Testament) in certain clear-cut cases. But there are many cases in modern society where marriage has broken down through incompatibility, drink, cruelty, and sundry other causes on which there are no explicit pronouncements of scripture. There are also many cases in society of divorcees marrying and subsequently being converted.
>
> Is the church to deny the right of marriage to the former group and to tell the latter to unscramble their marriages? This would be the logical consequence of the rigorist interpretation of Jesus' teaching. But this would not seem to represent the mind of Jesus. The foundation of his teaching – *"what God joined together let man not put asunder"* – is a formula for avoiding the breakdown of marriage, and not an iron law putting into equal bondage the callous, the innocent, and the penitent.
>
> In cases where a believing partner desires to remarry, we should follow the example of Jesus and examine the situation in the light of God's purposes in creation. In creating man and woman it was God's intention that man should not dwell alone (Ge 2:18), and, as we have seen from Paul's argument in 1 Co 7:1-9), the saving

knowledge of God was not intended as a substitute for normal human relationships. Just as the sabbath was made for man, and not man for the sabbath, so marriage was made for man. We do not cease to have the need of physical and person-affirming relationships, when marriage breaks down . . .

To those who would preclude the possibility of remarriage on the grounds that marriage is indissoluble, the question must be put:

"By what right do you, who enjoy the security and warmth of a happy marriage, deny the possibility to others who find that their former marriage has broken down irretrievably and that there is nothing that they can now do to restore it?"

To those who would seek remarriage, the question must be put:

"Do you believe in your hearts that in your new marriage you can love God, each other, and those around you more fully than if you were to remain as you are?" (95)

## MARRIAGE IN UTOPIA

That renowned "man for all seasons", Sir Thomas More, wrote in 1516 his equally famous book, *Utopia*. In it he gave some sage counsel on divorce and remarriage. It was counsel he had earned the right to give because of the idyllic quality

(95)    Dictionary of New Testament Theology, Vol 3, pages 542, 543; Zondervan Publishing House, Grand Rapids; 1978.

of his own home life. Here then, first, is an account of his two marriages; and, second, an extract from *Utopia* –

Having abandoned an early inclination to the priesthood, the young Thomas decided to marry and fixed his attention upon the three daughters of a certain John Colte. His heart was drawn to the second of the three girls, but then he reflected on the insult the eldest, Jane, would suffer if her younger sister were married first. Accordingly, he asked for Jane's hand, and they were duly wedded. She proved to be a fine wife, bore him four children, and they enjoyed surpassing happiness for six years, until her death in 1511.

A few weeks later he married again. But his second wife, Alice, was a querulous woman, rather shallow in understanding, and unable to bring him the gladness that he and Jane had known. Nonetheless, just as he had resolved to do his duty by Jane, and in it found great contentment, so More conducted himself impeccably toward Alice. Here is a passage from a letter about him written by another to Erasmus –

> There is not any man living so loving to his children as he (More), and he loveth his old wife as if she were a young maid, and such is the excellency of his temper, that whatsoever happeneth that could not be helped, he loveth it as if nothing could happen more happily. You would say there were in that place Plato's academy, – but I do the house injury in comparing it to Plato's academy, wherein there was only disputations of numbers, and geometrical figures, and sometimes of morals and virtues. I should rather call his house a school or university of Christian religion, for there is none therein but readeth and studieth the liberal sciences; their special care is piety and virtue; there is no quarrelling or

intemperate words heard, none seem idle; which household discipline that worthy gentleman doth not govern by proud and lofty words, but with all kind and courteous benevolence; everybody performeth his duty; yet is there always alacrity; neither is sober mirth anything wanting." [96]

**Second**, in *Utopia*, More expresses his opinion on how an enlightened society should handle divorce –

And this were they (the Utopians) constrained more earnestly to look upon, because they only of the nations in that part of the world be content every man with one wife apiece. And matrimony is there never broken but by death, except adultery break the bond, or else the intolerable wayward manners of either party. For if either of them find themself for any such cause grieved, they may by the license of the council change and take another. But the other party liveth ever after in infamy and out of wedlock. Howbeit, the husband to put away his wife for no other fault but for that some mishap is fallen to her body, this by no means they will suffer. For they judge it a great point of cruelty that anybody in their most need of help and comfort should be cast off and forsaken, and that old age, which both bringeth sickness with it and is a sickness itself, should unkindly and unfaithfully be dealt withal.

---

[96]    Utopia, by Sir Thomas More, Everyman's Library, 1965. Page vi.

But now and then it chanceth, whereas the man and the woman cannot well agree between themselves, both of them finding other, with whom they hope to live more quietly and merrily, that they by the full consent of them both be divorced asunder and married again to other. But that not without the authority of the council, which agreeth to no divorces before they and their wives have diligently tried and examined the matter. Yea, and then also they be loath to consent to it, because they know this to be the next way to break love between man and wife, to be in easy hope of a new marriage. [97]

Sir Thomas More retained the extraordinary nobility of his character throughout his life, until he was beheaded by order of King Henry VIII, on July 6, 1535. This remarkable account, by his son-in-law, Sir William Roper, expresses a charm, grace, and courage that every Christian might aspire to –

Ascending the scaffold, he seemed so weak [98] that he was ready to fall; whereupon he merrily said to the Lieutenant, "I pray you Mr. Lieutenant see me safe up, and for my coming down let me shift for myself." Then desired he all the people to pray for him, and to bear witness with him that he should suffer death in, and for the faith of the Holy Catholic Church, a faithful servant both of God and the King. Which done, he kneeled down, and after his

---

[97]    Ibid., page 100.

[98]    After 15 months of harsh imprisonment.

prayers ended, he turned to the executioner, and with a cheerful countenance, said, "Pluck up thy spirits, man, and be not afraid to do thine office. My neck is very short, take heed therefore thou strike not awry for saving thine honesty. Then laying his head upon the block he had the executioner stay until he had removed aside his beard, saying that that had never committed any treason. So with much cheerfulness he received the fatal blow of the axe, which at once severed his head from his body.

## END WITH A CHUCKLE

The same Sir Thomas More in *Utopia* recommended that young people should see each other naked before marriage, and so avoid later disappointment. It was a dictum he put into practice with his own daughters, as the following anecdote shows. It illustrates too how a happy marriage depends much more upon a decision to be happy than it does upon modern concepts of romance –

Sir William Roper came one morning, pretty early, to my lord, with a proposal to marry one of his daughters. My lord's daughters were then both together a-bed in a truckle bed in their father's chamber asleep. He carries Sir William into the chamber and takes the sheet by the corner and suddenly whips it off. They lay on their backs, and their smocks up as high as their armpits. This awakened them, and immediately they turned on their bellies. Quoth Roper, "I have seen both sides," and so gave a pat on the buttock to the one he made choice of, saying, "Thou art mine." Here was all the trouble of wooing! [99]

The young lady's name was Margaret, and she proved to be a woman of high character, distinguished accomplishments, and deep piety. The marriage was eminently successful. It is said that she purchased the head of her martyred father less than a month after it had been exposed on London Bridge and kept it preserved in spices until her death. It was buried with her, and when her vault was opened in 1715 she was found still clasping the leaden box containing the precious relic. The poet Tennyson alludes to this in the lines –

> Morn broaden'd on the borders of the dark
> Ere I saw her who clasp'd in her last trance
> Her murder'd father's head. [100]

As I have mentioned above, her self-appointed yet loved husband, Sir William Roper (1498-1578), of Lincoln's Inn, wrote a life of her father, Sir Thomas More, which was first published in Paris in 1626.

---

(99)   John Aubrey (1478-1535), Brief Lives - Sir Thomas More.

(100)  From *A Dream of Fair Women*, in which the poet eulogizes many famous women from across the span of history.

# PART TWO CONTINUED

# FROM THE *"LETTER"*

## SECTION TWO

## MARKETS AND CHARISMATICS

## *NINETEEN*

# MARKET

See *1 Corinthians 8:1-13.*

## THE PROBLEM

The Corinthians faced an issue that was far more complex than whether or not to be a vegetarian. In that deeply religious society, most of the meat sold in the shops came from what was left of an animal's carcase after the beast had been sacrificed in a temple. Should Christians buy meat that had come from a pagan altar? Some people gave an emphatic negative, because, said they, the meat was now tainted by demonic spirits. Others laughed, insisting that the idols were dead nothings, incapable of either good or evil.

The problem was further compounded by the many public festivals that used such meat to provide a free meal for the celebrants. For poorer citizens, this might be the only time they could enjoy meat with their meal. Were Christians to be denied this charity? What about family and neighbourhood festivities, communal meals, and the like? Because they included meat that had come from a temple, could Christians no longer participate in these happy occasions? Were Christians to become social pariahs, refusing to eat with family and friends who had no scruples on the matter?

Hardly, says Paul. Anyone who truly understands who they are in Christ, and the freedom that has come to them through Christ, will not be bound by such petty restraints. Yet at once he hastens to soften the seeming insult to those who lack such knowledge, or who are still struggling to grasp its meaning. He will not tolerate any sort of arrogant superiority of one Christian toward another. He draws a contrast between two groups – those who are *"strong"*, who have gained an inner revelation of their liberty in Christ; and those who are *"weak"*. The former know that they are free to eat whatever they like; the latter are fearful of becoming corrupted, or of dishonouring God, if they eat food that has been touched by demons in the temple (see also Ro 14:1-15:13, where Paul deals with the same two groups, and again contrasts the *"strong"* with the *"weak"*.) [101] But he will not allow the strong to scorn the weak. He is certainly on the side of the strong, for his very use of the word *"weak"* must have been an incentive to those people to overcome their problem and join the strong! Nonetheless, in the meantime he demands that equal honour should be given even to people who may seem to be weak.

## THE SOLUTION

Paul urged the Corinthians to learn the difference between two things: **knowledge** (which by itself merely *"puffs up"*); and **love** (which *"builds up"*) (vs. 1) –

### KNOWLEDGE (VS. 4-6)

People who are strong in faith understand that an idol is nothing, and that through the grace of God in Christ we are free from all bondage to mere ritual. Paul rejoices in that freedom, and wishes every believer to make the same discovery. We know that an idol is a mere thing, incapable of doing anything except stay where it is placed – deaf, mute, blind, paralysed, and lifeless (Ps 135:15-18). But Paul recognises that such knowledge, if it stands alone, may breed

---

(101) From the Jerome Biblical Commentary; pub. by Geoffrey Chapman, London, 1978; in loc.

arrogance, which could open the door to Satan's malice, or could cause needless offence to other people.

Paul also recognises the importance of heeding the voice of conscience, even if it is not always fully reliable. If a choice has to be made between violating conscience and yielding to it, always choose the latter. True, conscience sometimes misleads us, and sometimes conscience is *"weak"*, but it is God's gift to us, to guide us, and it should be obeyed. Paul insists that ignoring conscience is perilous (vs. 11-12). The solution to an unreliable conscience is not to ignore it, but to enlighten it. Or, if conscience continues to be a plague, even after one has grasped the full measure of the liberty we have in Christ, then wash away its *"evil"* influence by gaining confidence in the blood of the everlasting covenant (He 10:22, 19-23).

Paul is rather scornful of those who are troubled by eating certain foods. He calls them *"weak"*. Nonetheless, he insists that they are fellow Christians, and that those who are strong must respect their scruples.

Hence, he says, we should also walk in

## LOVE (VS. 7-13)

Not all have a strong grasp on the gospel; not all are vigorous in faith; so beware, Paul warns, that your claim of liberty in Christ does not become a stumbling block to another. Paul would rather starve than be guilty of such a fault against a fellow Christian! (vs. 13)

His comments raise a question – which is better: to know *about* God, or to be known *by* God? There are those, says Paul, who are proud of their vast knowledge about God, and reckon that this knowledge makes them superior to other Christians who, in their opinion, are ignorant or weak. They suppose that their knowledge gives them a high standing before God. But Paul mocks that idea. If a choice must be made, it is far better to be known *by* God than merely to know *about* him. Whom then does God know? Whom does he consider a friend? Only those who are motivated by divine love! (vs. 2-3).

Let us then determine two things — by all means to learn all we can about the gospel; but above all, to walk in humble love, both toward God and toward each brother and sister in Christ.

## TWENTY

# CHARISMATA

See *1 Corinthians 12:1-14:40.* [102]

Paul refers to a group of people and/or spiritual manifestations that he calls *"pneumatika"* – a Greek neuter noun, which means *"things of the spirit"* or *"spiritual happenings"* (1 Co 12:1). He is talking about that spiritual dimension, normally invisible in this world, in which strange phenomena occur, some of them wrought by the Holy Spirit, but many of them arising from other sources. Paul wishes the church not to be *"ignorant"* about these matters, nor does he want them to fall short in the proper use of the true gifts of the Holy Spirit (the *charismata*). [103] From the way in which Paul links these gifts to the human body (on which see more below), no rational argument can be raised against their value to the modern church. They should be as much a part of modern church life as ever they were during apostolic times.

In our present context, the apostle lists nine gifts, which are often conveniently divided as follows –

### *Three Revelation Gifts*

---

(102)  Portions of this section are drawn from material in my book Equipped To Serve, Vision Publishing, Ramona CA. For a more extensive commentary on these three chapters from *1 Corinthians* (that is, chapters *12, 13, & 14*), see that book.

(103)  There are at least three lists of spiritual gifts in the NT – 1 Co 12:7-11, 28-31; Ro 12:4-8; Ep 4:7-13; and other gifts are mentioned here and there.

- The Word of Wisdom; the Word of Knowledge; the Discerning of Spirits.

### *Three Power Gifts*

- Gifts of Healing; Working of Miracles; Faith.

### *Three Oracular Gifts*

- a Message in Tongues; a Message in Interpretation; a Message in Prophecy.

Added to those are certain special gifts of ministry, such as Apostle, Prophet, Evangelist, Pastor, Teacher, plus Administrators and diverse Servant roles, such as Presbyters (Bishops), Deacons, and others.

All these are needed if the church is to function fully in the manner intended by God. It is not my purpose here to examine these diverse ministries, gifts, and functions in any detail, [104] but to lay down some important principles relating to their place and use in the church, particularly the local church.

# A CHARISMATIC CHURCH

## WE CANNOT BE CONTENT WITH A DECEIVED CHURCH

There are true and false spiritual manifestations in the world and in the church, including those that are

---

(104) See my books, *Clothed with Power, Equipped to Serve,* and Barry Chant, *The Church*, all printed by Vision Publishing, Ramona CA.

- ***fabricated*** – like the mechanical contrivances both in the past and still today in some cultures, that made idols seem to move and speak. (105)

- ***demonic*** – like those we read about in the gospels, and in the *Acts of the Apostles*, and which can still happen today.

- ***ignorant*** – like those conjured up by false dreams, or by mental or bodily disturbances, caused by a crisis, or ill diet, and so on. (106)

- ***uncontrolled*** – like those Paul warns about, that bring chaos and confusion, not grace and godliness to the church.

- ***genuine*** – as described in the text passage at the head of this chapter.

Our task, therefore, is to use responsible discernment, based upon the Word of God, so that we can separate wheat from chaff, rejecting what is spurious and keeping only what is genuinely wrought by the Holy Spirit.

Rabbi Sirach, who flourished 200 years before Christ, knew about false dreams, omens, signs, and the like, and he warned the young men who were his students to avoid them as if they were poison. Instead, he said, wise servants of God would measure all things by the truth of scripture –

> Disaster will not overtake you if you fear the Lord; or, if things do go wrong, then you will be

---

(105) That ancient trickery, sadly, occurs sometimes even in the church. There have been preachers who contrived to have feathers fall from the ceiling, simulating the Holy Spirit; or who used radio technology to help them pretend to receive divinely revealed knowledge about people; and the like.

(106) Cp. Sirach 34:1-7, which is also cited just below.

> rescued again and again. Those who are wise will love the law of God; but if you are insincere you will find yourself being tossed about like a small boat in a squall. (107) If you are sensible, and put your trust in the law, you will find it just as reliable as the Urim and Thummin. (Sir 33:1-3)

Imagine that! God himself gave Israel the Urim and Thummin as a means of discovering his will. (108) Yet, says Sirach, the written Word is a better guide. The rabbi did not mean that God never uses a miracle to reveal to his people his divine purpose, but that everything must be measured by the Law – that is, by scripture. He says, "You will find the Law just as reliable as a divine oracle" – but he leaves a strong impression that, really, he thinks the Law is *more* reliable! He would prefer a verse of scripture to a dream, a passage from the Law to a magical sign, the Word of God to an angelic visitation (cp. Sir 34:1-7). This, of course, is because such signs may be unreliable – even the Urim and Thummin – but *scripture* can always be trusted and will endure for ever (1 Pe 1:23-25).

So let us desire spiritual gifts (1 Co 14:1), but never forget that pre-eminent authority belongs to the written Word of God, the Bible. No true gift, one that genuinely comes from

---

(107) Cp. James 1:5-7.

(108) See Ex 28:30; Le 8:8; Nu 27:21; De 33:8. They were probably a set of stones that the priest cast, either upon his lap, or upon the ground, as a means of obtaining either a "yes", "no", or "perhaps" from God. But there are other theories. No one really knows precisely what the Urim and Thummin were, nor how they worked. Their use in Israel was eventually abandoned. Indeed the desuetude of scripture concerning their use after the time of David, strongly suggests an abandonment of mechanical devices in favour of the spoken (and later written) words of the prophets.

God, will ever countermand, contradict, nullify or deny scripture.

## WE CANNOT BE CONTENT WITH A DISABLED CHURCH

Paul twice uses the word *tithemi* — "to set in place, appoint, ordain, establish" (vs. 18, 28) —

- in the first reference he uses the word in a general sense, and relates it to our bodily limbs;
- in the second, he takes hold of a technical meaning the word had in Bible days —

### *"TITHEMI" AS A TECHNICAL RELIGIOUS EXPRESSION*

Go back in imagination to 50 A.D., to the day when a new temple is about to be consecrated in Corinth, and an idol placed on its pedestal deep inside the sanctuary. Try to imagine all the pomp and splendour, the dancers and musicians, the flowers scattered everywhere, a grand parade, the priests in solemn procession bearing the sacred object. Perhaps, if the golden idol is too heavy to carry, it is in a cart, drawn by pure white oxen, which will be sacrificed at journey's end. The spectacle is dazzling and enthralling. The crowds are cheering and singing, dancing, feasting and making merry.

But then a hush falls upon the city.

The most sacred moment of all has come, when the idol is borne reverently into the temple and set in its proper place.

That act of formally installing the image of a god or goddess in a temple was called *"tithemi"*. [109] Before that *"tithemi"*

---

(109) *"Tithemi"* had other uses in the wider world, but "setting a god in place" was its special meaning in a religious context.

had taken place, the temple was simply a building, and had no special sanctity. But now it becomes a sacred place, protected from desecration by strict laws and powerful customs. Only the presence of the god could turn a building into a holy place, a house of prayer and worship. Without the sacred image, it was an empty shell, lacking purpose or power.

Against that background, notice how Paul contrasts the *"dumb"* idols that were *"set"* in the heathen temples, with the living manifestations of the Spirit that are *"set"* in the church (vs. 2). He is showing two things —

- despite the *"tithemi"*, the temples of the heathen were still hollow husks, for their gods were *"dumb"*; and

- God has performed a true *"tithemi"* by setting in his church the gifts of the Holy Spirit, which do speak and act with power.

But we may add another conclusion: just as surely as the purpose of the temple was void if the *"tithemi"* did not occur, so the church is made ineffectual if it does not allow the Spirit to *"set in place"* (tithemi) the charismata. What else can Paul mean when he says that —

> God has *set* (tithemi) in the church, first apostles, second prophets, third teachers, then miracles, gifts of healing, helpers, administrators, and various kinds of tongues (vs. 28).

The apostle was certainly aware of the meaning *tithemi* had in the minds of his readers in ancient Corinth. They would at once have grasped the idea that one of the reasons the church exists is to be a depository of the charismata. Without the presence of such spiritual gifts, the church becomes like a pagan temple, largely dumb and helpless.

Then the other way in which Paul uses *"tithemi"* is this -

## "TITHEMI" IN RELATION TO THE HUMAN BODY

As our limbs are to our bodies, so, says Paul, are the charismata to the church, for God has *"set"* (tithemi) them in the church just as he has *"set"* your limbs in your body (vs. 18).

How healthy, how effective, is a limbless man? Lacking arms, legs, ears, eyes, can any person be described as whole and fully functional? He may still be alive, but he is not much use, either to himself or anyone else!

Many years ago I read a story about old China. Apparently the standard punishment for a defaulting civil servant was to disembowel him, stuff his abdomen with straw, sew him up, and force him to go back to his desk and work until he died. He may have been holding brush and ink, but he could hardly have functioned effectively, torn with pain, knowing he could hardly survive beyond a day or two.

Paul, I think, would have said that a church deprived of some or all of the charismata, much resembles a disembowelled or dismembered person. Perhaps still alive. Perhaps still functioning. But hardly doing well, and far less than a fully equipped church should be.

Some have argued that the charismata were given to the church only during its formative years, but they were withdrawn by God after the death of the apostles. However, Paul's analogy of the human body precludes this. Has God's design and purpose for the human body changed? Do we need our limbs any less now than people did twenty centuries ago? Neither has the church changed, nor does it have any less need of the charismata today than we do of our sundry members. It is surely improbable that Paul would have used such an analogy if he had thought that the charismata were merely a temporary asset? By likening them to our limbs he is surely saying that they are as necessary to a fully functioning church as your arms and legs are to you.

Notice, too, how Paul says the charismata are *"profitable"* (vs. 7); that is, they serve *"the common good, they are advantageous, and beneficial"*. Would he speak any differently today? Would he say that the modern church is so strong, so well formed, so effective that it no longer needs any supernatural endowments? Hardly! What folly it is then to deny, disparage, or ignore these gifts!

## WE CANNOT BE CONTENT
## WITH A DISJOINTED CHURCH

Notice that *tithemi* is in the middle voice, which in grammar has the sense of *"for his own special purpose God has set"* diverse ministries and charismata in the church (vs. 28). Therefore, to ignore any of God's appointments is to thwart this divine purpose. Paul also says that, *"for his own special purpose,"* God has placed in the church <u>two groups</u> of ministries –

- those who depend upon careful planning and hard work; and

- those who depend upon supernatural revelation and divine action.

Notice how carelessly Paul intertwines the natural and the supernatural, the earthly and the heavenly, the human and the divine. He refuses to make any sharp distinctions between them; they are all vital to the good health of the church. So, there is a group of

- **<u>"natural" functions</u>** – *"apostles, teachers, helpers, administrators"*.

By "natural" I mean that such ministries depend as much upon human ability, natural temperament and skills, as they do upon divine calling or enabling. Some churches can be described wholly in these terms, which by themselves tend to create an arid intellectualism. But there is also a group of

- **"supernatural" functions** — "prophets, healers, miracle-workers, glossolalists".

These are divinely given and supernatural functions, which have much less connection with ordinary human skills or abilities. Some churches can be wholly described in these terms, which by themselves tend to create a shallow emotionalism.

A truly healthy, fully functional church, one that reflects the divine ideal, will be endowed with a balanced mixture of all those gifts and ministries. But Paul would never have separated them as I have just done! Rather, he mingled them easily, the natural with the supernatural, the miraculous with the mundane, for he knew that unless they all flourished together the church would fail in its mission.

To each is given his or her proper gift and/or function in the church (12:7-11), according to what kind of person we each are. So, says Paul,

> to one is given a word of wisdom,
> to another (person of the same kind, *allos*) a word of knowledge,
> to another (person of a different kind, *heteros*) faith,
> to another *(allos)* gifts of healing,
> to another *(allos)* working of miracles,
> to another *(allos)* prophecy,
> to another *(allos)* discerning of spirits,
> to another *(heteros)* tongues,
> to another *(allos)* interpretation of tongues.

By mixing up his pronouns (*allos* and *heteros*) Paul probably intends to highlight the idea that the Lord bestows his callings and gifts according to the capacity, qualities, abilities, and temperament of each person. Therefore, part of the secret of knowing what spiritual gifts you may rightly claim comes from honestly knowing *yourself*. Thus, it is unlikely that someone who is inarticulate will be gifted, say, with prophecy. Nor is it likely that someone who lacks empathy will be gifted with discerning of spirits. And so on. I do not say that such things are impossible (after all, remember Balaam's donkey), [110] only that they are improbable.

## WE CANNOT BE CONTENT
## WITH A DISORDERLY CHURCH

Despite the opinion of some people that any kind of worship practice is acceptable to God, so long as it is sincere, Paul insists that certain rules or principles must govern the way a local church structures its worship. In particular, he gives two rules in connection with using the charismata —

### *EVERYTHING DECENTLY AND IN ORDER*

See *1 Corinthians 14:39-40*. Mark how that injunction places upon the leaders of the church full responsibility for the manner in which it conducts itself in its public worship. Paul's rule certainly discredits the practice of quietism, [111] which abrogates human responsibility in giving direction to a worship service, and tries instead to make the Holy Spirit the initiator of all that happens. The role of the Holy Spirit is to guide and inspire, not control. Instead, control over a worship service is vested in the leaders of the church, and they will not, cannot please God, if they cast off that duty.

---

(110)  Numbers 22:21-31.

(111)  "Quietism" is discussed more fully in my book *Christian Life* (Vision Publishing). In brief, *quietism* describes a kind of religious mysticism that requires abandonment of the will, discarding all human effort, and entering a state of passive contemplation of God. The idea is to be rid of all sense of self, and to retain awareness only of God. In particular, quietism scorns any human interference in spiritual matters, including worship, which they say should be governed by God alone. But God has put leaders in the church, to lead, and he expects them to do so.

Paul wants a worship service that is redolent of grace, beauty, dignity, and reverence. But then, neither would the apostle have found any pleasure in a service that was so orderly, so dignified, so reverent as to be stuffy and void of any liveliness. As he says elsewhere, our rule should be moderation in all things (Ph 4:5, KJV). [112] We should avoid the solemnity of a cemetery, but neither do we want the rowdy chaos of a schoolyard. Paul puts it best – everything should be done properly, and in good order.

Is Paul seeking to control the Holy Spirit? Hardly! But he certainly wishes to control the *human* spirit, just as he does when he makes human choice the determinant of whether or not he will speak or sing in other tongues (vs. 14-16). We cannot control the Holy Spirit, nor should we ever wish to do so; but we *are* solely responsible for the actions of our human spirit, which includes the choices we make in connection with worship and the use of the charismata.

No doubt a great mystery lies here, in this matter of the relationship between the human spirit and the Holy Spirit. These sacred gifts *are* resident in us, and it places upon us an awesome responsibility to use them wisely, responsibly, and successfully. Part of that responsibility is to recognise the validity of Paul's second rule, namely –

## THEY MUST ACHIEVE THEIR PURPOSE

The glory of the charismata does not rest in the fact that they *exist* in a local church, but that they achieve their *purpose* in the church –

---

(112) The word is variously translated as gentle, forbearing, kind, reasonable, considerate, gracious, and so on. In other words, there is no real English equivalent for the Greek *epiekes*. But I think, in this place, it would be difficult to improve on the KJV choice of "moderation".

## THEIR PARTICULAR PURPOSE

See *verses. 3, 5* where Paul declares that the purpose of the spiritual gifts of prophecy and interpretation of tongues is to *build up, encourage* and *comfort* the local church. From which we may conclude that no one who uses those gifts properly will speak in a manner that is —

- *critical* (harsh, vindictive, condemnatory, for the purpose of the charismata is to comfort, encourage, and console the people)

- *negative* (failing to uplift and encourage the church, for Paul insists three times that every oracle must "build up" the church and the people)

- *directive* (taking command over the choices of the people, for they are royal priests before God, and have been set free in Christ).

Church leaders, says Paul, must *"judge"* by those criteria every use of the charismata in a local church, and bring under discipline or restraint anyone who misuses them (vs. 29).

## THEIR GENERAL PURPOSE

Arising from the above, we can say that the charismata are given to

- equip the church to be the body of Christ; that is, enabling it to do and be as Jesus himself would if he were here in the flesh; and to

- draw us into a closer relationship with Christ (12:3).

If the use of the charismata in a local church fails to achieve that two-fold divine purpose, then they are in some way disorderly, and must be corrected.

But now let me add an

## *EXCURSUS: ON THE USE OF THE FIRST PERSON*

In modern churches it is common to hear people giving a prophecy in the first person, that is, speaking as if it were God himself, thus *"I the Lord tell you my people that ...."* Or to put it differently, people speak in the same manner as the prophets of old Israel often did. This seems to me to be wrong. "Prophecy" in the local church differs from the kind of oracles that were spoken in old Israel. Those prophets were spokesmen for God, and were reckoned to be delivering the very words of God himself. They were *directly* inspired by the Holy Spirit.

But in the local church, a prophecy and/or an interpretation of tongues issue primarily out of the *human* spirit, and therefore it must be *"judged"* − that is, assessed as to whether or not the oracle speaks truly and in harmony with the rule of strengthening, encouraging, comforting, and building up the people.

The prophets of Israel would never have allowed such "judging". They *knew* that they were the mouthpiece of God, and they expected to be heard, believed, and obeyed. No one using the gift of prophecy in a local church has the right to arrogate to himself or herself such immediate and direct inspiration. At best modern oracles, spoken in a local church, are *indirectly* inspired by the Holy Spirit; but the actual utterance, as Paul insists, arises from the spirit of the speaker, and *must* be *"judged"*. (113)

---

(113) An exception may lie in those who possess the *ministry* gift of a prophet (Ep 4:11), which is distinct from the *spiritual* gift of prophecy. The former is a roaming ministry; the latter, one of the charismata set in the local church. Even so, in my opinion, whether an oracle arises from a *ministry* gift or a *spiritual* gift, neither sort speaks with the same authority as the

..........*continued on the next page.*

Therefore, it seems better to avoid the use of the first person. After all, if someone delivers (say) a prophecy as if God himself were speaking, he attaches an authority to his utterance that precludes the church from *"judging"* it. How can I presume to tell *God* that he is mistaken? So the speaker, by using the first person, removes from me the right to reject his or her oracle. Yet *scripture* obliges me to weigh up what is said, and to determine for myself whether or not the oracle is true. So I dislike it when a prophet tries (even if unconsciously) to take away from me that right and that duty by speaking as if it were God himself. Nonetheless, of course, no matter how an oracle is expressed, or who delivers it, I will most surely exercise my God-given right either to accept it, reject it, or leave it on hold until further evidence brings confirmation or denial.

So all prophecies, interpretations of tongues, words of knowledge, and the like, should be spoken in a way that leaves the hearers free to assess for themselves, whether or not these revelations come from God.

### *EXCURSUS: ON WOMEN PROPHESYING*

See *1 Corinthians 14:34, 35.*)

From the time Paul wrote those words until now, no one beyond the church in ancient Corinth has known what he meant by them, or why he wrote them; but notice that –

- his prohibition is against married women asking questions; and

---

..........*continued from previous page.*

Hebrew prophets possessed, and they must all be "judged" by the local church.

- he himself allowed women to prophesy (11:5), which had to be done in the church, subject to *"judgment"*, for the *"edifying"* of the church.

Whatever Paul intended when he told the ladies to keep silent in the church, he certainly did not mean to silence them altogether! You will find a full discussion of the ministry of women in a later section of this book.

## WE CANNOT BE CONTENT
## WITH A DISUNITED CHURCH

The charismata must be used from a motive of love, and their effect will be to unite the church in love (1 Co 13). Where they fail to do this, they must be reckoned out of order, and brought under discipline. Yet, properly used, the charismata will effectively bind the people more closely together in the love of Christ. Thus Paul concludes his poem on *"Love"* with an encouragement to seek spiritual gifts, (14:1), thus suggesting the close link between the charismata and a church flourishing in love. In particular, he urges them to pursue the gift of *"prophecy"* –

# A PROPHESYING CHURCH

Just as love is the mark of an individual Christian (Jn 13:35), so *"prophecy"* is the mark of the Spirit-filled church (Ac 2:17-18). Prophecy is also the key to spontaneous growth (1 Co 14:24-25).

Note, however, that the very power of this gift makes it a special target of Satan, therefore special care must be taken in its use –

## PROPHECY SHOULD NOT COME FROM MERE IMPULSE

See 12:1-2, " ... *you know how, when you were still pagans, you were governed by impulse, doing whatever you were moved to do ...*"

Paul highlights one of the major aspects of paganism, which is the loss of personal volition – people do whatever the pagan spirit drives them to do. That is, they lose self-control and perhaps self-awareness; they are compelled to do certain things; they fall into convulsions or frenzies; they lapse into a catatonic state, their limbs rigid, their minds are taken over by some uncontrollable force; they collapse into an unresponsive stupor; and the like. I don't mean that all pagan worshippers experience such things, nor that they experience them continually, but that such mindless behaviour is characteristic of paganism.

It should never be part of Christian worship, which should always have about it a quality of grace and beauty. Any kind of automatism should be unwelcome in the church. Yet some Christians feel that the pinnacle of happiness is indeed to *"lose"* oneself in the Lord, to be reduced to a state of spiritual catalepsy, prostrated in the Spirit, and the like.

Do we really want to emulate those pagans who surrender inertly to religious or emotional impulse; who do whatever they are *"moved"* by their god to do; who go wherever they are *"moved"* to go; who behave any way they are *"moved"* to behave? It is sad to see any Christian craving such experiences, as though they represent the quintessence of spiritual maturity and piety.

It does not reflect spiritual maturity to do things just because one feels *"led"* to do them. It is foolish to view each prompting as if it were the voice of God, which must be instantly obeyed. A wise Christian does not yearn to be *"taken over"* by the Spirit, to lose control, to lose self-awareness, to be *"slain"*, and the like. (114)

I do not mean that such experiences are necessarily wrong or evil; rather, they may be powerful, pleasant, enriching; but you should recognise that they are not intrinsically or specifically a work of the Holy Spirit, especially if they require a loss of volition.

By contrast, see *Galatians 5:22-23*, and note that one of the true marks of the presence of the Holy Spirit in a person's life is *self-control* (cp. Ez 2:1-2; 3:23-24). Hence Paul insists that we must take personal responsibility for what is happening in our own spirits (1 Co 14:32). We are not automatons, but

---

(114) Such phenomena, of course, are by no means limited to Pentecostals; they are part of the religious experience of mystics in all branches of the church, and also in the great non-Christian religions. For example, one of the greatest of the English Roman Catholic mystics was the illiterate, but very intelligent, Margery Kempe (c. 1373-c. 1440). Her experiences are described in her autobiography (which she dictated), The Book Of Margery Kempe. In it she talks about falling into compulsive weepings, howlings, shoutings, laughings, and the like. Here is one of many similar passages: "She told him *(her amanuensis)* how sometimes the Father of Heaven conversed with her soul as plainly and as certainly as one friend speaks to another through bodily speech. Sometimes the Second Person in the Trinity, sometimes all Three Persons in the Trinity and one substance in Godhead, spoke to her soul, and informed her in her faith and in his love – how she should love him, worship him, and dread him. ... Sometimes our Lady spoke to her mind; sometimes St Peter, sometimes St Paul, sometimes St Katherine, or whatever saint in heaven she was devoted to, appeared to her soul and taught her how she should love our Lord, and how she should please him. These conversations were so sweet, so holy and so devout, that often this creature could not bear it, but fell down and twisted and wrenched her body about, and made remarkable faces and gestures, with vehement sobbings and great abundance of tears, sometimes saying 'Jesus, mercy,' and sometimes, 'I die.'" (Tr. by B. A. Windeatt; Penguin Books, 1988; pg. 75.).

free-born children of the Lord. We are not pagans, to be driven around by wild impulses, but servants of the living God, who treats his children with respect and dignity. We are not mindless puppets, jumping on the end of a heavenly string, but people who are born of the Spirit and invited into wise partnership with the Lord (Jn 15:15; Ga 4:6; 1 Co 2:16).

## RECOGNISE THE FIVE LEVELS OF PROPHECY

Paul's language makes it clear that prophecy is a direct act of the *human* spirit, and only indirectly an act of the *Holy* Spirit (cp. again 1 Co 14:14, "*my spirit prays ... *").

This means that a prophetic gift can function with or without the presence or power of the Holy Spirit – see *1 Corinthians 12:1; 13:2; Deuteronomy 13:1-3.*

Hence we can observe *five* possible levels of prophecy:

- that which is merely **concocted**: a piece of human invention or imagination.

- that which is **demon-inspired**: a lie planted in a willing mind.

- that which is **sincere**, but **wrong**: honestly spoken, but not inspired by the Holy Spirit; arising from a mere impulse or fancy.

- that which is apparently **true**, but **wrong**: an oracle can be true, yet not necessarily inspired by God.

- that which is truly wrought by the **Holy Spirit**.

### *FOUR NECESSARY RULES*

Because of the difficulty of keeping prophecy pure, an anti-charismatic party soon arose in the church (1 Th 5:19-20). But we dare not lose our charismatic identity! So the following rules become imperative –

- Each prophet must remain under the authority of the church – any prophet who insists upon acting independently, or resents any kind of oversight, should be rejected as false.

- You must not surrender your liberty to any prophet. Beware of giving too much authority to any personal prophecy (cp. Ez 22:28b, " ... *although the Lord has not spoken, they still say, 'This is the word of the Lord!'"*) Listen to each oracle with respect, but then reserve an absolute right to decide for yourself how much heed you will give to it.

- Prophets should strive to *"excel"*, for the glory of God, and for the benefit of the church (Ro 12:6; 1 Co 14:12).

- All prophecy must be subject to judgment, by the leaders of the local church, by the church itself, and by any individual to whom an oracle is addressed (14:29).

Here, too, are some

### OTHER PRINCIPLES TO OBSERVE

- Sometimes a false prophecy may yet be true (De 13:1-5); so the spiritual content of the prophecy, its spiritual effect, are also important (cp. also 1 Kg 22; Je 28; Mt 7:15-23; 1 Jn 4:1).

- Sometimes a genuine prophecy, whether of blessing (Mi 3:9-12), or of judgment (Je 26:16-19), may be unfulfilled because certain conditions (whether stated or implied) are attached to it.

- Some prophecies involve a lesser and a greater fulfilment. For example, many Messianic prophecies were first fulfilled in Israel, and then later, in Christ. Some prophecies about David, or other biblical characters, had a later, and greater, fulfilment in

Christ. Many oracles about Israel's return from exile have had only a partial historical fulfilment; their greater realisation is yet to come.

- Prophecy can be misunderstood; e.g. was it Paul or his companions who misunderstood the Spirit's intent? (Ac 20:22-25, 37-38; 21:4, 9-14). Commentators differ in their reading of those stories. Personally, I think that Paul should have heeded the warnings, and not gone stubbornly on. However, I will also say emphatically, that right or wrong, Paul had *complete freedom* in Christ to make his own choice, and to expect that God would honour it. He chose to go on. He suffered the inevitable consequences. Yet the Lord did indeed honour him, and out of his imprisonment came some marvellous letters!

- Prophecy can have an unexpected fulfilment. For example, think about the surprising way some of the Messianic prophecies were fulfilled. The same is true of many of the prophecies dealing with Israel.

- Prophecy can be fulfilled in principle, but not in detail. There are many prophecies concerning Israel and the nations that have never been, and never can be, fulfilled in all their details. The old prophets couched their oracles in various literary forms, often replete with very colourful imagery and illustration. The predicted judgments certainly fell upon the hapless peoples, but seldom in exactly the manner foretold. [115]

---

(115) For a more extensive examination into the manner in which the old oracles were fulfilled in Israel and in the nations, see my book *Understanding Your Bible*.

It is simply true, even the best of prophets speak only *"in part ... (and) see through a dark glass"* (1 Co 13:12).

## CONCLUSION

Continual prophecy is the glory of the church. It is the special sign of the new era of the Spirit. Let us then never quench nor grieve the Spirit (1 Th 5:19-21). Let us rather fulfil *Romans 12:11*, never flagging in zeal, always aglow in the Spirit, serving the Lord in the full power of Pentecost until the day Jesus comes!

## WE CANNOT BE CONTENT
## WITH A DECLINING CHURCH

> *"Since you are eager to have spiritual gifts, strive to excel in your use of them so that you help the church to grow."* (1 Co 14:12)

The literal meaning of the opening clause is rather different to the translation I have given, which follows most other translations. Not that the rendering is wrong. It captures well enough the sense of the clause. Nonetheless, it is not what Paul himself wrote. He actually said, *"Since you are zealots of spirits ..."* Now that is a strange expression, which doesn't make much sense in English; hence translators usually paraphrase it as *"eager* (or zealous) *for spiritual gifts"*, or something like that. But let us rather stick with Paul, and try to discover what he meant.

### ZEALOTS

First, we are to be **"zealots"**, which is a noun that can have either a negative or a positive sense – in this case, of course, it is positive. Paul is spurring us to passion and urgency. Indeed, when we are dealing with the charismata, complacency is our worst enemy. The Corinthians had many faults, but in this he could commend them – when it came to spiritual gifts, they were zealots! *So keep the fire* *burning!* (116) Which means maintaining a zeal for the charismata, which in turn means that we should always be –

- Eager to see them <u>functioning</u> – never content with a church where there is no charismatic expression.

- Eager to see them <u>all</u> in action – never content with a church that welcomes only one or two of the gifts of the Spirit.

- Eager to receive them <u>personally</u> – never content with a life that is restricted to the mundane, wholly natural, never touching the supernatural.

### *SPIRITS*

Second, we are to be zealous for **"spirits"**. Now that is a surprise, for we would expect him to have written, *"zealous for the charismata"*. Instead, he uses *"pneumaton"* = breath, wind, that is, *"spirits"*, for it is plural in number. We cannot help but ask, "Why?" Paul probably means us to understand that –

**First**, we should break loose from the bonds of a secular viewpoint and reach into the supernatural world that lies beyond our natural environment. To many Christians cannot see further than this present, visible, tangible world. But outside this earthly dimension there is another vaster world, the realm of angels, of principalities, powers, and spiritual authorities, both good and evil. It is unseen, but we can see it; it is invisible, but the eye of faith can give it substance; it is spiritual, but it has enormous influence on the natural world. Indeed, Paul urges us to stop looking only at what can be seen, but to focus rather on what cannot be seen, for, as he

---

(116) *"Always aglow in the Spirit"* (Ro 12:11). The Greek word means *bubbling*, as in boiling water; hence burning hot, fervent, zealous.

says, *"what can be seen is temporary, but what cannot be seen is eternal!"* (2 Co 4:18). We should be zealous to gain access to that world, and all the resources it represents.

**Second**, we Christians are now citizens of the Kingdom of God, which is a supernatural kingdom, governed by supernatural law, and operating in supernatural power. It is a shame for us to be so earthbound that the realm of *"spirits"* is unknown to us, to live as if we have no access to heaven's resources, or as if there are no angels, no *"ministering spirits sent out to serve those who are the heirs of salvation"* (He 1:14). Yet from the moment of our new birth we became supernatural more than natural, spirit more than flesh, and of heaven more than earth. Let us then live like children of the King, utilising the riches that are ours to claim in the realm of spirits.

**Third**, Paul is probably trying to convey the idea that there is a great variety of spiritual gifts, many more than the nine we commonly call "the charismata" (which I have outlined at the beginning of this chapter, and are listed in 1 Co 12:8-10). The word *"spirits"* suggests that the charismata cannot be limited to those nine, for there are many additional functions in the church, such as those I have listed earlier –

- apostle; prophet; evangelist; pastor; elder; deacon; teacher; administrator; presbyter; overseer; "helper" (musician; secretary; treasurer; leader; counsellor; financier; nurturer); and so on (Ro 12:6-8; 1 Co 12:28; Ep 4:11; 1 Pe 4:10-11).

Those gifts, ministries, and functions, even if some depend more upon natural abilities than others, are all ultimately supernatural, based upon a divine gift and calling. That is why Paul calls them "spirits". Perhaps, too, by placing them all under the one term *"spirits"*, he means to show that we dare not call one gift or calling better than, or more important than, another. The good health and growth of the church depend upon them all being present and functioning properly.

## *STRIVERS*

*"Strive to excel in your use of the gifts."*

The Greek verb is in the present imperative tense – "seek!" – "strive!" – "struggle to find" – "earnestly desire" to excel in your use of the charismata, or in fulfilling the task the Lord has laid upon you. Which leads me to just one question – are you doing so?

## *ACHIEVERS*

*"So that you help the church to grow."*

If we are keen to see our churches grow, then here is a powerful key!

Growth comes, not just when the charismata exist, but when they are used wisely and well. That means –

- Prayerfully.
- Humbly.
- Faithfully.
- Obediently –

about which I could say many things, but instead, let me conclude this part of our study by the text (paraphrased a little) that began it –

> *"You should be zealots for the diverse gifts of the Spirit, and then strive to excel in your use of them so that you help the church to grow."*
> (1 Co 14:12)

# TWENTY-ONE

# GROWING THROUGH WORSHIP

Paul makes an arresting statement about the Corinthian church – *it was a* **growing** *church!* (1 Co 14:23-26). *"Unbelievers"* and *"outsiders"* were continually coming in to their worship services, falling flat on their faces, and crying out, "God is in this place!" The passage is fascinating, both because of the surprising report of outsiders falling prostrate and shouting, but also because it is the only description we have of a worship service in the apostolic churches.

So the church was growing. But why? Simply because the presence of God was manifest in their assemblies. But surely God is always present with his people? In a general sense, yes; but this was a special kind of presence, for it brought irresistible conviction of sin; it compelled a confession of faith; it continually attracted outsiders and unbelievers.

So here is a wonderful rule – people will always be irresistibly drawn to any place where they believe the presence of God can truly be found!

What was the source of this divine overshadowing in Corinth? Is it still possible to create an extraordinarily powerful worship service, which irresistibly attracts *"outsiders and unbelievers"*, and forces them to acknowledge the presence of God in the church?

It was a special quality in the way they *"came together"* (vs. 23a, 26a); from which we observe four things –

## PRODUCTIVE WORSHIP

The right kind of worship generates church growth. How can this be? Simply because there is *a release of life* in the assembly of the saints that is absent from individual Christians. And by a universal law of God, life always begets life; thus the spiritual life begotten out of worship irresistibly generates new life.

Thus the local church is pre-eminently a place of **worship**, not **evangelism**, except that it will do its best evangelism **through** excellent worship. In this connection, it is worth noting that both the so-called "gospel service" and the use of "altar calls" for salvation are recent innovations; they were unknown prior to the middle of the last century. On the contrary, across the centuries the church has existed primarily as a *worshipping* community, and its witness has arisen mostly out of its worship. In other words, lacking everything else, the church can still grow, and *will grow best*, through worship!

That is shown by the early church which, despite awful persecution, and lacking almost all the material items (buildings, printed literature, advertising, music, musicians, professional crusades, entertainments, outreaches, promotions, and so on, [117] that we deem essential for growth, still expanded mightily.

By contrast, see the effect of bad worship. When things are done badly, says Paul, visitors will simply walk away, mocking the Christians as madmen (vs. 23). That will always be the result when worship fails, or is poorly conducted, or falls into fanaticism, or is unbiblical, and the like. Worship done well, brings growth. Worship done badly brings rejection of the gospel.

---

(117) Note that the first known church building is dated about 230, and is a converted house, seating no more than 80 people; it is near Baghdad, on the banks of the Euphrates.

Notice how Paul twice mentions the *"coming together"* of the congregation, creating a kind of bracket (vs. 23, 26), in which he inserts the qualities of good and bad worship. Ruinous worship will be uncontrolled, graceless, disorderly, too emotional, causing observers to brand the worshippers as fools at best, and insane at worst. Fruitful worship will be marked by good order, and decency. The Greek word has the sense of gracious, seemly, becoming.

This does not mean that fruitful worship should be merely a lovely ceremony, lacking vitality and sparkle. Far from it. Paul wanted everyone to be actively involved in a lively manner – *"each one has a hymn, a lesson, a revelation, a tongue, or an interpretation"* (vs. 26). But he wanted them also to behave in such a way that the church would be *"built up"*, not pulled down by unruly charismata or tumultuous clamour.

## PASSIONATE WORSHIP

The Greek word translated as "come together" is *sunerchomai*, which comes from two words *erchomai* = to come, and *sun* = united. It was commonly used of sexual intercourse! – [118]

> I too am an ordinary man, just like all other men, for are we not all descended from the first man, who was made from the dust? In my mother's womb I was fashioned into flesh during the time of her pregnancy, nurtured in blood from the seed of her husband and the pleasure that is found in bed. (Wis 7:1-2)

---

(118) It also carried its literal meaning of "come together". Context had to determine what meaning it held in a given sentence.

Paul uses *sunerchomai* in the same sense just a couple of chapters earlier –

> *Married couples should not deny sex to each other, unless they agree to do so in order to spend time in prayer. But then they should* <u>come together</u> *again, so that Satan won't find an opportunity to tempt them.* (1 Co 7:5)

It seems very daring to apply the same word both to marital relations and to Christian worship! Why such boldness? I think Paul had two reasons –

- He wanted to show that a Christian *congregation* [119] should never be merely an *audience*; rather, he insisted upon their coming together in a warmth of love, and unity of heart. If love of God and neighbour does not envelop the worshipping community, then its praise will be a dull sound in the ear of God. Let worship be passionate, all-consuming, and adoring!

## PARADOXICAL WORSHIP

> *What am I to do? I will pray with my spirit, but I will pray with my mind also; I will sing praise with my spirit, but I will sing with my mind also.* (1 Co 14:15)

Paul there highlights two essential components of Spirit-filled worship –

---

[119] Like *sunerchomai*, "congregation" is a compound of three Latin expressions that mean "to gather a flock together", or "come together as a flock".

## THE IRRATIONAL

*"I will sing with my spirit ... I will praise with my spirit."*

He is speaking there, of course, about praying and praising God in other tongues, or glossolalia, the language of the human spirit. (14:2, 14) Glossolalia highlights the truth that there is an irrational dimension in God, that is, there are aspects of his nature and works that defy human reason. Some examples – his *self-generation* (if God made everything, who made God?); *eternity* (where time does not exist, and the passage of time is unknown); *infinity* (the many things that have no reasonable beginning nor end, such as the infinite series of numbers, the boundlessness of the cosmos); *foreknowledge* (how can even God know what has not yet been?); *sovereignty* (how can he allow free-will, yet retain absolute control?); and the like. In the end we must admit that to the human mind God is a profound mystery.

Yet that should not surprise us; after all, even at our level, the best things in life are irrational (cp. Pr 30:18-19); thus who can logically explain the beauty of a rose, the magic of a glorious sunset, the wonder of a child's laugh, the splendour of love, the mystery of pain, and a thousand other incomprehensibles of ordinary life?

Therefore we should spurn this world's idolatrous worship of human reason, its arrogant attempt to reduce all Christian doctrine and practice to logical propositions; to make our faith altogether "reasonable". And here is exactly one place where glossolalia is so useful. It has this peculiar and priceless value of injecting a dimension of illogic, of pure spirituality, of fathomless mystery, into Christian worship. Thus it prevents the church from settling into a comfortable respectability; it keeps us in touch with the infinite.

Furthermore, the presence of irrational glossolalia in worship keeps us open to the supernatural; it creates a channel through which constant miracles can flow into the church.

## THE RATIONAL

*"I will praise with my mind ... I will sing with my mind."*

No matter how many miracles it may be enjoying, nor how abundantly the charismata are flourishing, the church must remain zealous for good order (see 1 Co 14:6, 26, 33, 40). The "irrational" cannot be equated with the unreasonable nor the disorderly; it gives no licence to fanaticism nor chaos; it does not endorse ugliness; it allows no excuse to folly or stupidity.

Paul therefore, as I have mentioned before, insists upon a worship style that displays gracefulness, dignity, beauty, skilful arrangement, proper sequence, good order. The gorgeous ceremonial, the lavish robes, the splendid ritual that God ordained for the worship of ancient Israel show that he is not offended by order and beauty. Yet they were merry enough, and sometimes celebrated before God with song and dance, sacrifice and ceremony, that lasted across several days.

Enduring spiritual power in the end depends upon us achieving and sustaining such qualities in our worship. (vs. 12).

# PROPHETIC WORSHIP

Paul's saying about *"all prophesying"* [120] appears to contradict his instructions in vs. 29,31, where he insists that no more than two or three should prophesy, and then one by one, deferring to each other. But there he is talking about

---

[120] See 14:24, "Suppose you are all prophesying ... then the unbeliever will be convicted by all."

gifted people bringing a prophetic *oracle*. Here he is talking about a prophetic *mantle* that should rest upon the entire church – that is, the sound of prophecy, the voice of God, should echo in every part of the worship service. Does someone pray, or read a passage of scripture, give an announcement, sing a song, preach a sermon – no matter, it should all be infused with a divine accent, conveying an echo of heaven to the people. They should feel some divine impact; they should sense the presence of God. Or to put it differently, everything that is said, sung, and done in a worship service should carry a prophetic unction, a quality of divine grace that lifts it from the natural to the supernatural.

Where this prophetic quality is missing, the worship service must be deemed in some respect to have failed. The lack of a divine mantle must eventually reduce worship to the level of a human performance, an event contrived solely by human skill, not requiring any divine ability. Worship then becomes little more than a piece of religious entertainment, the Christian equivalent of a secular theatre performance or sing-along. Small wonder that *"unbelievers and outsiders"* stay out of such churches – they can have more fun in the concert hall!

Indeed, when it comes to entertainment, the world has vastly greater resources and expertise than the church can ever muster. For us, the tangible presence of God, and his voice speaking among his people, is the one thing Christian worship can create that the world cannot even begin to emulate.

Is this possible? Yes!

Simply note the prophetic quality of the Psalms, which shows how the worship of Israel, at its best, was clothed with this same mantle of prophecy! We are told that the musicians prophesied with their lyres, harps, and cymbals, and the choristers also, prophesied with their songs. (1 Ch 25:1-3)

Then there was Heman who, although he was chiefly a musician, was also *"the king's seer"*. He too prophesied, and managed to do so even through the names of his last nine sons, whose names together comprise a prophetic oracle. As well, the young men themselves sang prophetically in the temple! (vs. 4-6)

Here are their names, and the oracle that many commentators think arises out of them –

    Hananiah: ............................*Be gracious O Lord*

    Hanani: ..............................*Be gracious to me*

    Eliathah: .............................*You are my God*

    Giddalti: ..............................*I will exalt you*

    Ramamti-ezer: ....................*I will extol you, my Helper*

    Joshbekashah: ....................*(Though) I sit where trouble abounds*

    Mallothi: .............................*Give heed to my prayer*

    Hothir: ...............................*(And grant me) abundantly*

    Mahazioth: ..........................*(Your) visions.*

Did the Corinthians achieve such a prophetic quality in their worship? Did outsiders truly come in, only to fall down, stricken with guilt, repenting and crying out that God was overwhelmingly present? Probably not. Or at least, not very often. His words are likely hyperbolic, for such a dramatic response to the gospel was no doubt as uncommon then as it is now. But Paul is trying to show the *potential* that lies in true Spirit-filled worship – it can generate enormous spiritual energy; it can bring a wonderful sense of the presence of God; it can reach out like a magnet to draw a constant stream of visitors.

So the apostle was reaching for an ideal, revealing how worship, at its best, can carry us as near to Paradise as we can possibly come before the resurrection!

If the Corinthians did reach such heights of glory, how was it done? I suppose through the next quality in their *"coming together"*, which was

## PARTICIPATORY WORSHIP

Paul was able to describe them as *"all prophesying"* (vs. 26), because they were *"all participating"* –

> *When you come together, each one has a hymn, a lesson, a revelation, a tongue, or an interpretation.* (1 Co 14:26)

True worship, then, will include the entire congregation. Paul highlights the importance of this congregation-wide participation by the way in which he changes and uses the two pronouns: *each* and *all* (12:7,11,12,13,18,27; 14:24,26,31). *Each* person has some gift, function, or office; *all are* included, none may exclude themselves, nor be excluded by the church; *each* and *all* have their part to play.

Furthermore, they came together, not to be ministered to, but to minister. Their purpose was not to be amused, nor entertained, nor even inspired. Their primary desire was not to be made whole, nor to enjoy fellowship, nor any other self-focussed goal. They had but one main focus, to worship, honour, and glorify God, in all things giving pre-eminence to Christ (Cl 1:18). Those lesser things may all be valid benefits of worship; but they should never be the final aim of our assembling together.

The two pronouns, embracing both the entire congregation and each individual, show that there is no warrant for worship that is merely a performance by professional clergy, with the congregation acting mostly as passive spectators; nor for an irresponsible individualism that scorns the authority of those to whom God has given leadership in the church.

A local church can best achieve that splendour when it functions like a *living body* (1 Co 12:12-13), which is why Paul uses the two pronouns –

## *"EACH"* (12:7,11; 14:26)

Worship is like a symphony, [121] not a solo performance, but a harmony of many individuals brought into one melody. How much room is there in an orchestra for a silent musician, one who refuses to play? Such a worthless member will soon be dismissed. So Paul is insistent – **each** Christian must find some active part to play in the church, and especially in its worship. This is because each person is important, each person is called, each person has some gift from God; the Spirit has no favourites, and there are no exclusions. No matter how small or seemingly unimportant, there is always something a person can do, be, or say, that will enhance the worship of the whole church.

## *"ALL"* (12:13; 14:24)

Not even the most talented member of an orchestra is allowed to perform only at home, alone, rather than with his fellow musicians in the concert hall. So in the church – though **each** has a place, he or she must occupy it for the benefit of **all** (12:14-26), and **all** must play their part for the benefit of **each**. And each and all must do all and each for the glory of God.

Continuing the musical analogy, a good conductor will not allow any one musician to play his or her instrument either

---

(121) Think about Jesus' use of the Greek word *sumphoneo* (from which comes "symphony") in *Matthew 18:19,* and also Paul's use of the same word in *1 Corinthians 7:5,* where he mentions a married couple "agreeing together" (*sumphoneo*). So worship is like a couple "coming together" and "agreeing together", in a lovely harmony of praise.

too loudly or too softly, or at a different tempo, or in a wrong key. The great object of a symphony orchestra is to create a symphony, where all the sounds blend in perfect harmony and synchronicity, to create one unforgettable musical experience. Likewise, the leadership of the church must endeavour to create a similar harmony of praise, softening those who are too boisterous, encouraging those who are too timid, and preventing any one person from dominating or disturbing the worship, striving for a perfect blending of heart, mind, voice, and faith.

Nonetheless, place must also be allowed for any individual, great or small, to speak as an oracle of God to the church (vs. 26, 30). God is never obliged to act only through official channels; he is always free to choose any person through whom to convey his will and his word to the church. Good leadership will recognise this principle, and be sensitive to what the Spirit might be saying, from whatever source.

I have used an orchestra as an example of the "each – all" principle. Paul chose the human body – one body, but with many members, which must all function both individually and in union with the body. Think about that, and then ask yourself, then, "Am I a source of joy or of pain to my local church, to the body of Christ?"

Neutrality in this matter is impossible, for a **dysfunctional** limb is just as hurtful to the body as a **diseased** one. Rather, let us all be wholesome and active members in the body of Christ, the local church, for in the end, a Spirit-filled church truly functions only when we are all in our proper places, fulfilling our appointed tasks, using the gifts we have received, for the benefit of the entire church, and to the endless honour of our Lord.

# PAEANIC WORSHIP

*"Giving thanks well!"* (1 Co 14:17)

Our worship should comprise a single paean to the Lord, an extended act of praise, thanksgiving, rejoicing, and triumph in Christ. Indeed, worship that fails to express heartfelt gratitude and praise to God hardly deserves the name.

What is the chief image of God in us? Our voices, especially when they are aroused in praise to God! That is made clear by scripture, which says that men and women were made in the image of God (Ge 1:27) when the *only thing* known about God was that he had created all things by the spoken word alone.

Notice, too, the strange use of *kabod* (the ordinary Hebrew word for "glory") in *Psalms 16:9; 30:12; 57:8; 108:1, 3; 149:5, 6.* In each place, *kabod* is used as a synonym of the human voice, which is called the psalmist's *"glory"*. That usage may have arisen out of an early Hebrew experience of glossolalia, which the psalmist himself seems to have enjoyed (cp. 1 Sa 10:5-6, 10; and there are other similar references in the OT).

Such a use of *kabod* shows that the psalmists reckoned that their voices could attain no higher honour than to be raised in supernatural praise to God. This was their noblest dignity; this clothed them with eternal glory!

Our prayer should be that God will enable us to create such worship, which will be our highest "glory" – and his!

*PART TWO CONTINUED*

# FROM THE "LETTER"

*SECTION THREE*

## THE MINISTRY OF WOMEN

## TWENTY-TWO

# SILENCE PLEASE, LADIES?

> *As in all the churches of the saints, the women should keep silent. They are not permitted to speak, but should be in submission, as the Law also says. If there is anything they desire to learn, let them ask their husbands at home. It is disgraceful for a woman to speak in church. (1 Co 14:33b-35)*

Truly? A woman is not allowed even to *speak* in church, let alone *preach*? Did Paul really mean to say that?

It is a brave man, or a fool, who puts his foot into this quagmire of controversy! Perhaps I am both, but I am willing to venture an opinion, which I hope will be found to be in agreement with what the Bible teaches. However, I do not pretend that the following pages are infallible, nor do they contain an exhaustive treatment of the question about how far women can pursue diverse ministry roles in the church. But they do represent a compendium from both Testaments of most of the appropriate scriptures, and I hope they will provide a sufficient answer in the affirmative – that is, *I cannot see any incontestable biblical argument against women serving in diverse ministry and leadership levels in the church*.

First let us consider those Scriptures that favour the ministry of women –

## EXAMPLES IN THE OLD TESTAMENT

It seems reasonable to assume that women should have no less freedom in the New Covenant than they enjoyed under the old, which shows that while women were not permitted to officiate in the Temple, [122] nor to act as priests, they were certainly able to expound the Word of God, to prophesy, and by every means within their authority to lead the people to serve the Lord better.

## MIRIAM, DEBORAH, & JAEL

*Miriam the prophetess, who was the sister of Aaron, picked up her tambourine, and all the women followed her, playing tambourines and dancing. (Ex 15:20) ... Deborah was a prophetess. She was the wife of Lapidoth, and she judged Israel at that time. (Jg 4:4)*

Both ladies are called a *"prophetess"*. The word means "an inspired woman," that is, one who spoke or sang by the authority and inspiration of God, whether in prediction, discourse, or declamation. Deborah is described also as a *"judge"*; that is, she had the right to pronounce sentence for or against, to govern, to defend, to rule. The Bible shows that Deborah was richly anointed by the Lord and greatly honoured by the whole land.

As for Jael, she was God's servant in slaughtering Sisera, which seems considerably less feminine than merely delivering an oracle or preaching a sermon! (Jg 4:9 ff).

## HULDAH

*Hilkia the priest, Ahikam, Achbor, Shaphan, and Asahiah, consulted Huldah the prophetess, who was the wife of Shallum the son of Tikvah, the son of Harhas, Keeper of the Wardrobe.*

---

(122) Except as choristers, dancers, assistants, prophets, and the like.

> *She lived in the newer part of Jerusalem and they met together in her home. (2 Kg 22:14; 2 Ch 34:22)*

She too was a *"prophetess"*, apparently renowned for her wisdom, so that a group of high-ranking officials were happy to consult her on questions relating to scripture. She told them what God was saying and warned them about coming disasters. Note too –

## NOADIAH & ATHALIAH

Noadiah was a prophetess (Ne 6:14).

Then there was Athaliah, who, although wicked, ruled lawfully as regent over Israel (2 Kg 11:1-3).

## MANY WOMEN

> *"Afterward," says God, "I will pour out my Spirit upon everyone. Your sons and daughters will prophesy. Your old men will dream dreams. Your young men will see visions." (Jl 2:28-29)*

We are told that *"your daughters shall prophesy"*; that is, by inspiration of God they will speak out the Word of God; they will utter predictions; they will exhort the people to follow God (which meanings are all included in the verb "to prophesy"). [123]

> *As for you, son of man, set your face against the daughters of your people who insist on prophesying out of their own minds. (Ez 13:17)*

---

(123) The Hebrew word is defined by Strong as "to speak (or sing) by inspiration (in prediction or simple discourse); prophesy (-ing); make oneself a prophet."

Though that passage speaks of women who prophesied falsely, it nonetheless shows that the prophetic (and therefore preaching) ministry of women was generally accepted in Israel.

> *Then a wise woman called out from the city walls. "Hear me! Hear me! Please tell Joab to come near so that I may speak with him."* ... *Then she spoke (and Joab listened to her counsel)* ... *Then the woman spoke to all the citizens in her wisdom* (and the city of Abel of Beth-maachah was saved because of her shrewd words and actions)." (2 Sa 20:14-22; and compare also 14:2-21)

Joab should have enquired of God before besieging the city (De 20:10,11; cp. 1 Sa 23:2; 30:8), but, when he failed to do so, God used a woman to set him right and to save the city. She was called a *"wise"* woman. The word means to be wise in mind, word or act; to be able to teach wisdom, to be intelligent. Her wisdom and authority were plainly respected and heeded by the people of the city.

## ANNA

> *There was a lady called Anna, a prophetess, the daughter of Phanuel, of the tribe of Asher, who was very old. Her husband had died after only seven years of marriage, and she was now a widow of 84. She refused to leave the temple, and served God with fasting and prayer night and day. Simeon had barely stopped speaking before she came in and at once began to give thanks to God and to speak about the child Jesus to all who were waiting for the redemption of Jerusalem. (Lu 2:36-38)*

Though this is a NT reference, it deals with OT circumstances, and a woman, Anna, who was a *"prophetess"*.

Notice –

- She served God in the temple; that is, she ministered before the Lord.

- She *"spoke"* about Christ to all who looked for redemption. The word *"spoke"* means to talk, to preach, to give an extended discourse, or to make a random speech to a crowd (whether large or small).

That is, Anna witnessed constantly of Jesus to the people who thronged the Temple, which certainly may include preaching.

From such Scriptures, it is evident, under the old covenant, that while women could not officiate as priests nor establish any new ritual of worship, they were clearly employed by God to bring the people back to holy service, to expound the Law, to deliver prophecies, to teach, to rule in temporal matters, to guide, to correct faults, to give instruction.

Surely the New Testament will not allow Christian women **less** liberty than this?

## EXAMPLES IN THE NEW TESTAMENT

### MATTHEW 28:19-20

*Go therefore and make disciples in every nation. Baptise them in the name of the Father, and of the Son, and of the Holy Spirit. Teach them to observe everything that I have commanded you. And never doubt that I am with you always, even to the very end of the age.*

Jesus commanded the apostles to go and *"make disciples"* (lit.) in every nation, teaching them to practise everything that he had commanded them. Those words were spoken on a mountain (vs. 16), which is almost certainly the same hillside and the same occasion upon which he appeared to 500 people (1 Co 15:6). There can be no serious doubt that many women were included in that large crowd, and that the Saviour therefore commanded them too, along with the men, to preach, to heal the sick, and to fulfil many other aspects of gospel ministry.

### MARK 16:17-20

*These signs will follow those who believe – in my name they will cast out devils; they will speak with new tongues; they will pick up snakes; and if they drink any deadly thing, it will not hurt them; they will lay hands on the sick, and they will get well. After the Lord had said all these things, he was received up into heaven, where he sat down on the right hand of God. And the disciples went out and preached everywhere, while the Lord worked with them, and confirmed the word with signs following.*

Both men and women who have believed and have been baptised are here given a commission to cast out devils and heal the sick – a commission that must be associated with preaching as, in fact, it always was by Jesus – *Matthew 10:7-8; Luke 9:1-2,6; 10:19* etc.

Some claim that the passage was not a part of Mark's original gospel, but is a later addition, and should not be treated as scripture. Even if that is true, the witness of the passage is still powerful. For if it does not in fact convey to us Mark's opinion, it still reveals the doctrine held by the early church, right on the heels of the apostolic age.

## JOHN 4:39,42

*Many of the Samaritans in that town believed in Jesus because of the testimony of the woman who told them, "He revealed everything that I ever did!"*

The Lord, well knowing the character and background of this woman, was yet pleased to have her testify about him and to make of her one of the first "evangelists". Jesus used her witness to bring many people to trust him.

Notice ...

- The city believed in Christ because of the *"testimony"* (124) of the woman, which must have involved some kind of public proclamation. The word used here is the same as the one used in *Acts 1:1* (treatise) and see Luke's own explanation of this word in *Luke 1:1-4.*

- The men of the city later said to the woman, *"We do not believe because of your speech ..."* (Greek: *lalia*). Here the word is the same as *"spoke"* in *Luke 2:38* – that is, it suggests that the woman, when she went into the city, called out to the crowd and preached to them the wonder of Jesus' knowledge of her past life and his claim to be the Messiah.

- It says she *"testified"* (Greek: *martureo*); that is, she bore witness of Christ, or gave an account of his knowledge and power.

---

(124) The Greek word is *"logos"*, which has a wide variety of meanings, including teaching and preaching.

## ACTS 1:8

*You will receive power when the Holy Spirit
has come upon you, and you will bear witness
for me both in Jerusalem, and in all Judaea,
and in Samaria, and to the most distant lands
on earth.*

Women are included in this commission (compare vs. 14,15).
Therefore, women are able to be *"witnesses"* of Christ. The
word *"witness"* (Greek: *martureo*) means to *"bear testimony
of"*, *"to give evidence concerning"*, to *"attest to the truth of"*
something. The Greek word also carries the sense of
*"martyrdom"* – that is, to so witness as to give one's life for
the sake of the gospel.

## ACTS 2:1-4

*When the day of Pentecost dawned, they were
all gathered together in one place. Suddenly
there was a noise from heaven like a roaring
gale, and it filled the house where they were
meeting. Then they saw something like
tongues of fire falling down and sitting upon
each of them. They were all filled with the Holy
Spirit and, as the Spirit inspired them, began
to speak in other tongues.*

Both men and women were filled with the Spirit and spoke in
other tongues in a public assembly.

## ACTS 2:17-18

*"This is what will happen in the last days,"
says God. "I will pour out my Spirit upon
every land. Your sons and your daughters will
prophesy, your young men will see visions,
and your old men will dream dreams. I will*

*pour out my Spirit upon my servants, both
men and women, and they will prophesy."*

Peter quotes Joel's oracle (which was fulfilled in Ac 2:1-4)
and says that both *"sons and daughters, ... men and women
will prophesy"* – that is, "will speak or sing by inspiration of
God, either in prediction or in simple discourse." [125]

## ACTS 18:26

*Apollos began to speak boldly in the
synagogue. But when Aquila and Priscilla
heard him, they took him aside and explained
the way of God to him more correctly.*

Priscilla, it seems, was equally adept as her husband at laying
open the meaning of the Word of God, even to a highly
effective preacher. See the use of the same word in *Acts 11:4;
28:23.*

Together with her husband, Priscilla was Paul's fellow-
worker (Ac 18:2, 18; Ro 16:3), a teacher (Ac 18:26) and a
leader of a local church (Ro 16:3-5 1 Co 16:19).

## ACTS 21:9

*Philip had four daughters, all unmarried, who
prophesied.*

The word *"prophesy"* cannot be limited to its narrow
meaning of foretelling the future. It means basically "to

---

(125) Thayer defines the word (*propheteuo*) as to prophesy, to be a prophet,
speak forth by divine inspiration, to predict future events pertaining
especially to the kingdom of God, to declare a thing that can only be
known by divine revelation, to break forth under sudden impulse in lofty
discourse or praise of the divine counsels, or, under like prompting, to
teach, refute, reprove, admonish, comfort others.

forth-tell", especially under the impulse of divine revelation. Some translations render it as *"prophesied"*, but others have *"proclaimed God's message"* (GNB); *"speak what God has revealed"* (GW); *"spoke by the Spirit of God"* (Moffatt). So the idea cannot be excluded that they addressed the people under inspiration of the Lord and brought exhortation and edification to the Church of God.

### ROMANS 12:6-8

*We have received gifts that differ according to the grace that has been given to us. If prophecy, prophesy; if ministry, minister; if teaching, teach; if exhortation, exhort; sharing, with simplicity; ruling, with diligence; showing mercy, with cheerfulness.*

That is a more or less literal translation, especially in its staccato, all-inclusive style. No space is left for any gender discrimination. Both men and women can and do receive grace from God to serve him in each of the ways Paul lists, which include *"prophesying, ministering, teaching, exhorting and ruling"*. If women must be excluded from those functions, then they must also be excluded from *"sharing"* and *"showing mercy"*, which would be absurd.

Thus there was ***Phoebe***, who was a deacon, and who apparently delivered Paul's letter to the Romans (Ro 16:1-2, 12-13). And ***Tryphena***, another of Paul's fellow-workers (Ro 16:12). And ***Tryphosa***, another fellow-worker (Ro 16:12). And ***Persis***, another *"worker"* (Ro 16:12).

### ROMANS 16:7

*Greet Andronicus and Junia, who are my relatives. They are prisoners like me and they are prominent among the apostles. They were Christians before I was.*

Although Andronicus and Junia are both Greek names, they were apparently Jews since Paul calls them his *"relatives"* (literally *"fellow-countrymen"*). Junia is a girl's name (the masculine form is Junias, which some translations use even though the Greek text certainly requires *"Junia"*). [126]

Andronicus and Junia were presumably either husband and wife or brother and sister. If this assumption is correct (and the weight of evidence is much in its favour) then Paul lists a woman among the apostles and calls her *"prominent"* (literally, "eminent" or "remarkable"). Not only that, she and Andronicus were apparently apostles before Paul was!

As Peter Lampe (*Anchor Bible Dictionary* 3:1127) writes –

> Without exception, the Church Fathers in late antiquity identified Andronicus' partner in *Romans 16:7* as a woman, as did Minuscule 33 in the 9th century which records *iounia* with an acute accent. Only later medieval copyists of *Romans 16:7* could not imagine a woman being an apostle and wrote the masculine name "Junias." This latter name did not exist in antiquity; its explanation as a Greek abbreviation of the Latin name "Junianus" is unlikely.

Another writer says –

> The English versions (of the Bible) move from a consistent feminine understanding of "Junia" for the first three centuries (1526 to 1833,

---

(126) Thayer defines Junia as "a Christian woman at Rome, mentioned by Paul as one of his kinsfolk and fellow prisoners". I wonder why Thayer omits Paul's description of her also as a fellow "apostle"? Inadvertent, or a display of prejudice?

though the 1833 Dickinson version is an anomaly); then a second, fairly consistent masculine period of about a century (1870s to 1960s, with a few exceptions); followed by nearly three decades (1970 to 1996) of alternation between masculine and feminine, but with an increasing trend of returning to the feminine. [127]

And another –

A recent study reveals over 250 examples of (Junia) in Greek literature, not one of which is masculine! This seems to be early incontrovertible evidence that the name is feminine, which would make the pair husband and wife (or perhaps brother and sister). If the name is feminine, then Paul's referring to Andronicus and Junia **as outstanding among the apostles**, who **were in Christ before I was**, is very significant. It would indicate that (1) **apostles** refers to a group larger than the original Twelve, (2) among whom was to be counted a woman, (3) and probably a wife, (4) who had been an apostle before Paul was. [128]

A check of various commentaries and Bible dictionaries will show many different opinions about Junia. Some insist that the name is indeed masculine; others insist that the phrase *"prominent among the apostles"* means only that she was

[127] Eldon Jay Epp, Junia: The First Woman Apostle; Fortress Press, Minneapolis, 2005; pg. 65

[128] James E. Edwards, Commentary on Romans; Hendrickson Publishers, 1992; pg. 355.

admired *by* the apostles (but was not herself an apostle); and the like.

I am inclined to feel that if there had been no controversy about women in ministry neither would there be one about the meaning of "Junia"! The quarrel arises because of prejudice against a woman being an apostle. I am personally satisfied that Junia was indeed a woman, and that she was recognised as an apostle by Paul, and that this is the natural and most likely reading of the verse. [129] I cannot deny anyone a right to dispute that claim; but neither can anyone say that it is against either reason or scripture. Each person must decide for himself or herself.

### 1 CORINTHIANS 11:5

*Every woman who prays or prophesies with her head uncovered dishonours her head. It is just as offensive as if she had shaved her head.*

Here it is shown that women may pray or prophesy in a public assembly. Notice also *"every woman"*, which indicates it was a general practice for women to so behave.

Remember too that "prophesy" can have a wide application, from delivering an oracle to any kind of divinely inspired preaching or teaching.

### 1 CORINTHIANS 14:5, 23-24, 26, 31

*I would that you all spoke in tongues, but rather that you prophesied, for those who prophesy are greater than those who speak in*

---

(129) The word "apostle" had a broader meaning then than it does now. It was not restricted to the famous Twelve Apostles, but could be applied to any anointed messenger of the gospel.

> *tongues, unless they interpret, so that the church may be edified. ... When you come together, each one has a hymn, a lesson, a revelation, a tongue, or an interpretation. Let everything be done in a way that builds up the church. ... You may all prophesy one by one, so that all may learn, and all may be comforted.*

It would be irrational to limit that instruction to men alone. From those verses, we learn that women, along with men, may speak in tongues, prophesy, interpret, bring a Psalm, call the attention of the church to a doctrine, receive revelation from God and, by their ministry, bring learning and comfort to the assembled church.

### PHILIPIANS 4:2-3

> *I entreat and advise you, Euodia and Syntyche, to agree together and to work in harmony with the Lord. And I exhort you too, my genuine yokefellow, help these two women to keep co-operating, for they have toiled along with me in the spreading of the gospel, as have Clement and the rest of my fellow-workers whose names are in the book of life.* (Amplified N.T.)

Those verses imply that the two women actually worked with Paul in spreading the good news of the gospel. They were *"fellow-labourers"* with Paul; that is, they were his *"companions"*, *"assistants and fellow-helpers"*, *"associates with him in his ministry"*. The word also carries the sense of being empowered or appointed to perform the duties of another. In other words, Paul delegated something of his ministry to them.

## 1 TIMOTHY 2:8-10

*In every church, the men should be men of prayer, lifting up holy hands without anger or quarrelling. Likewise, women should clothe themselves sensibly and modestly, with restraint, not depending upon fancy hair styles, gold, pearls, nor expensive gowns. Rather they should be adorned with good works, which are proper for women who profess godliness.*

Paul here instructs women on how they should dress themselves for public prayer, thus showing that public speech was not denied them.

Notice also the phrase *"women who profess godliness"*. The word *"profess"* may mean no more than a claim to be godly, but it could also imply a public declaration or an open acknowledgment of the gospel, that is, *"those who <u>preach</u> godliness."*

## TITUS 2:3-4

*The older women should display godly behaviour as people who claim to be holy. They should not share in malicious gossip, nor indulge in too much wine. Rather, they should be teachers of virtue and good examples of Christian conduct and so be able to show younger women how to be self-controlled, to love their husbands, and to love their children.*

The older women were to be –

- *"<u>Teachers</u>"*: that is, they were to give instruction in Christian living, to open up the meaning of the gospel to their hearers, to answer the questions of any inquirer. Nothing in the context demands that this teaching be done only in private.

- They were to be teachers of *"virtue"* (literally, "good things"); that is, of those things that are right and noble and proper for a Christian to observe and do.

- They were to *"teach the young women"*. This word "teach" is different in Greek from the former one, and means to make of a sound mind, to discipline, to correct, to train.

There is no essential reason to restrict this teaching function to private encounters. It may easily include house meetings, other groups (whether formal or informal), and even the public worship services of the church.

## REVELATION 2:20

*I (Jesus) have a few things against you, because you tolerate that woman Jezebel, who calls herself a prophetess, and allow her to teach my servants and to seduce them into committing fornication, and into eating things sacrificed to idols.*

Though Jezebel was a false prophetess, we may still infer that women acting in the capacity of a prophet were accepted in the Church and that their message was acknowledged as of the Lord. It says that Jezebel *"prophesied"* and *"taught"*, which implies that a woman who was a prophetess was permitted to preach the Word of God, to prophesy under the inspiration of the Holy Spirit, to break open the meaning of the gospel, to give instruction and information concerning the Christian walk.

## REVELATION 22:17

*And the Spirit and the bride say, Come. And let him that heareth say, Come. And let him that is athirst come. And whosoever will, let him take of the water of life freely. (KJV)*

*"Let him that heareth say, Come"* – which is a definite command of Christ that all those who hear the gospel should proclaim the gospel and invite sinners to repent and to come to the cross. As women are numbered among those who hear the gospel, they must also be numbered among those who are commanded to preach the gospel.

Thus scripture shows the following areas of ministry all clearly open to women –

- prophesying – Ac 2:17-18; 21:9; 1 Co 11:5; 14:31.

- evangelism – Ac 8:1-4; Ro 16:7; Ph 4:3.

- teaching – Ac 18:26; Tit 2:3-4.

- public prayer – 1 Co 11:5; Ac 16:13ff.

- pastoral ministry – Ro 16:3-5; 1 Co 16:19.

- serving as a deacon – Ro 16:1-2; 1 Ti 3:11 (taking *"women"* here as *"women deacons"*, not *"wives of deacons"*)

- apostolic ministry – possibly implied by the references to Junia (Ro 16:7), Priscilla (16:3; 1 Co 16:19), Euodia and Syntyche (Ph 4:2-3).

- spiritual gifts – there is nothing in the key passages on this subject (Ro 12:3 ff; 1 Co 12:7 ff) to suggest that such gifts were restricted only to men. Indeed, on the basis of Jl 2:28 ff and Ac 2:17 ff, together with Ac 1:14 and 2:1-4, we may well believe exactly the opposite. [130]

The inference from all of those passages is that women are permitted to expound the Word of God, to speak out a prophecy, to teach, to rule in temporal matters, to guide, to correct faults, and to give instruction. They may do this under the new covenant just as they were able to under the old. The only difference is that their activity is now within the framework of the Christian Church instead of within the framework of the Temple.

---

(130) The above list was taken from The Church, by Dr Barry Chant, ch. 8; Vision Publishing, Ramona Ca.

### TWENTY-THREE

# OBJECTIONS

There are two other Scriptures we must now consider, both of which may seem to preclude women from preaching the gospel or accepting the role of pastor or teacher in the church.

## I CORINTHIANS 14:34-35

*Your women should maintain silence in the churches. They are not permitted to speak; rather, they should be in submission, which the Law also commands. If they want to learn something, they should ask their husbands at home. It is a shame for women to speak in the church.*

Notice in this passage, Paul is dealing with the question of authority. And concerning the authority of women, he says –

*They should be under submission, which the Law also commands (cp. Gen 3:15 and 1 Co 11:3,8-9) –*

*I want you to know that the head of every man is Christ, and the head of the woman is the man ... for the man did not come from the woman, but the woman from the man. Neither was the man created for the woman; but the woman for the man.*

How can we reconcile those injunctions with the many Scripture passages that adequately confirm the propriety of a woman speaking, even in the church? Surely, by recognising that Paul's intention here is to confirm that, while women may be active in ministry, they are still to be under authority. But then, men too are under authority of one sort or another, as indeed are we all. So there is no intention of demeaning women nor of making men superior to them in some way. We are all fully equal in Christ, though we obviously do have different functions and offices in the family, society, and church.

In this passage too, the apostle is dealing, not with preaching, but with asking questions – *"If they want to learn something ..."* The Amplified New Testament renders it - *"But if there is anything they want to learn, they should ask their husbands at home, for it is disgraceful for a woman to talk in church."*

So the issue is not the public ministry of women but rather the appropriate time to ask questions.

The prohibition given in this passage is also addressed specifically to married women – *"Your women"* should probably be translated as *"your wives"*. [131] He tells them to *"ask their husbands at home"*. It is certainly making the passage say too much to construe it as a prohibition against any kind of public speaking by women, especially given the many other places where women are shown as vigorously speaking in public.

The subject of discussion in the whole chapter (1 Co 14) is *"confusion"* versus *"peace"* in public worship. Bearing this in mind, we infer that Paul is not laying down a general prohibition of women preaching, but is insisting that only those with a recognised ministry should speak, or they

---

(131) So it is translated by Weymouth, the World English Bible, the Anchor Bible; etc. The Greek word is *gune*, and it is translated *"wife"* some 80 times in the NT, so to render it as "wife" here is hardly unreasonable.

should speak only in an approved manner. But neither men nor women were permitted to indulge in mere gossip, to speak out of turn, to ask irrelevant questions, or in any way to disturb the worship service, and the like.

The Greek verb translated *"speak"* is in both places *"laleo"*. It <u>can</u> be used of preaching, but it refers generally to any kind of speech, including idle chatter as well as formal declamation. The two most common words for "preach" in the NT are *"euaggelidzo"* and *"kerusso"*, both of which have much the same usage as "preach" has in English, and both of them are used in the NT in contexts that may in several places be readily construed as including women. So too with *"propheteuo"* (1 Co 11:4-5), which cannot be limited to uttering a prophecy but must and does include any kind of divinely inspired speaking, teaching, preaching, or declamation.

As concerning love, fellowship, worship and service, women have an equal standing with men. But they should remember that, as concerning office and authority, from the beginning God has ordained that they stand in a special relationship with men – *"man was not created on account of or for the benefit of woman, but woman on account of and for the benefit of man"* (1 Co 11:9, Amplified N.T. and Ge 2:18). Especially does this hold true in respect of husband and wife (Ep 5:22-24). Does that make her greater or lesser than he? Of course not. It simply means that each of them have a proper duty to the other, of mutual love and service.

Even so, Paul throughout is not trying to establish some kind of rigid rule, but to define principles of good order in the home and in the church. He insists that Christian behaviour should be such as not to give unnecessary offence to the ungodly.

Just in what way some of the ladies in Corinth were unusually disruptive in their conduct is unclear. It has been suggested that men and women were separated from each other, and that the ladies were calling across the aisle to their menfolk. But there is not a shred of evidence for that. [132] However, it *is* plain that Paul was reaching for a level of behaviour in public worship that displayed grace and dignity (vs. 40). The ladies (or at least some of the married women) were somehow, and for some unknown reason, violating that rule. At this time, twenty centuries later, we cannot tell exactly what the problem was, but it enabled Paul to demand that worship should be *"decent and orderly"* (KJV), which in the end, was the main point of the discussion.

It is also conceivable that if Paul were writing a similar letter today (at least in Western culture), he would express himself differently. After all, in our time it is offensive to the ungodly to insist on female subjugation or that she must wear a hat, and the like.

I suggest that it is very easy to fall into the ancient error of straining at gnats while swallowing camels. It would be, I think, wiser to major on the principle of good order rather than on the shape Paul gave that principle to suit his time. Indeed, given the diversity of cultures [133] into which the gospel has now gone it is plain that Paul's rules will have to take many different shapes if they are to be truly effective.

## I TIMOTHY 2:11-14

*Women should learn quietly with all submissiveness. I do not permit a woman to teach or to exercise authority over a man.;*

---

(132) It is true that in later centuries men and women sat in different parts of the church, but there is no evidence of them doing so in early Corinth.

(133) Women have very diverse roles around the world; in some lands quite lofty, while in others they are hardly better than slaves.

*rather, she should remain silent. Remember that Adam was made first, then Eve; nor was Adam first deceived, but the woman was deceived and so broke God's law.*

In view of all that we have before discussed, it seems evident that this passage deals again primarily with the matter of authority. The woman is not to teach so that she usurps the rightful authority of the man; on the contrary, she is to learn in quiet submissiveness. But then, so must we all, as indeed **all** of us must be *"subject, one to the other"* (Ep 5:21).

However, this is a difficult passage, and any reasonable understanding of it would say that Paul does seem to be forbidding women to teach or preach. If the passage in Corinthians about *"women keeping quiet in the church"* has puzzled commentators from the Church Fathers onward, this one has been impossible almost from the day Paul wrote it!

Is he just reflecting the prejudice of his time? Can we endure the thought today of compelling all women in the church to keep quiet, never to speak, only to learn, no matter what gifting or callings have come to them from God? [134]

Many commentators do endure such a doctrine, and indeed, insist upon it! But others soften the blow by drawing attention to the very restricted role that women had in religious circles (Roman, Greek, and Jewish) in Paul's day, and that he was trying to be sensitive to those cultural pressures.

Yet it is difficult to restrict the saying to a mere cultural ban, because Paul goes right back to the beginning of creation in

---

(134) Women can have just as strong a sense of vocation as any man, and it is unreasonable never to question a man's sense of a divine call while scorning a woman's claim to the same.

order to enforce his argument. He calls upon the example of Adam and Eve and thus gives his injunction the shape of an eternal principle built deeply into the economy of God.

Yet the passage seems so contrary to the generally affirmative approach of the gospel to women that it grates on one's spiritual sensitivity. Hence some say that Paul himself modifies his meaning. He does not (they say) insist that women cannot teach at all (which certainly seems ridiculous), but that women cannot teach in such a way as to usurp authority over the man. That is (as someone has said), women must not "lord it over" men. But then, I would say, neither should men "lord it over" women!

Others modify Paul to mean that women may teach and preach but not in such a way as to establish doctrine or to seize control over the church. They claim that women are unable to develop doctrine safely. However, given the record of *male* theologians and teachers over the centuries it is hard to believe that the ladies could have done much worse!

Others argue that Paul makes no mention of the church in the passage, and that he is in fact referring primarily to the conduct of married women, especially in the home. But that seems too restrictive. The apostle does seem to be speaking about women generally, and in a context of teaching, especially teaching men.

Others claim that he was not referring to all the ladies in the church, but only to recent converts from paganism, who had yet to learn the godly qualities of meekness, serenity, and submission. But that, too, seems somewhat tortuous.

In the end, one must say that there is no clear answer. Taking the passage as it stands, not considering any other references, nor any sort of cultural context, it seems bluntly to forbid women to teach (which one presumes includes preaching). Yet within the context of many other verses I simply cannot accept that reading. If a woman preaching offends some people, then I have to say that Paul's injunction, if it is strictly read, offends me! Therefore I also feel obliged to assume that there must have been some local reason, or cultural imperative of the time, that moved Paul to write as he did. What that pressure was can only be guessed now, but it was obviously very strong. In our time, cultural mores demand the opposite. Nor is that cultural demand, as we have seen, contrary in this case to scripture. Many passages clearly allow, even encourage women to participate in the teaching of the Word or the preaching of the gospel, and in leadership of the church, at many different levels.

If that were not so, and if this passage stood alone in scripture, then, no matter how reluctantly, I would have to take it literally, in its narrowest meaning. For in the end, scripture must be accepted as the final authority. Mere cultural mores cannot ever be allowed to override the Word of God. But as it happens, there *are* all those other passages, and they show how active women were in many different roles in the church. They cannot be ignored, and Paul's words to Timothy must be modified by them.

So I conclude with this. May the Lord indeed continue to pour out his Spirit upon his servants and handmaidens. May both our sons and our daughters continue to prophesy powerfully and passionately, impelled, called, and gifted by the Holy Spirit. May he continue to give us apostles, prophets, missionaries, pastors, teachers, both men and women (Ep 4:11-12), who will prepare us to serve the Lord and to build up the body of Christ.

# PART TWO CONTINUED

# FROM THE *"LETTER"*

## SECTION FOUR

## RESURRECTION AND GIVING

## TWENTY-FOUR

# WHAT A SILLY QUESTION!

Plainly, Paul did not do ministerial ethics at school. In violation of the best rules of decent pastoral behaviour, he insults his parishioners and bluntly calls them *"fools"* ! –

> *Some of you have asked, "How will the dead be raised to life? What kind of bodies will they have?" What a stupid question!* (135) (1 Co 15:35-36)

Well, to Paul it might seem like a foolish question, but I think it is quite reasonable to ask about the resurrection of the dead! How can it possibly happen? What shape will we have? When will we rise? What will be the aftermath? And the like. Those questions sound sensible to me, and along with a multitude of other people, I crave answers to them

Perhaps, during an earlier visit to Corinth, the apostle had already explained these matters. Perhaps he was exasperated by their continuing uncertainty. In any case, while deeming the questioners "fools" (which is not recommended by any pastoral theology course that I ever heard of), Paul nonetheless provides them with some wonderful answers – see *1 Corinthians 15:1-58*.

Since any hope that we may one day rise from the dead depends upon the victory of Christ over death, Paul begins

---

(135) The Greek word is *aphron*, which Strong defines as "mindless, that is, stupid". In the Greek world, it had a general meaning of unwise, or foolish.

his great discourse on the resurrection by stating the evidence for Christ's escape from the tomb –

> *I delivered to you as of first importance what I also received: that Christ died for our sins in accordance with the Scriptures, that he was buried, that he was raised on the third day in accordance with the Scriptures, and that he appeared to Cephas, then to the twelve. Then he appeared to more than five hundred brothers at one time, most of whom are still alive, though some have fallen asleep. Then he appeared to James, then to all the apostles. Last of all, as to one untimely born, he appeared also to me.* (1 Co 15:3-8, ESV)

Paul had no doubts about the visible, bodily triumph of Christ over death. The Saviour died. He was buried. He rose again three days later. All this was in agreement with scripture. [136] Upon this our sure sense of immortality is built.

However, there are people who try to keep the *values* of the resurrection while denying its *historicity*. They say that the gospel stories are symbols, or myths, used by the apostles to describe their spiritual experience of the glorified Christ. The stories are not true (they say), but they nonetheless enshrine the truth that Christ is alive in the spirit, and is able to commune with his people.

At once we encounter both the great strength and the terrible weakness of our religion. Christianity, uniquely, is a religion that is founded on fact, not fiction. Its dogmas are rooted in

---

(136) Psalm 2:7; 16:10-11; Isaiah 53:11-12; Hosea 6:2; Matthew 12:40; Luke 24:26.

history not myth, and in objective truth, not abstract theory. Every element of our faith rests ultimately upon God's actions among men and women. Other religions might rely upon human religious speculation, but all the great concepts in Christianity arise out of words that God actually spoke to our forefathers and things that he actually did among them. So much is this true, that if the history can be proven false, then the dogmas that rest on them also become fictitious. So this is our great strength – our faith does not depend upon the vagaries of human thought, but upon rock solid history. But that is also our terrible weakness – for if the history proves after all to have no more substance than a fairy tale, then all our doctrines too must be called worthless fables.

Paul was aware of this peril, so he begins his argument by citing the many witnesses to the resurrection of Jesus – people who knew him when he was alive, who saw him crucified and buried, and then later saw him again, living, walking, talking, and eating. Jesus was not some kind of ghost or apparition. People were able to touch him and confirm that this was indeed the same Jesus whom they had known before. He was substantial, real, yet possessed amazing powers.

I will come back to those ideas, but in the meantime, let us look at some of the objections raised by sceptics against the possibility of a man truly living again after he has been put to death.

## MIRACLES DON'T HAPPEN

It is said that nature is everywhere uniform; therefore, any event discontinuous with normal experience is impossible. But those who make such claims are making, not a statement of *fact* but of *faith*. Simply, the proposition that natural law is uniform throughout the universe is unproven and unprovable! It may be a reasonable *assumption*, but the only way to *prove* it would be to visit every place that exists in every galaxy everywhere.

So, people who make such assertions are engaging in an act of *faith*, which they expect everyone to believe. I'm happy to believe it. But then, don't mock me when – also by an act of faith – I assert my belief in God, and therefore that anything is possible, even the dead living again!

Further, why should I give more weight to an assumption (about the uniformity of nature), which is based on limited observation, than to the testimony of several hundred eye witnesses, who saw Jesus alive after he had lain in the tomb for three days? Should philosophy determine history, or vice versa? Indeed, from a Christian point of view, the life, death, and resurrection of Jesus have actually been a part of nature, and therefore of natural law, ever since the first promise about the Messiah was spoken in *Genesis 3:15*.

Surely, too, our knowledge is too sparse for us to say with certainty what the limits of natural uniformity may be. Time and again science has shown that things once thought absurdly impossible are in fact quite natural.

Likewise, those who claim that no miracle has ever happened, or can happen, cannot possibly *prove* such an assertion, especially when it is contrary to a mass of evidence.

God is deeply involved in nature, and his will is the final arbiter of what is or is not possible (Jn 5:17).

Hence, the resurrection of Christ, while it was a unique event, was neither isolated nor unannounced, nor contrary to any proven tenet of science. Rather, it was the necessary culmination of a series of events going right back to the beginning of creation.

## THE GOSPELS ARE FICTITIOUS

Some people claim that the gospel writers mainly invented the story of Jesus. But what could they have hoped to gain. Persecution and violent death? Certainly, none of the gospel writers could ever have thought that their efforts would bring them fame, or riches, or any other kind of worldly benefit. The story, if it were merely a piece of fiction, was too bizarre, and the person of Jesus too revolutionary, to arouse popular acclaim, or to attract financial gain.

Perhaps such a story might be invented by some kind of religious fanatic, one who cared nothing for cursing, rejection, and persecution. But can the same accusation be reasonably made against *four* men, all writing independently, in different places, at different times, and for different reasons (cp. Lu 1:1-4)? Further, how can it be supposed that men renowned for honesty and virtue could have perpetrated such a deception? No! They told the story of Jesus as they did, because it was simply true. They told what they had seen and heard. No other sensible reason for the existence of the four gospels can be found.

The Evangelists do seem to have drawn their material from similar sources, but they show no signs of collusion, which would be expected if they were fictitious. Indeed, the numerous and often absurd apocryphal gospels that were written during the second century, show what kind of stories impostors would have invented. But the four Evangelists show a restraint, a compulsion for truth, a sense of recording only what the writers had truly observed, that is quite lacking from those later spurious effusions.

Further, how can it be supposed that men renowned for honesty and virtue could have perpetrated the foul deception of colluding together, and of presenting to the world as truth, a wholly invented fiction? Given the environment of those times, such men could not have supposed that their fable was harmless. They would have known it could mean awful suffering for anyone who chose to believe it, and that they themselves would be among the first to die terribly!

## THE APOSTLES WERE DECEIVED

The argument here is that the gospel writers suffered an illusion or hallucination, caused by their intense longing for Jesus to rise from the dead. Hence, while they themselves truly believed that they had encountered the risen Christ, in reality he was only some kind of phantasm. But could 500 people hallucinate in the same way and at the same time? (1 Co 15:6)

Further, they were *not* expecting his resurrection (Mk 16:14), and even failed to recognise him when he did appear to them (Lu 24:13-31; Jn 20:15; 21:4). In fact, there is nothing about the gospel account of the resurrection of Christ, and of his several appearances to his disciples before his ascension, that carry any of the marks of some kind of hallucinatory dream or fantasy.

## THE NARRATIVES ARE LEGENDARY

It is said that the gospels were written long after Jesus' death, and therefore they merely enshrine legends that had grown around his name. But that cannot apply to Paul's letters, which were incontestably written within 35 years or less of the event (cp. 1 Co 15:6).

## CHRIST REVIVED FROM A SWOON

This has been a frequent suggestion over the centuries that Jesus did not rise from the dead because he had not died. On the contrary, he had only lapsed into unconsciousness after his side was pierced by the spear, but revived again while he was lying in the tomb, rolled away the stone, and escaped.

But how could a man suffering from the wounds inflicted upon Christ have survived three days in the grave? How could he have moved the massive stone unaided? How could he have persuaded others that he had actually triumphed over death? And how could his unavoidable subsequent death have been hidden from them? Are we to suppose that the disciples conspired with Jesus to deceive the world? If so, why? What could they possibly gain by such a lie?

## THE BODY WAS STOLEN

This too has been a common argument, that the body of the dead Jesus was stolen, thus giving rise to a rumour that he had in fact risen from the dead. Yet the Jews had no reason to steal his body (Mt 28:65-66); the Romans had no interest in his body (Lu 23:52-53); and the disciples could not have stolen it, because of the guard, and would not have stolen it, because of their own fear.

The fact is, it is easier to believe that Jesus really did rise from the dead after three days in the tomb than it is to believe the foolish arguments that are raised against his triumph.

# PROOF OF THE RESURRECTION

Luke claimed *"many infallible proofs"* (Ac 1:3, KJV). What are they?

## THE DOCTRINE ITSELF

*Resurrection*, as distinct from *resuscitation*, was a radical new idea? What was its source? Was it merely a human invention? Yet that seems impossible. Why would anyone do so, and it is extremely hard, if not impossible, to conceive an idea that has never before entered a human mind (cp. Ec 1:9).

Further, a religion without relics was another startling innovation. Why did the early church have no relics of Christ? Simply because there were none to be had! He rose from the dead and ascended back to the Father, leaving nothing behind to be turned into a relic. Additionally, those first Christians felt no need for any relic of Jesus. They lived in daily fellowship with the ascended and living Christ himself. Only much later, when faith had decayed into religious superstition, did people begin to yearn for something tangible to cling to, such as a splinter from the cross, or the finger of a saint.

Much the same is still true today. When people have no real experience of the power of the resurrection of Christ, they turn to icons, images of saints, religious ceremony, indeed, almost anything, if it can help fill the awful gap, the emptiness, that loss of any sense of the resurrection causes. That is why Paul said that he would pay any price, just to know Christ and the power of his resurrection (Ph 3:8, 10). That perhaps is the reason why people don't experience resurrection power – they are unwilling to pay a price, or to make any special effort to know what Paul elsewhere calls *"the law of the Spirit of life"*! (Ro 8:2).

Yet Christ is indeed risen from the dead, and we may truly experience the power of his resurrection, for which says Paul he would toss everything into the trash can, deeming it as worthless as dung (137) compared to the treasure to be found in Christ!

---

(137) The Greek word used in Ph 3:8 is *skubalon*. It is a compound of two other words that create a sense of something fit only to be thrown to the dogs. Hence it came to mean anything worthless, and particularly ordure, or dung. It was a crude and vulgar word, and Paul probably intended to shock his readers, forcing them to take sharper notice of what he was saying. You can imagine the impolite and offensive English word that

..........continued on the next page.

Now, to some proofs that Jesus did indeed conquer the grave
— (138)

## THE CHURCH

The problems associated with the resurrection are less than those of trying to explain the church *without* the resurrection. The history of the church defies the canons of normal human social relationships and human psychology, except in one circumstance –the resurrection was known to be true! Then the behaviour of the early Christians, the awful suffering they embraced with joy, their astounding confidence, all become reasonable, indeed, inevitable.

The church has depended for its growth, not upon the sword (as in Islam), but upon the integrity of its witnesses (1 Jn 1:1-3; 1 Co 15:14-15). If that integrity could have been destroyed, it would have been. But everywhere, Christians who had felt the power of the resurrection of Christ withstood hideous torture, refusing to deny the Christ who for them was more real than life or death.

Associated with the above is the question, how could the NT have been written if Jesus had perished? Unless he truly had shown himself alive after death, and confirmed it with *"many infallible proofs"* (Ac 1:3, KJV), why would the disciples have bothered to write anything? What would have been the point in dying for a lie? How could a falsehood have driven the apostles to their incredible evangelistic endeavours? Can an illusion create such passion for years on

---

..........*continued from previous page.*

would convey its meaning better than "dung" does – but I am too polite to write it here.

(138) I cannot claim any originality for these proofs. They have been often suggested in many different studies, books, and discourses.

end? Can self-deception be carried so far in costly effort and world-shaking accomplishments? Do people abandon a lifetime of faith for a new religion, when there is any sort of uncertainty about the basic tenet of the new creed?

All such questions demand a negative response. Those first Christians simply *knew* that their Lord was alive. The proofs were more than adequate. Across the world they shouted, "A man has died and lived again!" – and all who believe in him will likewise conquer death and inherit Paradise for ever!

So great was the transformation people experienced when they encountered the living Christ, that before the year 100 even Jewish Christians had forsaken the Jewish Sabbath. Instead, along with the church everywhere, they chose to worship on Sunday, "the eighth day ... the Lord's Day," the day of the resurrection.

Think also about the Eucharist ("thanksgiving"), which used the emblems of death as symbols of joy. How could the crucifixion – an act of ugly brutality, and foul murder, accompanied by sickening torture – have been so transformed, if Jesus were still in the grave? But of course, the tomb was empty. And the early church knew it. So they celebrated the cross as a symbol, not of ghastly defeat, but of abounding gladness, for it spoke of pardon, and heaven, and everlasting life.

## THE CHRISTIAN COMMUNITY

The early Christians differed about many things, but on the resurrection of Christ they were adamantly unanimous.
Men, women, and children endured excruciating torments rather than deny that Jesus had risen from the dead.

Notice, too, Paul's list of witnesses in 1 Co 15:3-8 –

## CEPHAS

"Cephas" means a stone or a rock. It is the nickname Jesus gave to Peter (Mt 16:18; Jn 1:42). Yet how miserably he failed to live up to his name! But how stunningly he was changed by the resurrection! (Ac 4:1-2, 8-10)

When did Peter first meet the risen Christ? Paul says Peter was the first witness of the resurrection; but the four Evangelists all write that the two Marys were the first to see the empty tomb. Why this discrepancy? Perhaps it was a concession to the ancient prejudice against accepting women as witnesses (note that Paul was writing to the Romans).

There is also, despite the declaration by Mark that Mary Magdalene was the first to see the risen Christ (16:9), a hint in Luke of a private meeting that Peter had with the Lord (24:34); but just when this happened is unknown.

At any rate, about one thing there is no doubt – Peter saw Jesus alive again after he had been buried, and he was no phantom, but a real person.

## THE TWELVE

*On the evening of that day, the first day of the week, the doors being locked where the disciples were for fear of the Jews, Jesus came and stood among them and said to them, "Peace be with you." When he had said this, he showed them his hands and his side. Then the disciples were glad when they saw the Lord. (Jn 20:19-20; ESV)*

Someone may object that it is not valid to use the gospel to prove the gospel, and at first sight it seems to be a strong objection. But think about it. We have no other source but the gospels, which were all written at different times, in different places, and by different writers, none of whom could hope to gain any worldly profit by their efforts. Further, there were scores of people who could easily have given the lie to the gospels if Jesus were indeed still buried. Similar evidence, if offered in connection with any other matter today, would probably be accepted as conclusive. People refuse to accept the evidence of Christ's resurrection, not because it is weak, but because the ramifications are too awful! If Jesus truly did conquer death on behalf of us sinners, then we owe him an incalculable debt, and he has every right to demand our love, loyalty, and absolute obedience. To an unbeliever, those demands are intolerable. To us who believe, they are a source of endless love, hope, and joy.

However, even among the disciples, especially those who had not seen the risen Christ, there remained some doubt about the reports of his resurrection. Incredibly, even among those who *had* seen him there were sceptics (Mt 28:17). So further proof was given. Jesus himself linked his resurrection with a promise that the Holy Spirit would be poured out upon the church (vs. 22). This indeed was one of John's favourite themes (7:39; 14:16, 18, 19.26, 28, 29; 15:26; 16:7, 16). It was fulfilled on the Day of Pentecost (Acts 2:1-8), and provided the final proof to the apostles that they had not been dreaming, nor hallucinating, nor deceived by spurious apparitions of Christ – Jesus truly had demolished death! Hence Peter stood up boldly in a public place in Jerusalem and shouted –

> *God has raised up Jesus from the dead, and of this we are all witnesses. And now, after being exalted to the right hand of God, and having received from the Father the promise of the Holy Spirit, he has poured out this that you yourselves are seeing and hearing.* (Ac 2:32-33)

We can still "see" and "hear" him pouring out his Spirit upon people today, with the same sign (glossolalia) as marked the outpouring on the Day of Pentecost. Just as the 120 who were present in the Upper Room in old Jerusalem on that great day discovered beyond doubt that Jesus truly is alive for ever, so all who receive the heavenly gift today encounter the risen Christ tangibly. We see it happening; we hear it happening; we feel it happening – we know that he who gives us his Spirit is indestructible!

## THE FIVE HUNDRED

After his resurrection, Christ instructed his disciples to go to a place in Galilee, where he promised to appear to them. They did as he commanded, and quickly more than 500 people gathered there (Mt 28:7-20; 1 Co 15:6), most of whom, says Paul, were still alive when he wrote to the Corinthians.

## NOTE PAUL'S CONFIDENCE

There is no record in secular or sacred writings of any query being raised during Paul's lifetime about the existence of those 500 witnesses. There were too many of them for any sceptic to risk making a fool of himself by denying that they ever existed. But notice also that Paul's record of this event provides

### *A VERY EARLY WITNESS*

The letter to the Corinthians was written about 55 A.D.; Paul had probably told the Corinthians personally about the 500 no later than A.D. 50. Even earlier, Paul probably got his information about Peter and James and the 500 when he visited Jerusalem in A.D. 40.

So here is a strong witness going back to within only ten years of the event, which makes the claim that the whole thing was a piece of fiction even more foolish.

## NOTE THAT THE 500

- disprove the hallucination theory; for it is unimaginable that so many could be forced into some kind of delusory mania at the same time.

- disprove that the gospels are later myths, for they were all written within the lifetime of many people who were contemporaries of Jesus and the apostles.

- disprove the "spiritual" resurrection theory, for many of the witnesses of the resurrection spoke with the Saviour, touched him, and had no doubt that they were conversing, not with a phantom, but a real person.

- disprove the "swoon" theory, for how could a mere man, so savagely wounded and brutalised as Jesus had been, make his way to Galilee and there convince people, many of whom had known him previously, that he had in fact died and was risen from the dead?

- disprove the "stolen body" theory, for there he was, bodily, visible, audible, still wounded, but unaffected by those wounds (cp. Jn 20:27).

### JAMES

James (1 Co 15:7) was Jesus' half-brother, who had once thought Jesus was insane (Mk 3:21; 6:4; Jn 7:5). But now we find him a pillar of the church, and author of a NT letter (cp. Ja 1:1; 2:1; 5:7-8). How did that happen?

The story of his conversion is told in *The Gospel Of the Hebrews* (dated c. 130) –

The gospel which is named according to the Hebrews, and which was recently translated by me (Jerome) into Greek and Latin, which Origen too often used, refers to the time after the resurrection of the Saviour. It says, "Now the Lord, after he had given his burial cloths to the servant of the priest, found James and appeared to him, for James had sworn that he would not eat bread from that hour when he had last drunk from the Lord's cup, until he saw him risen from among those who sleep." [139] A little further along, this gospel has the Lord saying, "Bring out a table and bread." And then straight away it adds, "He took up the bread, blessed it, and broke it, and gave it to James the Just, and said to him, "My brother, eat your bread, because the son of man is indeed risen from among those who sleep." [140]

Whether or not that story is true, we know that within a few days of the resurrection he was among the disciples (Ac 1:14), that Jesus did appear to him, and shortly after that he was head of the Jerusalem church (15:13). Presumably, Paul heard the story of his meeting with Jesus from James himself (Ga 1:18, 19).

An early churchman, Hegesippus, referred to James in his history. Only a few fragments remain, but they tell how James became revered in Jerusalem for his extraordinary piety and fair-dealing –

> This one was holy from his mother's womb. He drank no wine or other intoxicating liquor nor did he eat flesh; no razor came upon his head;

---

(139) The writer here seems to be confusing James, the son of Mary, and half-brother of Jesus, with the apostle, James the brother of John. James and John were the sons of Zebedee. The latter were with the other apostles in the Upper Room with Jesus on his last night; the former was not.

(140) From Jerome, *De Viris Inlustribus* ("On Famous Men"), ch. 2, "James."

he did not anoint himself with oil, nor make use of the bath. He alone was permitted to enter the holy place: for he did not wear any woolen garment, but fine linen only. He alone, *I say*, was wont to go into the temple: and he used to be found kneeling on his knees, begging forgiveness for the people – so that the skin of his knees became horny like that of a camel's, by reason of his constantly bending the knee in adoration to God, and begging forgiveness for the people. [141]

Hegesippus continues the tale, telling how James, because of his popularity and huge influence, was urged by the Jewish authorities to turn the people away from Christ. Instead he preached a passionate sermon on the return of Christ, which so infuriated the leaders that they cast him down from a high place in the temple. Both his legs were broken, but he was not killed, so they began to stone him, until someone struck him with a club and brought his sufferings to an end. Then Hegesippus adds the telling comment –

and shortly after Vespasian besieged Judaea, taking them captive.

## ALL THE APOSTLES

This (1 Co 15:7) is probably the appearance mentioned in *Acts 1:3, 14*. The group included "Mary his mother and his brothers" (and presumably also his "sisters", included among "the women"). Over a period of six weeks, he appeared from time to time to these people, leaving no room for even the

---

(141) From his five-volume Commentaries on the Acts of the Church (c.170), of which only fragments are still extant. See http://www.earlychristianwritings.com, *in loc.*

least uncertainty about the fact he had died but was now fully alive again.

Note how they had all been embarrassed by his ministry and claims (Mt 12:46-48; 13:53-57, and note Jesus' implication that he had been rejected not only in the village, but also in his own house).

They had thought him insane (Mk 3:21; Jn 10:20; Jn 7:5, 20). Then his family and friends had to endure the humiliation of seeing him condemned as a criminal and hanging naked on the cross. Yet barely six weeks later his former family and many others are gladly worshipping him as their Lord and God! (Jn 20:28)

Surely only *"many infallible proofs"* (Ac 1:3, KJV) could have effected such a transformation.

## PAUL

See again the text, vs. 8-10, which means literally, *"Even to me, Paul, who was like an aborted foetus, Christ appeared."*

Here was the greatest and most inexplicable change of all – the passionate Jew, the furious persecutor, the hater of Christ and Christians (Ac 8:1-3), became an apostle – yet with no possible material or social benefit to be gained, nor with any reason except that he could not deny the evidence that Jesus had conquered death. How vigorously he argues his case, emphatically insisting that Christ was truly victorious over the grave, and hence the guarantor that we too shall surmount death –

> *If we have told you that Christ has been brought back to life, how can some of you say that coming back from the dead is impossible? If the dead can't be brought back to life, then Christ hasn't come back to life. If Christ hasn't come back to life, our message has no meaning and your faith also has no meaning. In*

*addition, we are obviously witnesses who lied about God because we testified that he brought Christ back to life. But if it's true that the dead don't come back to life, then God didn't bring Christ back to life. Certainly, if the dead don't come back to life, then Christ hasn't come back to life either. If Christ hasn't come back to life, your faith is worthless and sin still has you in its power. Then those who have died as believers in Christ no longer exist. If Christ is our hope in this life only, we deserve more pity than any other people. But now Christ has come back from the dead. He is the very first person of those who have died to come back to life* (1 Co 15:12-20).

## CONCLUSION

The contemporary, documented evidence for the resurrection of Christ is more extensive than that available for any other event of the first century. If the resurrection cannot be believed, then there are scant grounds for believing any record of those times.

But if Christ did rise again in fulfilment of his own promise, and by his own power (Jn 10:18), then it is inconceivable that his promise to return to this earth one day will fail. If we know he is risen, then we also know that he is coming!

Are you ready to meet him when he comes? (142)

---

(142) For further study of the resurrection, and the details of *1 Corinthians 15*, see my books *Cross and the Crown*, and *When the Trumpet Sounds*. Both are available from Vision Publishing.

## TWENTY-FIVE

# AT THE LAST TRUMPET!

> *Listen! I will tell you a mystery. We shall not all sleep, but we shall all be changed — in a moment, in the blinking of an eye, at the last trumpet. For the trumpet will sound, and the dead will be raised incorruptible, and we will be changed* (1 Co 15:51-52).

Here is a mystery indeed! So much is *said* about the sounding of the Last Trumpet and the day of Christ's return, but so little is *known!* Countless books have been written, innumerable sermons have been preached, a legion of "last days" conferences have attracted millions of curious attendees, but still no one can say for sure just when the Lord will come, or in what manner.

But we *can* say that certain principles are at work, which *do* control the time of his coming, and which should also shape our attitude toward that great event –

## THE PRINCIPLE OF CERTAINTY

Paul said that he was disclosing a *"mystery"*, about which much will remain mysterious until the day comes. But he has no uncertainty about its *happening*. With absolute assurance he declares –

- The trumpet of the Archangel **will** sound!

- The dead **will** rise from their graves!

- We **shall** all be transformed into creatures of splendour!

We are in the same place. We cannot tell just when the Lord will return, nor precisely how he will do so (for it is difficult sometimes to separate metaphor from reality), but we do know this – he **is** coming! And as for me, I pray that on that day, whether I am called out of my grave or am still alive when Jesus comes, I will truly be ready to meet my God (Am 4:12).

## THE PRINCIPLE OF UNCERTAINTY

That uncertainty about the time of Christ's return has been a cause of much frustration. How people have struggled to penetrate the veil and to gain some inside information on it! As a result, a great many absurd books have been written and sermons preached, confidently predicting that Jesus must come soon. So far, they have all been wrong. In the end, we can do no more than keep on looking for his appearing, and waiting for it patiently, while never allowing our confidence in the promise to waver –

> *You need to stay patient, and keep on doing God's will, so that you will be sure to receive what he has promised; for in just a short time he who is coming will come; he will not delay* (He 10:36-37).

Of course, our problem is that what God deems a "short time" has so far extended some twenty centuries! But, as Peter tells us in a similar context, a thousand years to God is no more than a day! (2 Pe 3:8) Hence he adds –

> *The Lord is not tardy in fulfilling his promise, as some people accuse him; rather, he is patient toward you, because he does not want anyone to perish. Instead, he desires that they should all turn away from their sin. (vs.9)*

Nonetheless, says Peter, when the Day of the Lord does come, it will be unexpected, like a thief in the night. The sky above will be torn apart with a cacophonous roar, the earth will be scorched from pole to pole, and in its place will appear God's new heaven and new earth! (vs. 10-13)

But then he adds a surprising aspect to the event. On one hand he warns us that the time is unpredictable. On the other, says he, we can hurry things along! He makes this arresting statement –

> As you wait for the Day of God, _you should do_ _your best to make it come soon_ – I mean that Day when the heavens will be destroyed by fire, and all heavenly bodies will melt away. (vs. 12)

How can we do such a seemingly impossible thing as hasten the day of the Lord's return?

In fact, there are many things we can do. Jesus himself gives us one of them – pray! Pray that the will of God will be done on earth as surely as it is in heaven (Mt 6:10; Lu 11:2). There the Lord invites us into partnership with himself in creating the future, and in bringing about Paradise on earth. To prayer, we might add planting churches, converting the lost, reaching out through world missions, and the like, for he will assuredly come when the number of the redeemed has been reached! (Re 6:11; 7:4)

For those very reasons, and despite popular opinion, and much hunting for "signs of the times", there is in fact no sure way of telling when that day is near. Daniel declared that the "Book" will remain sealed until the "end" actually comes (12:9). Jesus insisted that there are _"no signs you can observe"_ that will reveal when the Day is at hand (Lu 17:20). Both Christ and the apostles averred that the Last Day would come as unexpectedly as _"a thief in the night"_ (Mt 24:43; Lu 12:39; 1 Th 5:2-4; 2 Pe 3:10; Re 3:3; 16:15).

Furthermore, Christ says that life will continue normally right up to the very last minute, with no special warning of his coming (Mt 24:37-39; Lu 17:26-30).

Also consider the *Olivet Discourse* of the Lord (Mt 24:3-8; Mk 13:3-8), where he lists six things that are commonly taken as "signs of the times", [143] but which Jesus clearly states should not be so taken. He said –

> *Make sure that that no one leads you astray (by these signs) ... **the end is not yet** ... these are but the beginning of the birth pangs ... do not believe it (when they point to the "signs").* (Mt 24:4, 6, 8; Mk 13:5, 7, 21; Lu 21:11)

It is astonishing how many preachers do point to the "six signs", asserting that they are sure indicators of the end of the age. Yet Jesus expressly said, when you see them, you should say to yourself, *"The end is not yet!"* Indeed, the history of the interpretation of Bible prophecy, and of countless attempts across the centuries to predict the time of the end, [144] shows the futility of looking for "signs".

## THE PRINCIPLE OF DELAY

Family tradition has it that my forefathers were French Protestants, some of whom suffered horribly when Roman Catholic authorities persecuted the Huguenots during the 17th century. By the early 18th century perhaps as many as 500,000 Protestants had fled France, of which some 50,000

---

(143) They are: false prophets; wars and broken alliances; earthquakes; famines; floods; persecution. To which (from Luke) may also be added, pestilence.

(144) See my booklet, Oracles Galore (Vision Publishing), which summaries 20 centuries of failed predictions about the nearness of Christ's return.

migrated to England. Among them were my ancestors, who settled in Yeovil in Somerset, where many of their descendants remain to this day.

But not all the persecuted people were sufficiently affluent to be able to escape their torment. They had to remain in France and could not escape their tormentors. Among those martyrs were probably some distant relatives of mine. Their sufferings were horrible – tortured with every imaginable cruelty, burnt to death at the stake, flogged, raped, broken on the wheel, torn apart by foul machines, racked and broken. Still they resolutely clung to their faith. Nothing, no pain however hideous, could force them to recant and embrace the authority of the Pope. They died, staunch in their loyalty to their God.

They also died believing they were in the Last Days, that the Pope was the Antichrist, and that Christ would come again any moment, overthrow the Beast and the False Prophet, and establish everlasting Paradise on earth. How often they cried, *"How long, O Lord, how long?"* (Re 6:10) How passionately they yearned for the Lord to come and to end their pain. But heaven remained silent. The trumpet of God was not heard. Jesus did not appear in the clouds above. And the years rolled relentlessly on.

Perhaps some of them were made bitter by this delay (cp. 2 Pe 3:4, 8), and shook an angry fist at God. Perhaps some, whom torture could not break, were broken by this delay, and came to reject the promise and to lose all hope of the Lord's return and of a new heaven and a new earth. Perhaps some, crushed by torture, demoralised by the delay in the Second Advent, came even to scorn the gospel and to reject Christ altogether.

Yet, while I feel their anguish deeply, I remain glad that the Lord did not heed their pleas! I am glad that his return did not happen then! Suppose the Second Advent had taken place 400 years ago. How many would not have been born and never found the joy of salvation in Christ? How many churches would not have been planted? How many inventions and advances would not have been made? How much love and laughter, song and happiness would never have been experienced? You would certainly not be reading this book! The family of God would be less than half what it now is.

Despite all the hurt that has also been part of the past 400 years, none of us would wish that Christ had come before the day of our own birth! So the apparent delay in fulfilling the promise is not an act of divine weakness, as some have scornfully suggested, but rather of divine mercy. It means, and do mark this, God is not motivated by a principle of haste, but rather by a ***principle of delay***. He is determined to postpone the Last Day for as long as possible!

Now, to many people, that will be a surprising thought. They think that God should be in as much of a hurry as they are for the end of the age to arrive. But he is no hurry at all. Instead, he is governed by two loves –

## THE HEART OF A FATHER FOR HIS CHILDREN

When our first child was born to me and Alison, I loved that little boy fiercely, and it felt like my very heart was swelling. So full was this love, that when my wife was carrying our second child, I became anxious that I would not be able to love him or her as much as I loved our first-born. It seemed impossible that there could be any room left to love another child with anything like the same intensity.

How wrong I was!

Our daughter was born, and then two more sons. I found it quite easy to love them all to the same measure. I made this (to me) startling discovery, that no limit can be placed upon a father's love. Apart from inescapable physical limitations, I came to realise that if I had a hundred or a thousand children, I could love them all equally. As an ordinary man, *I* had to accept natural and social restraints, but *love* had no limits nor any boundaries. Alison's health, too, and other circumstances, obliged us to restrict our family to four children. But, had it been practical, we would have delighted in several more sons and daughters. Parents yearn for children!

Then I realised that our Father in heaven is the same. He desires as many children as he can bring into his family, and he loves them all with an everlasting and unquenchable love. He is still adding members to his family; he still loves each new child as much as he ever loved any of them. He will not hasten the time of the end while a prospect remains of adding a yet greater multitude of souls to the Kingdom. That idea is implicit in what Paul wrote –

> *So Christ came and preached the Good News of peace to all –to you Gentiles, who were far away from God, and to the Jews, who were near to him. It is through Christ that all of us, Jews and Gentiles, are able to come in the one Spirit into the presence of the Father. So then, you Gentiles are not foreigners or strangers any longer; you are now citizens together with God's people and <u>members of the family of God</u> (Ep 2:17-19, GNB).*

Which leads to the Father's second love –

## THE HEART OF A KING FOR HIS KINGDOM

*"A king's greatness depends upon how many people he rules; without them any prince is worthless."* So said

Solomon (Pr 14:28). That maxim is just as true (at least in its earthly expression) for the Kingdom of God, as it is for any earthly principality. [145]

Thus, not only as a Father, but also as a King, the apostle can say that

> God does not want anyone to perish, but rather that everyone should come to repentance (2 Pe 3:9).

So, while *we* may think him dilatory in fulfilling his promises about the return of Christ, in God's reckoning, only a couple of "days" have gone by, and he has plenty of time to add many citizens to his Kingdom and children to his Family.

Nonetheless, the day will finally come when Christ can delay no longer. The archangel will stir, the trumpet will sound, and

> *the Lord Jesus, coming in blazing fire, will be revealed from heaven with his mighty angels. Vengeance will be inflicted upon those who do not know God and do not obey the gospel of our Lord Jesus.* (2 Th 1:7-8).

In the meantime, let us redeem the time!

## THE PRINCIPLE OF EVANGELISM

One way that the church can *"hasten"* the coming of the Lord is to fulfil its missionary mandate. In fact, this is the only sure sign of the *"end"* (Mt 24:14). We see three things –

- The gospel of the kingdom will be proclaimed throughout the whole world

---

(145) God himself, of course, can never be considered either ruined or impotent.

- As a testimony to all nations; and

- Then the end will come.

Because of those three indicators, many think they can calculate the nearness of Christ's return by tabulating the success of the church in fulfilling its missionary mandate. "At last," they cry, "we have a sure sign of just when Jesus will come again."

But is that a valid way to use this promise?

Consider the lack of precision in Christ's words. Although the oracle may at first sight seem to be clear, it does raise five questions –

- *When is the gospel **preached**?* Are radio, TV, literature, a sufficient witness; or does it require a living *"messenger"* with *"beautiful feet"* to appear upon the *"mountains"* of every nation? (Ro 10:14-17)

- *When is the gospel **sufficiently** preached?* Is it enough for preachers to appear in a few main locations; or must it be preached in every city, village, hamlet, community? And how many times must each person hear the gospel (for not all preachers communicate well) before they can be rightly judged to have rejected it?

- *What exactly is the "gospel of the **kingdom**"?* Consult the commentaries and you will discover that there is much disagreement about this!

- *What does it mean, as a **"witness"**?* Or, it could be translated, *"with"* a witness. Perhaps God requires that the gospel be preached as Paul specified (Ro 15:18-19; and cp. Mk 16:15-20; He 2:4), with mighty signs, wonders, and miracles. If so, then perhaps in God's reckoning not a single nation has yet had a proper witness brought to it!

- *What **response** must the gospel produce?* How deeply must it penetrate the life and culture of each society before the justice of God will be satisfied?

In the end, an oracle that we first thought would tell us everything tells us almost nothing! In fact, it becomes clear that Jesus' statement cannot be used as a basis upon which to count nations and missionaries in order to arrive at a "sign" of the end of the age. Only God knows when the provisions of the oracle will be adequately fulfilled. Our task is simply to go on bearing witness for Christ until the end comes.

## VASTLY IMPORTANT

Is the oracle then a mockery? No, because it has a far greater importance to the church than a way of predicting when Christ will come. In it there stands

### *A PROMISE OF THE INDESTRUCTIBILITY OF THE CHURCH*

The question asked by the disciples is still being asked –

> *"Tell us, when will these things be, and what will be the sign of your coming and of the end of the age?" ... Jesus replied, "You must not be afraid! ... This gospel of the kingdom will be proclaimed throughout the whole world as a witness to all nations, and then the end will come."* (Mt 24:3, 6, 14)

Among the first responses Jesus gave, was an admonition not to be afraid, that is, they should not be troubled when they see all manner of disasters coming upon the world. Such things, said he, are inevitable in a fallen planet. They are not necessarily signs of the end, but just a sort of birth pang, [146] which the earth must endure as it writhes toward the Last Day.

Is the prediction he made about the gospel going to every nation close to being fulfilled. It may be, but probably not. Only God knows.

In any case, the greatest thing we learn from it is that _the church is indestructible_ and _its mission is certain_. For, until the very end, declares Christ, _the church will still be bearing witness for him_!

Whatever else may crumble into dust, ruined by war, devastated by earthquakes, scorched by fire, overwhelmed by floods, or ravaged by a shaking planet, the church will remain strong!

> Crowns and thrones may perish,
> Kingdoms rise and wane;
> But the Church of Jesus
> Constant will remain.
> Gates of hell can never
> 'Gainst the Church prevail;
> We have Christ's own promise,
> And that will never fail. [147]

### A PROMISE OF MISSIONARY SUCCESS

Jesus declared, _"The gospel of the kingdom **will** be preached throughout the entire world!"_

---

(146)  That is, in the womb of the present age; the birth pangs that will eventually produce the new age.

(147)  Hymn _Onward Christian Soldiers_, by S. Baring-Gould, 1834-1924; stanza 4.

The Second Coming cannot occur until the church has fulfilled this missionary command, this divine mandate that no power on earth can finally prevent. In every nation, throughout every nation, the gospel __*will*__ be preached! No power of darkness can silence the clarion call to repentance, nor the joyful announcement of the Good News we preach in Christ. Oh! They may hinder us from time to time. They may even imprison and kill us. They may proscribe us with their laws. They may try, as the 18th century French Revolutionaries did, to ban religion altogether and replace it with some secular creed – but they will fail.

> *The Lord gave his Word, and great is the company of those who proclaim the good tidings!* (Ps 68:11) [148]

Prior to the return of Christ, nothing on earth nor in hell can still that glad sound!

So, two strong things do indeed come out of Jesus' oracle. Perhaps we cannot find there any clear sign of the nearness of his return; but instead, rejoice in this – Christ guarantees the _indestructibility of the church_, and the success of its _missionary mandate_. Those two things, in fact, demonstrate the true purpose of Bible prophecy – not to satisfy curiosity about *"times and dates"* (Ac 1:6-8), [149] but rather, to provide an ethical and moral dimension to events both past, present, and future. Or, we may say that the oracles are spiritual in character, not material.

---

(148) I am more or less following the KJV here. The original text actually says, *"The Lord gives a word; the women who publish the good news are a great host!"* But that was more than the rather chauvinistic KJV translators could bear!

(149) Notice how this passage parallels Mt 24:3, 14. There as here, the disciples asked for a sign of the end. Jesus refused to give them one. He told them only to keep pressing on with the task of world evangelism.

# THE PRINCIPLE OF PREPAREDNESS

I have already remarked that the Bible several times uses the expression *"a thief in the night"* to describe the unpredictability of the time of Christ's return. Therefore we should be constantly ready. He may come today!

We may learn here from past generations of Christians. They were wrong in their interpretations of the prophecies, for, despite their confident expectations, the Lord did not come in glory during their lifetime. But there is also another and better sense in which they were right. If anyone had told the people, say, a thousand years ago, that the return of Christ was still many centuries distant, they would not have believed it, any more than we are willing to believe it today.

Consider my own attitude. In my *head*, I have to acknowledge that the return of Christ may yet be distant by another millennium, or more. But in my *heart*, I hope to see him come before I die! One part of me says, "Surely, when the human race is just now emerging from darkness and ignorance to the amazing achievements of modern science, and is on the verge of even more astonishing discoveries, this is not the time for it all to end!" Just as any father is glad to see his children grow up, discover their skills and abilities, and begin to utilise them in maturing adulthood, so the heavenly Father must be proud of what his children today are learning and doing. We are barely into the dawn of our wonderful new world. I find it hard to believe that it will all be swiftly burned to ashes before the best has been achieved!

Yet I still cast my eye skyward, and I still strain my ear for the first echo of the Last Trump!

Why is this? It is because the kingdom of God is already born within us; we are already citizens of heaven; we dwell daily on the edge of eternity; the rays of the rising Sun of Righteousness have brightly touched us, and we cannot help but live constantly with excitement, sensing the imminent appearing of Christ. Hence the apostle says that we *"love"* his appearing (2 Ti 4:8), and we irresistibly yearn for it and believe it to be near. [150]

After reading so many foolish books and hearing so many ignorant sermons on the subject over the years, I confess that I have grown a little cynical about attempts to pin down even the decade – or rather, the century! – in which the Lord must come, let alone the year. Even so, I truly do find myself often scanning the sky above, trying to penetrate the clouds, while asking, *"Is it today, Lord? Will I see my Saviour coming today?"* I could almost say that here is a mark of the true Christian, as distinct from those whose religion is nothing more than form and habit. Those who truly love the Lord, who deeply know him, and who have felt the power of his resurrection (Ph 3:10), are already more in heaven than on earth, and already more eternal than time-bound. We *know* the Lord is near. We yearn for his appearing. We crave his coming. We are hastening toward it, and doing all we can to hasten it. We shudder to think that marvellous day may yet be far distant. We cry with saints of old, *"Come quickly, Lord Jesus!"* (Re 22:20)

And in this, we and they do no more than echo the promise of the Lord, who himself four times affirmed, *"Surely, I come quickly!"* (Re 3:11; 22:7, 12, 20)

## WHAT OUR RESPONSE SHOULD BE

Peter gives a simple but emphatic response to all these things – *"Since everything will be destroyed by fire, what kind of*

---

(150) Think of a young maiden, unsure when her lover will appear, but waiting keenly for the sound of his coming.

*people ought you to be? You ought to live holy and godly lives, while you keep on waiting eagerly for the day of God to come."* (2 Pe 3:11).

# TWENTY-SIX

# ON GETTING READY

*Just as we have borne the image of the man of dust, we will also bear the image of the man of heaven.* (1 Co 15:59)

When you get down to basics, very little separates us from the animals around us. They eat, drink, sleep, copulate, and feel pleasure and pain. They also labour, fight, build, communicate, make music, and even invent.

Yet there are some things that are unique to us, who are made in the image of God – thus, we can recognise a joke and laugh; we admire beauty and scorn ugliness; we can create by the spoken word, just as God does; and we have what no animal truly has, a sense of time, and especially of the future. Time is both our bane and our blessing. We curse its imprisoning chains; we rejoice that we can see beyond it to a timeless splendour. As Tennyson wrote –

> For though from out our bourne of Time and Place
> The flood may bear me far,
> I hope to see my Pilot face to face
> When I have crossed the bar. [151]

The poet knows that one day he will escape the limiting boundaries of time and space, and that he will cross the bar that presently blocks the way to eternity. The journey may be long; yet, at its end, he hopes to see his Pilot (Christ) face to face.

---

(151) Alfred, Lord Tennyson (1809-1892), *Crossing the Bar*, last stanza.

That phrase, "I hope to see," marks perhaps the most striking difference between us and all other earthly creatures. We alone are able to look beyond today and to anticipate tomorrow; we alone are compelled to make a decision about our final destiny. Some, of course, simply deny that there is any future after death, but that is still a decision. No rational person can avoid making some kind of determination about what lies ahead, about whether or not there is life after death. We Christians, of course, embrace the gospel assurance that death is far from the end. Rather, it is a glorious new beginning. We live with confidence, knowing that we shall either rise up from the earth when Jesus comes, or out of our graves, all together to meet the Lord in the air, and to enter with him into his everlasting dominion.

Unbelievers scoff at our hope. Yet they cannot avoid thinking about tomorrow; they cannot avoid choosing whether or not to believe that we exist beyond the grave.

Here are some principles that should guide our thinking about that great day for which we Christians are destined – the day of resurrection when Christ returns –

## AN INDEFINABLE PARAMETER

The angel who spoke to Daniel gave him three spans of time – 1260 "days", 1290, and 1335 (Da 12:5-13). What do those peculiar time sequences mean?

### A LONG TIME

Across the centuries there have been many attempts to apply those periods to the calendar, and to calculate the time of the end. When do they each begin? When do they each end? Many adventurous Bible readers have posited sundry dates. So far, they have all proved wrong. There is not much likelihood that the present crop of prognosticators will be any more correct than their forefathers.

Does the prophecy then have no meaning?

It certainly does not permit us to calculate dates, which not even Jesus was able to do, nor the angels in heaven. (Mk 13:32-33) It seems a bit presumptuous, with our limited knowledge, to attempt something that defies even angelic wisdom! I think it is wiser to accept that while the scriptures show how *God* will determine the end-time, they do not allow *us* to do so (vs. 34-36).

We can say with certainty only that the 1260, 1290, and 1335 days show a long period of time! How long, is a question that even Jesus had to speak about it vaguely (Mt 25:19, *"long time"*; also Lu 20:9; and cp. 19:12). And indeed, just how many centuries would pass before the *"end"* arrived, no one could have guessed! I think even the apostles would have scorned the suggestion that at least two more millennia would first have to come and go. They were apparently all sure that the Second Coming would occur fairly soon (1 Co 1:7-8; Ja 5:7-9; etc.).

## A LIMITED TIME

Actually, for all we truly know, the end may still be far removed even from our time. But we do know this – the day is assuredly fixed by God! (cp. Ac 1:6-7).

That being so, there are three things we should all do –

### WAIT

*Therefore, dear friends, wait patiently until the day of the Lord's coming* (Ja 5:7).

Many people were deeply disappointed when the year 2000 came and went with no sign of Jesus appearing in the clouds above. Prophecy 'tragics' at once redid all their calculations, and began setting new dates, placing the end a decade or more into the 21st century. I expect they will prove to be as wrong as all those who have gone before them. Undoubtedly, one group of soothsayers will one day get it right, but only because they will be lucky enough to choose the year that actually does see the coming of Christ. However it will not be a result of their superior skills in understanding Bible prophecy, but simply a piece of good fortune. Indeed, when prophecy buffs do set up dates for prophecy to be fulfilled, they simply show that they lack any real skill in eschatology!

So stop calculating, and wait patiently!

### WORK

We are enjoined to keep busy as we wait for the Lord to come – see *1 Corinthians 7:29-31; Ephesians 5:14b-18; 1 Th 4:11*, which Paul spoke just before his dramatic oracle about the coming of Christ (vs. 16-17). He did not encourage frenzied searching for signs of the times, but rather, a quiet, steady life, with each family working diligently and paying its own way (2 Th 3:10-12).

Christ gave a similar warning. After stating that neither he nor the angels knew the day the Father appointed for his return, he said –

> *Since you do not know the time, stay alert and*
> *be ready!* (Mk 13:32-33; and vs. 23).

In the year 1854, when she was only 18 years old, the Canadian poet Anna Walker was inspired by some words spoken by Jesus (*"Work, for the night is coming when no one can work"* – Jn 9:4), and she wrote these lines –

Work, for the night is coming,
Under the sunset skies;
While their bright tints are glowing,
Work, for daylight flies.
Work till the last beam fadeth,
Fadeth to shine no more;
Work, while the night is darkening,

When man's work is o'er. [152]

## WATCH

What should we watch? Not the newspapers, but ourselves!

The purpose of Bible prophecy is not to satisfy curiosity, but to inspire holiness and witness (Lu 21:34-36; 2 Pe 3:11-14; Ac 1:6-8).

Nor is there any use in turning the interpretation of Bible prophecy into soothsaying. We need to realise that in all his dealings the Lord

- ### *sets his own agenda*

Please read *Hebrews 10:35-38*. The promise is affirmed, but we must wait patiently, firm in faith, steadfast in witness, all the while realising that we cannot know the Lord's timing. He marches to his own drum beat, which is neither tardy nor quick, and keeps steadily to the programme he has already decreed. It is just because we do not know how the programme of the Almighty will unfold that we need to watch, always on guard, pursuing holiness, ready at all times to meet the Lord should he come.

- ### *follows his own method*

Please read *Isaiah 55:8-11,* which tells us that the ways and means of God are inscrutable to the human mind, so that we cannot know how or when he will fulfil his promise. But we do know that he *will* fulfil it, and it will neither be a day too early nor a day too late.

---

(152)  Hymn, Work for the Night is Coming, stanza 3.

# AN IRRESISTIBLE JUDGMENT

When Jesus spoke about vultures falling upon a carcase (Mt 24:27-28), he used a familiar Jewish *proverb of inevitability*. All languages have such proverbs –

- Turkey: "Death is a black camel that kneels at every door."

- Romania: "The sun will rise, whether or not the cock crows."

- Kashmir: "Where there is sunshine, there must also be shade."

- English: "The tide that goes out always comes in again."

- England: "When death chooses to come, no power can deny it."

Likewise, the Jews said that some things were as inevitable as vultures falling upon a rotting carcass. Jesus applied the proverb to

## JERUSALEM

Indeed, it had a terrible fulfilment in AD 70, when the city was overthrown by the Roman Army, and left scorched and ruined. It also had a literal fulfilment, for the Roman soldiers carried their "Eagle" (153) standards into battle; they saw them as being "alive", inhabited by a divine spirit, which Josephus describes thus –

---

(153) In Greek, the same expression can be used either for a vulture or for an eagle.

Now the Romans ... brought their ensigns into the temple, and set them alongside its eastern gate, and there they offered sacrifices to (the eagles), and proclaimed Titus as the emperor, with loud and joyful acclamations. And the soldiers collected such vast quantities of plunder that in Syria a pound of gold now fetched only half of its former value. (154)

So when Jerusalem, morally and spiritually, had taken on the aspect of a rotting carcase, the "vultures" came. And they came within that generation, as Jesus had predicted (Mt 24:34).

## THE WORLD

*On that day two workers will be in the field; one will be taken, and the other left. Two women will be grinding at the mill; one will be taken, and the other left. So be alert! You don't know just when your Lord will come.* (Mt 24:40-42)

*The last day is coming, when Christ will hand over the kingdom to God the Father. But first, he will destroy every ruler, every authority, and every power. For he must reign until he has put all his enemies under his feet. So wake up from your delusions, come to a right frame of mind, and stop sinning. For, to your shame, I have to say that some of you have no true knowledge of God.* (1 Co 15:24-25, 34)

---

(154) The Jewish Wars, 6:6.

As happened to Jerusalem of old, so one day the world will come to that same state of corruption. On that day, the Lord will summon no human army. Rather he will muster the angels of heaven to inflict vengeance upon a decadent race –

> *The Son of Man will send his angels, and they will pluck out of his kingdom whatever causes people to sin and all who defy the law of God. The angels will throw them into a blazing furnace. Then there will be much weeping and many groans of despair. Then the righteous will shine like the sun in their Father's kingdom. Do you have ears? Then heed what I say!* (Mt 13:41-43).

## AN IRREVERSIBLE DESTINY

Only a Jew could have asked the question recorded in the gospels –

> *The disciples came to Jesus privately, and asked him, "Tell us, when will these things be, and what will be the sign of your coming and of the close of the age?"* (Mt 24:3)

It is improbable that any Roman or Greek would have raised such an enquiry, because it pre-supposes a linear view of time, and that time is ultimately under the control of God. The Greeks and the Romans usually held to some sort of circular view of time, seeing it a series of vast cycles that repeat themselves, so that everything that *has* happened will happen again, in exactly the same way, and again and again, endlessly.

The Jews, moulded by scripture, saw time, not as a huge wheel, going around and around, but as a straight line, beginning with God's creation of the earth and ending with its destruction. Time, of course, remains a great mystery. We all know what it is, until someone asks us to define it. Does the past exist? Apparently not, except in our memories. Does the future exist? Apparently not, except in our anticipation of it. We have in fact only the present moment, and as soon as we try to focus on *that*, it vanishes!

Our planet, and indeed the whole universe, seems to be rolling along just on the present moment, which is endlessly coming to us, seemingly from nowhere, and going from us, seemingly to nowhere, and will continue doing so until the Lord God brings time to an end and carries us into eternity.

The past we can do nothing about, except trust in the grace of God in Christ to obliterate all that offends heaven, and make us fit for his Kingdom. But the future, as it rolls toward us, we can and must embrace, setting ourselves to please God and to capture the promised crown of glory (2 Ti 4:8).

Perhaps, then, the greatest folly of our time is the failure of so many people to have any sense of the future. Supposing that they can do nothing to alter yesterday nor to change tomorrow, they live as if there were indeed only today. Yet how paltry is such a life! We can be truly alive only as we live with a vision of

## HEAVEN

How wonderful are the rewards promised by God (Re 2:26-29; 3:5-6, 11-13, 21-22; etc.); but now, not tomorrow, is the time to prepare for, and become worthy of, these treasures! It may be later than you think!

In April 1914, the Canadian poet Robert Service was sitting alone in a Paris café, penniless, meditating on the strangeness of life –

> I have no illusions about myself. I am not fool enough to think I am a poet, but I have a knack of rhyme, and I love to make verses. Mine is a tootling, tin-whistle music ... (Tonight) I am at the end of my tether. I wish I knew where

tomorrow's breakfast was coming from. Well, since rhyming's been my ruin, let me rhyme to the bitter end –

(Then he composed a poem whose title has now entered into common speech – *It Is Later Than You Think*. He describes the passing parade – a band of merry students; a willing young blonde; a successful playwright; a beggar destroyed by alcohol. He warns them all – then finally turns to his readers) –

> Lastly, you who read; aye, you
> Who this very line may scan;
> Think of all you planned to do ...
> Have you done the best you can?
> See! the tavern lights are low,
> Black's the night, and how you shrink!
> God! and is it time to go?
> Ah! the clock is always slow;
> It is later than you think;
> Sadly later than you think;
> Far, far later than you think. [155]

## HELL

About sixty years ago a grizzled old seaman named Commander Harvey used to patrol Adelaide in a colourful gypsy van, drawn by a massive draft horse. He would pull up outside the gates of one of Adelaide's public schools, loudly clang a brass ship's bell, and when the children had gathered, fervently preach the gospel of Christ. He held their attention, for they were enraptured by the brightly painted van of many colours, the shiny brass bell, the scary sword, and the other

---

[155] Ballads of a Bohemian, Bk. One, *Spring*; T. Fisher Unwin Ltd., London, 1921; pg. 29, last stanza.

sea artefacts that were hanging on it. But mostly he held them with his raspy, deep, powerful voice, resonating with the thunder and howl of countless storms endured while skippering windjammers around the world.

His was no saccharine gospel. He was like those described by the Psalmist –

> *Those who go down to the sea in ships, bearing their cargo across the vast ocean, see the works of God, his wondrous deeds in the deep. He gives an order for a storm to blow up, and it arouses the waves of the sea. They reach up to heaven, they plunge into the abyss. The courage of the sailors melts before the horror; they reel and stagger like drunk men; all their skill avails them nothing. So they cry out to the LORD in their distress, and he delivers them from their troubles* (Ps 107:23-28).

Those same gales were in the Commander's declamations; the lightning flashed in his thunderous tones; the wind roared in his resonance; terrors of the Almighty echoed in his sermons. I first heard him when I was about eight or nine years old, and stood trembling and excited beneath his words. I can still see him, standing up on his van, ancient and hoary, massive beard and many wrinkles, his features carved by the battering winds and driving spray, but his body tough and well-muscled. I still remember, as I walked home clutching a *Gospel of John* he had given me, how much I feared that any moment the jaws of Hell would open at my feet and swallow me up for ever! Happily, they didn't. Instead, I got home safely, read my gospel, and signed the confession of faith in Christ that was printed on its last page.

I became a Christian.

But as scripture says, the wisdom born in me that day was built upon the fear of God, which is the best kind of wisdom (Ps 111:10; Pr 9:10). In turn, that wisdom led me to a deep trust in Christ as Saviour. Faith built upon the fear of God is the best kind of faith. Indeed, if people do not at some point in their Christian lives learn the fear of the Lord, they are unlikely to have enough strength to weather the gales of life. Backsliders are usually those who have never truly learnt to fear God, else how could they fall away? Nor can it be denied that the apostles preached a similarly stern gospel –

> *The Lord Jesus will be revealed from heaven with his mighty angels, coming in flaming fire to inflict vengeance on those who do not know God and on those who do not obey the gospel of our Lord Jesus. They will suffer the punishment of eternal damnation, condemned to be for ever separated from the Lord. ... It is a terrible thing to fall into the hands of the Living God!* (2 Th 1:7-10a; He 10:31; and see also Re 19:11-16; 20:11-13;).

But this should not be gloomy news; it should not darken your joy in the gospel. Rather, it can be the greatest word you will ever hear: there will be requitement! Jesus warned us about hell, not to kill all happiness, but to open the door to indestructible happiness by repentance and faith (Mt 18:8, 11).

## AN INEXCUSABLE FOLLY

> *Just as it was in the time of Noah, so the coming of the Son of Man will be. In those days before the flood, people were eating and drinking, marrying and giving in marriage, buying and selling, planting and building, until the day Noah entered the ark. They knew*

*nothing, until the flood came and took them all away. It will be the same at the coming of the Son of Man.* (Mt 24:36-39; Lu 17:26-30).

It is often supposed that the people destroyed by the Flood were terribly wicked. But Jesus does not say so. He describes them as doing ordinary, everyday things, the things that everyone does as a normal part of life – eating, drinking, marrying, buying, selling, planting, building. Why then were they all so pitilessly drowned? Why that ghastly spectacle, as far as they eye could see, of bobbing corpses – men, women, teenagers, even little children and infants? When they hammered on the sides of the ark, begging Noah to take them up, why were the doors not opened?

What awful indictment did God have against them?

Jesus tells us. *"They knew nothing!"*

They were possibly nice people doing kindly things, but they lived as if a man were no better than a dog, a woman no better than a goat, children of no more worth than sheep. They lived for themselves alone. They were totally focussed on earth and had no view of heaven; their bellies were their gods (Ph 3:18-19).

But they *should* have known.

Noah had been preaching for 120 years (He 11:7; 1 Pe 2:20; 2 Pe 2:5). Had they listened to him, they *would* have known that a day of judgment was coming.

The world today is still full of such people. Well-mannered, good neighbours, usually honest, upright citizens, hard workers – but they have no horizon beyond today, no vision past earth, no time for God, nor any interest in Christ. They know nothing. But they *should* know. They have no excuse. For them, the last Day will be like the day of Noah. The coming of the Son of Man will bring them no joy, but only fearful judgment, without mercy, without recourse, and too late for repentance.

So the setting for judgment is not one of universal wickedness, but rather of universal indifference. The only way to escape the doom of God is to discover the will of God *now*, and do it!

## AN INELUCTABLE GLORY

> *I will tell you a secret. Not all of us will die, but we will all be changed. It will happen in a moment, in the twinkling of an eye, when the last trumpet sounds. Indeed, that trumpet will sound, and then the dead will be raised without corruption, and we will be transformed ... (for) everyone in heaven will have a body like the body of the one who came from heaven. (1 Co 15:51-52, 48).*

Who can imagine the splendour of that hour! We may not be certain about the exact transformation that will take place as we rise from off the earth or out of our graves, but we do know this – we shall be like Jesus! And what higher splendour could we desire? (1 Jn 3:2; and cp. Re 1:13-17a).

## CONCLUSION

We are a people in the presence of eternity, carried along toward a meeting with God. Where is your eye fixed? On earth, or heaven; on today, or tomorrow?

One of the greatest English poets was Robert Browning (1812-1899), who was also a devout Christian. In one of his poems he contrasts a butcher who was an artist, a baker who was a poet, and a candle maker who was a musician, with a dismal man who lived only for his shop. The poet cries out in protest against such a dismal state, and prays that his heart may be kept far away from any such moribund and earthbound captivity. Your prayer, and mine, should be the same.

> Because a man has shop to mind
> In time and place, since flesh must live,
> Needs spirit lack all life behind,
> All stray thoughts, fancies fugitive,
> All loves except what trade can give?
>
> I want to know a butcher paints,
> A baker rhymes for his pursuit,
> Candlestick-maker much acquaints
> His soul with song, or, haply mute,
> Blows out his brains upon the flute!
>
> But – shop each day and all day long?
> Friend, your good angel slept, your star
> Suffered eclipse, fate did you wrong!
> From where those sorts of treasures are,
> There should our hearts be – Christ, how far!

## TWENTY-SEVEN

# GIVING

Some readers may wonder why a chapter on the earthy subject of giving follows so hard upon the heels of the sublime theme of the resurrection, or why I have put two such seemingly disparate subjects (*Resurrection* and *Giving*) into the same Section. I'm only following the example set by Paul, who immediately goes from his exalted declaration of our triumph in Christ to the prosaic statement –

> *Now concerning the collection for the saints, you should do just what I told the churches in Galatia to do"* (1 Co 16:1-4).

This *was* typical of Paul, who often mixed the mundane with the heavenly, the earthly with the spiritual, and the natural with the supernatural. He did this because he saw no final distinction between them – they are all part of the universal kingdom of God, and subject to the same spiritual principles.

So Paul easily moves from his shout of victory over death to the weekly offerings in the church! If we are indeed destined to rise from the dead and to reign with Christ for ever, then let us show our joy by the measure of our giving!

Paul encourages regular, cheerful, and generous giving, based primarily on the level of affluence each person has received from God (vs. 2). Yet at once we face a problem. Nothing about our faith is as offensive to the ungodly as our giving to the Lord through church offerings. Christians married to unbelievers often make that discovery. The unbelieving spouse may accept prayer, Bible reading, worship – but if the believer wants to tithe the family's income, what a storm of protest is often aroused!

Despite any difficulties that may be in the way, every Christian must try to find a way to give sacrificially to the church, for by our giving we demonstrate two equally necessary and important things –

## OUR BELIEF THAT GOD EXISTS

Nobody will give to the work of God, risking worldly security, without a profound belief that God exists and that he must be obeyed. If people have any doubt about the reality of God, then they will cling to their worldly possessions, for wealth becomes their only security. By our giving we show that our confidence is in God, that we trust him alone as the source of our supply, and that we have a heart to obey him. The world may mock us as fools for tossing good money into what they deem an empty hole, but we can do no other. Our God is real. His demands are imperative. His promises are magnificent. So we give joyfully.

## OUR BELIEF IN THE SPIRITUAL ABOVE THE MATERIAL

See *2 Corinthians 4:16-18*. Christian giving is a proclamation of our belief that spiritual law is stronger than natural law; spiritual pleasures are more delightful than physical; the spiritual dimension is more apparent to us than the material; the flesh will perish, but the spirit abides forever.

How then should we give? Contrary to popular opinion, Christian giving cannot be reduced to a rule, or a law, not even about a tithe. The only "rules" set down for the church in this matter, are that Christian giving should be free, generous, and in accordance with each person's affluence.

Nonetheless, there are some principles that can guide us in deciding how much we should give and to whom –

## PURPOSE

*1 Corinthians 16:1-3*

I read somewhere that a large mental research hospital sent out an appeal for funds, and also asked people to put in their will that they wanted to donate their brain to the hospital. The appeal went on to say, "Every donation will be welcome, no matter how small!" That may not have been precisely what they wanted to say. But the idea was good, that people should think ahead, weigh up their resources, seek the mind of God, and give with the intention of doing good.

God-directed giving will not be aimless, but will be motivated by a sense of obedience to the Lord and of divine purpose. Hence it will be apportioned as scripture indicates –

### *TO THE CHURCH*

Every Sunday, says Paul, we should put aside a portion of what we earned in the previous week. (1 Co 16:2) This money belongs to God's people, both in the local church and beyond it. Elsewhere, too, scripture enjoins support for the church and its ministers – *Malachi 3:10-11; Romans 12:13; 1 Corinthians 9:9; 1 Timothy 5:17-18*. The whole is delightfully summed up by Sirach –

> Love your Maker with all your might and do not leave his ministers without support. Fear the Lord and honour the priest and give him his dues, as you have been commanded ... Be open-handed also with the poor, so that your own well-being may be complete. Every living man appreciates generosity; do not withhold your kindness even when a man is dead (7:30-33, NEB).

How can you be kind to a dead man? By ensuring (especially if he is poor) that he has a decent burial, that all necessary comfort is offered to his grieving friends and family (vs. 34), that his widow and children are cared for, and the like.

Indeed, wherever you turn in scripture, open-hearted and open-handed generosity is expected from God's people, especially toward those who are fellow worshippers, and toward his servants and ministers.

### TO WORLD-WIDE MISSIONS

*"Tell every nation on earth,"* cried the Psalmist, *"that the Lord is wonderful, and he does amazing things!"* (96:3). Jesus, too, commanded his disciples to go out into all the world, and to preach the gospel everywhere to everyone (Mt 28:19; Mk 16:15). That mission cannot be fulfilled unless adequate funds are available. Hence Paul himself, having bade the Corinthians to be regular and generous in their church offerings, asked them to help him financially as he continued on his way to another city (1 Co 16:6).

Missions support, then, both in our own land and worldwide, must be a regular component of our giving. And those who do so, giving to expand the gospel beyond their home and church, come into alignment with a powerful spiritual dynamic. Such giving is –

### AN ACT OF OVERCOMING

Many great promises are given to those who *"overcome"* (Rev 2:7,11,17,26; 3:5,12,21; 21:7; KJV). There is probably nowhere more than in the control of their finances, where Christians need to show this overcoming grace. Those who gain spiritual victory in the matter of money are likely to be strong everywhere. When our lives are characterized by generosity, we show that we have overcome carnal greed, selfishness, and the naturalistic temper of the world. That is especially true of missionary giving, where the benefits of our giving are distant from us and may never be personally known to us.

There is a perfect altruism about missionary giving, especially when it is done with joyful faith, that more nearly reflects the heart of Christ than any other form of giving. Indeed, most of the great New Testament passages on Christian giving deal with offerings taken up in one church to assist churches in other places (Ro 15:15-27; 1 Co 16:1-4; 2 Co 8 & 9; Ph 4:10-18).

## A DECLARATION OF TRIUMPH

Missionary giving is an emphatic way of displaying confidence in the ultimate triumph of the kingdom of God. Who wants to give to a losing cause? We give because we believe *Matthew 16:18*. The church is the only indestructible thing on this planet! (He 12:25-29) Those who give to propagate the gospel include themselves in that church and share in its indestructibility.

Missionary giving is an act of faith. It shows that we believe what scripture says about the church. It shows our assurance that only one thing has any future: the kingdom of God. It shows our certainty that we who are bonded to that kingdom and who have laboured to establish it, will forever share its magnificent dominion (Re 2:26-29).

## TO THE POOR

When it comes to giving, I have heard it said, some people stop at nothing!

Depending on how familiar you are with English idiom, you will see that statement, either as a description of people who will allow nothing to deter them from giving richly and sacrificially, or as a humorous dig at the parsimonious. Our aim, of course, should be to emulate the former and scorn the latter.

There is a sense in which giving to the *poor* displays greater trust in the promise of God than does giving to the *church*. This is because giving to the church brings a present reward (both spiritually and financially), whereas giving to the poor may have its reward only in heaven. Those who are kind to the poor, expecting nothing back from them, are in effect *"lending to the Lord"*, and on God's great day of reckoning that loan will be repaid with splendid interest (Pr 19:17; Mt 5:7; 10:40-42; Ph 4:17; He 6:10).

Note, however, that the command to be *charitable* does not oblige you to be *cheated*. Jesus did say, *"Give to him who begs from you, and do not refuse him who would borrow from you"* (Mt 5:42). That demands more from us than doling out money to every scrounger who tries to take advantage of our Christian charity. You should not be a "soft touch" for every unscrupulous lay-about, nor every cunning beggar. To give money to some people is simply to worsen their moral and spiritual state, to encourage them in sloth, to squander the resources over which God has made you his steward.

Christian love does require that you never turn your back on any person, that you remain compassionate even toward the worst people. But it also requires that you show your concern for them (especially if they ask for your help) by trying to discover their real need, and by offering them help at that point. Their real need may in fact not be money. In many cases it will rather be counseling in how to handle money, re-training for employment, building up self-confidence, and the like. Nothing in the command of Christ requires us to support people in laziness and irresponsibility.

Do not allow your charity to be controlled by mere sentiment, nor by a misguided sense of duty, but rather by a sense of responsible stewardship and a mature and sensitive expression of genuine Christian love. Then mark the promise God gives to those who remember the poor in their giving –

> *Happy are those who are concerned for the poor; the Lord will help them when they are in*

*trouble. The Lord will protect them and preserve their lives; he will make them happy in the land; he will not abandon them to the power of their enemies. The Lord will help them when they are sick and will restore them to health* (Ps 41:1-3).

### FINAL COMMENTS

Christian giving should be governed by a **_right motive_** (one of loving joy and faith); it should have the **_right method_** (giving to the church, to missions, and to the poor); and it should have the **_right measure_** (giving generously and sacrificially). Indeed, the faith of those who do not give bravely, continuously, and expectantly may surely be doubted.

All three of those rules should at heart be altruistic – that is, we give, not just with an expectation of present personal benefit, but because we who believe cannot help but give. Giving is simply a natural expression of our faith in Christ, in scripture, and in the kingdom of God. Even if no reward were offered, nor any present or future benefit, true Christians would still hasten to give. Yet a reward **_is_** offered, and we should be bold in believing the promise and in expecting its rich fulfilment, so that greater glory may come to Christ.

## FINALE

There are many treasures in Paul's extraordinary *Letter to the* Corinthians that I have omitted from these pages, but I have room for no more. So let Paul himself write the last words in this book (1 Co 16:21-24) –

*With my own hand I write these words – Greetings from me, Paul. Whoever does not love the Lord –a curse on him! Maranatha! – O Lord, come soon! The grace of the Lord*

*Jesus be with you. My love be with you all in Christ Jesus.*

# INDEX OF TEXTS FROM 1 CORINTHIANS

# GLOSSARY

A continent man – a sober man

Abrogate – to end an agreement, to do away with something.

Antinomian – a person who believes salvation depends on faith alone, without any need to observe the moral law.

Apocalyptic – dealing with a revelation of the future or the last things; predicting disaster.

Areopagus, Mars Hill – a place of debate in ancient Athens.

Bourn, bourne – a boundary.

Cacophonous – harsh, discordant and loud noise.

Casuist – someone, especially a theologian, who tries to settle questions of ethics or morals by applying general principles to them.

Casuistry – application of general principles or rules to particular persons or cases, especially in relation to moral questions.

Catatonic - in a state resembling a trance.

Charismata – gifts or powers believed to be divinely bestowed; especially, the nine gifts listed by Paul in *1 Corinthians 11:8-10.*

Collude – to work secretly with somebody.

Compendium – a short comprehensive account.

Consanguineous – of the same blood, descended from the same ancestor.

Cultural mores – established customs of a culture.

Desuetude – the condition of not being in use.

Dictum – a formal authoritative pronouncement of a principle proposition or opinion.

Doctrinaire – determined to use a specific theory or method and refusing to accept that there might be a better approach.

The Dunciad – Alexander Pope's series of poems about foolish people.

Endemic – restricted to one place, living in a defined geographical area.

Eponymous – giving a name to something, having a name that is used as the title or name of something else.

Eschatology – a branch of theology concerned with the final events of the history of the world.

Ethical – conforming to accepted standards.

Glossolalists – those who speak in tongues.

Hegemony – authority or control, control or dominating influence by one person or group.

Indict – to formally charge an accused person.

Ineluctable – cannot be avoided, changed or resisted.

Inviolable – unbreakable, secure from being infringed, breached, or broken.

Layabout – someone considered idle or lazy.

Moribund – approaching death.

Oxymoron – a combination of contradictory words

Paean –joyful exultant song

Parsimonious - stingy

Paucity – smallness of quantity.

Polyandry – having many husbands.

Polygamy – having more than one mate.

Posit – to assume or affirm the existence of anything; to present an idea or proposition.

Presumptuous – overstepping due bounds, taking liberties.

Prophecy tragic – one who has an excessive passion for, or devotion to, prophecy.

Prophecy buff – a prophecy enthusiast.

Prognosticator – one who foretells from signs or symptoms.

Propagate – to increase, extend.

Pseudepigrapha – a body of Jewish and/or Christian literature written between 200 B.C. and 200 A.D., but not reckoned to have canonical authority.

Quintessence – the essence of a thing in its purest form.

Talismanic - relating to an object or charm that is supposed to possess occult or magical powers.

Thaumaturgy – to do with healing the sick and the performance of miracles.

# BIBLIOGRAPHY

Aubrey, John, .(1478-1535). *Brief Lives-Sir Thomas More*
Avery, Peter and John Heath-Stubbs. Tr. *The Ruba'iyat of Omar Khayyam*. Penguin Classics: 1983.
Bettenson, Henry (Selected and Edited) *Documents of the Christian Church*. Oxford University Press; London, 1973.
Blake, William (1757-1827); Poem; *The Everlasting Gospel*.
*Book of Verses*. pub. D. Nutt: London.
Carlyle, Thomas, *Sartor Resartus*. J. M. Dent & Sons Ltd., London, 1913.
Chant, Barry. *The Church*. Vision Publishing.
Chant, Ken, *Clothed With Power*. Vision Publishing.
_____. *Equipped to Serve*. Vision Publishing.
_____. *Understanding Your Bible*. Vision Publishing.
_____. *When the Trumpet Sounds*. Vision Publishing.
Charlesworth, J. H. Editor. *The Old Testament Pseudepigrapha* tr. by E. Isaac. Doubleday & Co., New York, 1983.
Clover, L. L. Thesis. *Evil Spirits – Intellectualism and Logic*. Louisiana Missionary Baptist Institute & Seminary. 1974. (Wikipedia).
*Commentaries on the Acts of the Church*; http://www.earlychristianwritings.com
Cranmer, Thomas. (16th Century) *Book of Common Prayer*.
*Dictionary of New Testament Theology;* Zondervan Pub. House. Grand Rapids, 1978.
Edwards, James E. *Commentary on Romans*. Hendrickson Publications: 1992.
Elliot, George (1819-1880) *The Mill on the Floss*.
Epp, Eldon J. *Junia: The First Woman Apostle*. Fortress Press. Minneapolis, 2005.
Fadiman, Clifton. Editor. *The Book of Anecdotes*. Little, Brown & Co., Boston, 1985.
Gibran, Kahlil, *The Prophet*. Pub. Alfred A. Knopf; New York, 1968.
Hill, Robert W. Jnr. Editor. *Tennyson's Poetry*. W.W. Norton & Co. New York, London, 1971.
Johnson, B. W. *The People's New Testament Commentary*. Word Search Corporation: Nashville, Tennessee, 2010.

Lampe, Peter. *Anchor Bible Dictionary*. Art. *Junia*.

Larson, David. *Interview Christianity Today*. November 23; 1992.

Lewis, C. Day. Editor. *The Poems of Robert Browning*. The Heritage Press. Norwalk, Connecticut, 1971.

Luther, Martin. *A Commentary on Paul's Epistle to the Galatians*. James Clarke & Co. Ltd., London, 1956.

Mackenzie, K. R. Tr. *The Georgics-Book One*. Folio Society. London, 1969.

More, Thomas. *Utopia*. Everyman's Library: 1965.

Roberts, A. and J. Donaldson. Editors. *Ante-Nicene Fathers*. Eerdman's Pub. Co., Grand Rapids, Michigan, 1979.

Russell, Bertrand. *The History of Western Philosophy*. Simon & Schuster; New York. 1945.

Schaff, Philip. Editor. *The Nicene & Post – Nicene Fathers*. Eerdman's Pub. Co., Michigan, reprint 1979.

Service, Robert. *The Best of Robert Service*. Dodd, Mead & Co., New York, 1953.

Suetonius, *The Twelve Caesars* tr. by Robert Graves. Folio Society: London, 1964.

Vasari, Georgio (1511- 1574) *Lives of the Artists*. tr. by George Bull. Folio Society: London, 1993.

Watling, E. F. Tr. *Phaedra*. Penguin Books. London, 1970.

Windeatt, B. A. Tr. *The Book of Margery Kempe*. Penguin Books: 1988.

Zipes, Jack. Tr. *The Complete Fairy Tales of the Brothers Grimm*. Bantam Books. New York, London, 1987.

## BIBLE COMMENTARIES

*The Interpreter's Bible;* Abingdon Press, New York, 1952.

*The Anchor Bible;* Doubleday & Co., New York; 1966.

Anders, Max., Editor. *Holman New Testament Commentary*; B & H Publishing Group; Nashville, Tennessee, 2004.

Baker's Publishing House., *The New Testament Commentary;* Grand Rapids, Michigan, 1987.

Barnes, Albert., (1798-1870).*Notes on the Bible*.

Bruce, F. F., gen. ed.; *The New International Commentary on the New Testament; Wm. B. Eerdman's Pub. Co.,* Grand

Rapids, Michigan; 1977.

Calvin, John., (1509-1564) *Calvin's Commentaries.*

Clarke, Adam., (1715-1832) *Commentary on the Bible.*

Excell, Joseph S. & Spence-Jones, H. D. M. Editors. *The Pulpit Commentary*; 1881.

Gaebelein, Frank E., Editor. *The Expositor's Bible Commentary*; Zondervan Publishers, Grand Rapids, Michigan.

Gill, John., (1690-1771) *Exposition of the Entire Bible.*

Hawker, Robert., *The Poor Man's Commentary On The Whole Bible;* 1850.

Hendriksen, William., *The New Testament Commentary*; Baker Book House, Grand Rapids, Michigan; 1972.

Henry, Matthew., *Commentary On The Whole Bible*; Marshall, Morgan, and Scott; London, 1953.

Hodge, Charles., (1797-1878) *A Commentary on Ephesians* Intervarsity Press.

Hubbard, David A., gen. ed.; *Word Biblical Commentary;* Word Books, Waco, Texas; 1987.

*Bible Background Commentary;* Nottingham, UK, 1993.

Intervarsity Press., *The IVP New Testament Commentary Series,* Nottingham, UK.

Ironside, H. A., *Expository Commentary* (1876-1951).

Jamieson, Robert; Fausset, A. R.; & Brown, David., *A Commentary on the Old and New Testaments,* 1871.

Johnson B. W., *The People's New Testament* 1891.

_____. *The People's New Testament Commentary*; 1891.

Joplin., *The College Press NIV Commentary;* Missouri, 1996.

Macdonald, William., *Believer's Bible Commentary*; Thomas Nelson Publishers; 1989.

Poole, Matthew., *Matthew Poole's Commentary*; 1685

Robertson A. T., *Word Pictures in the New Testament*; 1933.

Stern, David H., *Jewish New Testament Commentary*; Jewish New Testament Publications, Inc., Clarksville, Maryland; 1982.

Thomas Nelson Inc., *Nelson's New Illustrated Bible Commentary;* New York; 1999.

Tasker, R. V. G., *Tyndale New Testament Commentaries;* Tyndale Press, London; 1964

Trapp, John., *Commentary On The Old And New Testaments*

(1601-1669).
Vincent, Marvin R., *Vincent's Word Studies*; 1886
Walvoord, John & Zuck, Roy., *The Bible Knowledge Commentary;* Cook Communications; Colorado Springs, Colorado, 1989.
Wesley, John., *Explanatory Notes on the Whole Bible*; (1703-1791).
Wiersbe, Warren W., *Wiersbe's Expository Outlines*; Publisher, David C. Cook, Colorado Springs, Colorado.
Wiseman, D. J. General editor. *Tyndale Old Testament Commentaries*. Intervarsity Press.
Word Search Corporation., *Preacher's Outline and Sermon Bible*; Nashville, Tennessee, 2010.
Word Inc., *The Preacher's Commentary;* Nashville, Tennessee, 1992.

## BIBLE VERSIONS

In addition to the *KJV* or *Authorised Version* of the Bible, the following versions or translations are cited, or were consulted by the author of this work.

CEV – *Contemporary English Version*; the American Bible Society, New York, NY; 1995.

ESV – *English Standard Version*; Crossway Bibles, a publishing ministry of Good News Publishers; Wheaton, Illinois; 2001.

GNB – *Good News Bible*; Second Edition, by the American Bible Society; New York, NY; 1992.

GW – *God's* Word; God's Word to the Nations Bible Society; Cleveland, Ohio; 1995.

JPS – *The JPS* Bible; the Jewish Publication Society; Philadelphia, PA; 1995.

ISV – *International Standard Version*, v. 1.2.2; The ISV Foundation, La Mirada, CA; 2001.

NET – *The Net Bible*; Biblical Studies Press; Richardson, Texas; 2006.

NIV – *New International Version*; Zondervan Bible Publishers, Grand Rapids, Michigan; 1978.

NJB – *New Jerusalem Bible*; Doubleday & Co. Inc.; Garden City, New York; 1985

NRSV – *New Revised Standard Version*; the Division of Christian Education of the National Council of the Churches of Christ in the USA; 1989.

REB – *Revised English Bible with Apocrypha*; Oxford University Press; 1989.

RSV – *Revised Standard Version*, Thomas Nelson Inc., New York; 1959.

YLT – *Young's Literal Translation*; by NJ Young; 1898.